Building on Strength: Language and Literacy in Latino Families and Communities
ANA CELIA ZENTELLA, Ed.

Powerful Magic: Learning from Children's Responses to Fantasy Literature
NINA MIKKELSEN

On the Case: Approaches to Language and Literacy Research (An NCRLL Volume)*
ANNE HAAS DYSON and CELIA GENISHI

New Literacies in Action: Teaching and Learning in Multiple Media
WILLIAM KIST

On Qualitative Inquiry: Approaches to Language and Literacy Research (An NCRLL Volume)*
GEORGE KAMBERELIS and GREG DIMITRIADIS

Teaching English Today: Advocating Change in the Secondary Curriculum
BARRIE R.C. BARRELL, ROBERTA F. HAMMETT, JOHN S. MAYHER, and GORDON M. PRADL, Eds.

Bridging the Literacy Achievement Gap, 4–12
DOROTHY S. STRICKLAND and DONNA ALVERMANN, Eds.

Crossing the Digital Divide: Race, Writing, and Technology in the Classroom
BARBARA MONROE

Out of this World: Why Literature Matters to Girls
HOLLY VIRGINIA BLACKFORD

Critical Passages: Teaching the Transition to College Composition
KRISTIN DOMBEK and SCOTT HERNDON

Making Race Visible: Literary Research for Cultural Understanding
STUART GREENE and DAWN ABT-PERKINS, Eds.

The Child as Critic: Developing Literacy through Literature, K–8, Fourth Edition
GLENNA SLOAN

Room for Talk: Teaching and Learning in a Multilingual Kindergarten
REBEKAH FASSLER

Give Them Poetry! A Guide for Sharing Poetry with Children K–8
GLENNA SLOAN

The Brothers and Sisters Learn to Write: Popular Literacies in Childhood and School Cultures
ANNE HAAS DYSON

"Just Playing the Part": Engaging Adolescents in Drama and Literacy
CHRISTOPHER WORTHMAN

The Testing Trap: How State Writing Assessments Control Learning
GEORGE HILLOCKS, JR.

The Administration and Supervision of Reading Programs, Third Edition
SHELLEY B. WEPNER, DOROTHY S. STRICKLAND, and JOAN T. FEELEY, Eds.

School's Out! Bridging Out-of-School Literacies with Classroom Practice
GLYNDA HULL and KATHERINE SCHULTZ, Eds.

Reading Lives: Working-Class Children and Literacy Learning
DEBORAH HICKS

Inquiry Into Meaning: An Investigation of Learning to Read, Revised Edition
EDWARD CHITTENDEN and TERRY SALINGER, with ANNE M. BUSSIS

"Why Don't They Learn English?" Separating Fact from Fallacy in the U.S. Language Debate
LUCY TSE

Conversational Borderlands: Language and Identity in an Alternative Urban High School
BETSY RYMES

Inquiry-Based English Instruction
RICHARD BEACH and JAMIE MYERS

The Best for Our Children: Critical Perspectives on Literacy for Latino Students
MARÍA DE LA LUZ REYES and JOHN J. HALCÓN, Eds.

Language Crossings
KAREN L. OGULNICK, Ed.

What Counts as Literacy?
MARGARET GALLEGO and SANDRA HOLLINGSWORTH, Eds.

Critical Encounters in High School English: Teaching Literary Theory to Adolescents
DEBORAH APPLEMAN

Beginning Reading and Writing
DOROTHY S. STRICKLAND and LESLEY M. MORROW, Eds.

Reading for Meaning
BARBARA M. TAYLOR, MICHAEL F. GRAVES, and PAUL VAN DEN BROEK, Eds.

Writing in the Real World
ANNE BEAUFORT

Young Adult Literature and the New Literary Theories
ANNA O. SOTER

---

* Volumes with an asterisk following the title are a part of the NCRLL set: Approaches to Language and Literacy Research, edited by JoBeth Allen and Donna Alvermann.

(Continued)

Building on Strength

LANGUAGE and LITERACY
in LATINO FAMILIES
and COMMUNITIES

edited by *Ana Celia Zentella*

Teachers College
Columbia University
New York and London

California Association for
Bilingual Education
Covina, California

Published simultaneously by Teachers College Press, 1234 Amsterdam Avenue, New York, New York 10027 and the California Association for Bilingual Education, 16033 E. San Bernardino Road, Covina, California 91722-3900

The collaboration of the authors of this collection was facilitated with the support of a grant from the Center for the Study of Race and Ethnicity, University of California at San Diego, Ramón Gutiérrez, Director.

Library of Congress Cataloging-in-Publication Data

Building on strength : language and literacy in Latino families and communities / edited by Ana Celia Zentella.
        p. cm. — (Language and literacy series)
        Includes bibliographical references and index.
        ISBN 0-8077-4604-5 (alk. paper) — ISBN 0-8077-4603-7 (pbk. : alk. paper)
        1. Hispanic American families—Language. 2. Hispanic Americans—Socialization. 3. Hispanic Americans—Education. 4. Sociolinguistics—United States. I. Zentella, Ana Celia. II. Language and literacy series (New York, N.Y.)

P40.5.H57B85 2005

2005048540

ISBN 0-8077-4603-7 (paper)
ISBN 0-8077-4604-5 (cloth)

Printed on acid-free paper

Manufactured in the United States of America

12   11   10   09   08   07   06   05   8   7   6   5   4   3   2   1

*Con agradecimiento y orgullo, para todas las madres
luchadoras—las nuestras y las de la juventud latina
de los Estados Unidos.*

With gratitude and pride, for every mother in the
struggle—our own, and the mothers of young Latinas
and Latinos in the United States.

Contents

Acknowledgments

The collaboration that produced this volume, facilitated by a grant from the Center for the Study of Race and Ethnicity at the University of California, San Diego, is a testament to the willingness of its junior and senior authors to listen to and learn from each other, over many days and at several conferences. Despite endless revisions and painful cuts, we have remained friends, united in our commitment to bilingual excellence in the education of Latinas and Latinos in the United States and in our hope that the families that welcomed us into their lives achieve their dreams. Special thanks to another friend, Joan Manes, for helping me think things through when I got stuck. *Y para mi papito querido, mi amor sin límite por acompañarme* through thick and thin. *Que Dios me los bendiga a todos.*

About CABE

The **California Association for Bilingual Education** (CABE) is a state-wide nonprofit organization established in 1976. CABE is recognized at the state level, as well as nationally and internationally, as a premier source of professional development for educators, parents, and the wider community. CABE's vision is "Biliteracy and Educational Equity for All." This vision is based on the premise that students in the 21st century, in order to succeed and be powerful forces in our communities, have to be: 1) academically prepared; 2) multilingual; 3) knowledgeable of the diversity in our multicultural global society; 4) information and technology literate; and 5) civically oriented and active advocates for their communities. As a statewide advocacy-based organization, CABE's mission is to : "Promote and Support Educational Excellence and Social Justice for All."

Perspectives on Language and Literacy in Latino Families and Communities

Ana Celia Zentella

LATINOS NOW TOP MINORITY [*Los Angeles Times* headline]
Census Bureau estimates group's U.S. population at 38.8 million, ahead of blacks for the first time. Demographers see even more growth ahead.

(*Alonso-Zaldívar*, 2003)

The U.S. Census Bureau began forecasting a Hispanic 21st century several decades before the Latino majority among minorities became official in 2003. Comedian John Leguizamo jokingly refers to mainstream America's reaction as "His-panic," preferring *Latino* as a result. Whether the label is the one employed by the federal government (*Hispanic*) or the one favored by community activists (*Latino/a*), the repercussions of Hispanophobia are no laughing matter.[1] Destructive media images of "torrents," "hordes," "engulfing waves," and "a brown tide rising" (Santa Ana, 2002) inflame national fears of displacement and degeneration, amidst the most repressive anti-immigrant and English-only legislation since the xenophobic era of World War I (Crawford, 1992). Most worrisome are the outrageous denunciations of the depletion of the nation's favorable genetic pool by inferior immigrant stock (Brimelow, 1995; Herrnstein & Murray, 1994; Huntington, 2004; Lamm & Imhoff, 1985). Unscientific notions of race and language, and essentialized views of "Americans" versus "others," impede crucial national conversations about immigrants and their children.

Latinos have been construed as a monolithic bloc that threatens the future of the English language in the United States and as an unrelenting drain on the nation's resources. In reality, most Latino youth prefer to speak and read English, and Latino buying power is growing at a rate that is nearly three times that of non-Hispanic Whites, reaching $580.5 billion in 2002

(*Getting the Message Out to Young Latinos*, 2002, p. C1). Latino parents, portrayed as unwilling or unable to adopt the language and behaviors that guarantee success, are blamed for the high Hispanic dropout rate, which is double that of White students and one-third more than the African American rate (Fry, 2003). Even Latino spokespersons, including the first Hispanic secretary of education, Lauro Cavazos, and Linda Chavez, the former executive director of U.S. English, have accused Hispanic parents of being uninterested in their children's education (Chavez, 2000). In this negative climate, which constructs Latino parents and children as deficient and unwilling to assimilate, educators and other professionals in social work, health, and law are hard-pressed to find the encouragement, knowledge, and support required for their jobs.

This book views the rich language and literacy beliefs and practices of Latinos through the lens of the powerful historical, economic, and political contexts that shape them. The contributors to this volume highlight the inter- and intragroup diversity of Latino communities and the efforts that families make to cross linguistic and cultural frontiers. Children of Mexican, Caribbean, and Central American origin are socialized to speak and read—and to value speaking and reading—by negotiating overlapping or conflicting cultural models. Some lessons about language and literacy at home are the same as those learned in school, while others differ from the ways in which teachers expect children to perform in class. We suggest a variety of approaches that can help professionals and parents appreciate and build on the strength of Latino youngsters' skills. Though the bad news is that there is no one magic bullet, the good news is that there are many ways to intervene—including tapping into productive resources that students bring from home.

UNDERSTANDING LATINO COMPLEXITY

The number of Hispanics in the United States is expected to reach 60 million by 2020, amounting to 18% of the total population (Alonso-Zaldivar, 2003), and expanding far beyond the southwest. New Mexico remains the state with the largest Latino population: 42% in 2000 (see Table I.1). In some parts of New England, such as Maine and Vermont, the Latino percentage of the population is less than 1%, but growing rapidly. In other states, for example Texas and California, Latinos represent one third of the state's population. Furthermore, since Latinos are not a homogeneous group, educators everywhere are teaching more and different Latino students every year.

One of every five students in U.S. public schools is either an immigrant or the child of an immigrant, mostly from Latin America (Ochoa, 2003). Because 66.9% of U.S. Latinos trace their origin to Mexico, most statistics reflect the situation of Mexicans. Less is known about Central and South Americans (14% of U.S. Latinos) or Puerto Ricans, all of whom are U.S. citizens (9%, excluding more than 3 million on the island), Cubans (4%), and other Hispanics (6%) (Ramírez & de la Cruz, 2003). Due to the predominance of U.S.-born Mexicans and Puerto Ricans, the majority of the nation's Latinos were born in the United States. Inter- and intragroup diversity becomes greater with each decade, yet monolithic views persist.

The 11 authors of this collection strive to break down the monolithic wall that Latinos represent for many Americans, preventing us from joining hands. Based on extensive experience in the communities they write about, they encourage reaching out to Latino families by providing a historical, political, and cultural context for the language attitudes and socialization practices that help determine what and how the children speak, read, and write. The result is a fascinatingly complex portrait of adult caregivers of Mexican, Salvadoran, Guatemalan, Puerto Rican, Dominican, and Cuban backgrounds—including immigrants and native-born, monolinguals and bilinguals, working- and middle-class members in the West, Midwest, Southwest, Southeast, and Northeast—that contests homogeneous views of Latino culture. Up-close analyses of the two-way socialization of children and adults at home, in church, at school, and in a community organization reveal idiosyncrasies that distinguish Latinos from each other and the dominant society as well as similarities that unite them. *Mexicanos* in San Antonio, northern California, and Chicago are similar to Dominicans in New York in espousing contradictory views toward the role of schools in maintaining Spanish. An upper-class South American mother and middle-class Puerto Rican parents stress biliteracy equally, while some working-class Puerto Ricans across the generations are more passionate about behavior and *educación* (education that emphasizes respect) than books. Inevitably, readers must reject a view of Latino parents as monolithic and unconcerned about education or unwilling to help their children succeed, contrasted with an idealistic model of an equally monolithic but always caring and concerned Anglo middle class.

THE VALUE OF A LANGUAGE SOCIALIZATION FOCUS

This book represents a radical departure from the ways in which most educators have been taught to think about first-language acquisition and second-language learning. Biological, psychological, and linguistic approaches have concentrated on stages of development in pronunciation and grammar in the first language and on possible areas of structural conflict with the second language (Malmkjaer, 1991, summarizes two centuries of research). Researchers have proven that the processes and stages of acquisition are similar

TABLE I.1. Latino Population in the United States by
State, 2000

State	Total Population	Latino Population, Percentage of Total
Alabama	4,447,100	1.7
Alaska	626,932	4.1
Arizona	5,130,632	25.3
Arkansas	2,673,400	3.2
California	33,871,648	32.4
Colorado	4,301,261	17.1
Connecticut	3,405,565	9.4
Delaware	783,600	4.8
District of Columbia	572,059	7.9
Florida	15,982,378	16.8
Georgia	8,186,453	5.3
Hawaii	1,211,537	7.2
Idaho	1,293,953	7.9
Illinois	12,419,293	12.3
Indiana	6,080,485	3.5
Iowa	2,962,324	2.8
Kansas	2,686,418	7.0
Kentucky	4,041,769	1.5
Louisiana	4,468,976	2.4
Maine	1,274,923	0.7
Maryland	5,296,486	4.3
Massachusetts	6,349,097	6.8
Michigan	9,938,444	3.3
Minnesota	4,919,479	2.9
Mississippi	2,844,658	1.4
Missouri	5,595,211	2.1

Montana	902,195	2.0
Nebraska	1,711,263	5.5
Nevada	1,998,257	19.7
New Hampshire	1,235,786	1.7
New Jersey	8,414,350	13.3
New Mexico	1,819,046	42.1
New York	18,976,457	15.1
North Carolina	8,049,313	4.7
North Dakota	642,200	1.2
Ohio	11,353,140	1.9
Oklahoma	3,450,654	5.2
Oregon	3,421,399	8.0
Pennsylvania	12,281,054	3.2
Rhode Island	1,048,319	8.7
South Carolina	4,012,012	2.4
South Dakota	754,844	1.4
Tennessee	5,689,283	2.2
Texas	20,851,820	32.0
Utah	2,233,169	9.0
Vermont	608,827	0.9
Virginia	7,078,515	4.7
Washington	5,894,121	7.5
West Virginia	1,808,344	0.7
Wisconsin	5,363,675	3.6
Wyoming	493,782	6.4
Puerto Rico (U.S. Territory)	3,808,610	98.8

Source: U.S. Bureau of the Census (2000e).

in one or two languages and that bilingualism, which is the norm in most of the world, does not cause language delay or cognitive deficiency. Some may argue the pros and cons of initially learning to read in the first or second language, or the extent to which concepts and skills are transferable from one language to the other (see Cummins, 2000), but all linguists agree that "there is no reason why parents who wish to bring up their children bilingually should not do so" (Malmkjaer, 1991, p. 61). Unfortunately, this information has not reached all parents and educators, and the perspective we offer in this book is even less widely known.

Since the late 20th century, there has been a growing emphasis on the social context in language acquisition and the learning of language(s) as a key part of cultural apprenticeship (i.e., essential to how one learns to be a member of culture). Hymes (1974) in particular argued against the linguists' limited notion of grammatical competence in favor of communicative competence. A robot or machine might learn the grammatical structures of a language and even how to pronounce it perfectly, but in order to communicate effectively, a human has to know what, when, where, how, and why to speak—patterns that are rooted in each speaker's culture. Partly as a result of Hymes and others in his ethnolinguistic tradition, the divisions between the biological, psychological, linguistic, and cultural approaches have become blurred; the interaction "between the child's internal system and the linguistic environment" is now a given (Malmkjaer, 1991, p. 249).

Building on the contributions of the preceding traditions, language socialization researchers go beyond studying adults' verbal input and children's output to include how the activities of caretakers and their charges are socially and linguistically organized, involving "the structuring of knowledge, emotion, and social action" (Ochs, 2001, p. 227). The vocabulary children pick up and the structures they produce require cognitive and linguistic maturation, but they are also evidence of their cultural group's worldview. If a community consistently reports that the first word of infants is "*papi*" (daddy) and considers "*qué?*" (what?) an inappropriate reply to an elder's call, as is true in many Latino families, those patterns signal beliefs about appropriate gender and age roles that may affect how children learn. Getting at the "architecture" of parent–child collaboration that is socialization, as Ochs suggests, and adopting a comparative perspective will open doors to more effective communication across languages and cultures. This approach is worlds apart from the repetitive oral–aural drills in English designed to produce automatic responses and from the contrastive analysis of the rules of Spanish and English pronunciation, word formation, and sentence structure. Children who are taught to memorize routines for greeting and leave-taking that conflict with child-appropriate patterns in their culture may rile their elders if they use them at home. Similarly, effort devoted to replacing the trilled Spanish *r* with the retroflex English *r* or double with single negatives ("can't do nothing"), while helpful, may miss more fundamental differences in communication.

Language socialization research sheds light on the subtle yet significant contrasts between the cultural ways that students use language in their communities and the language genres of the classroom, whether the languages are the same or different. As described in Chapter 1, the best of this research was inspired by Heath's (1983) impressive work with White and Black working- and middle-class communities that differed in the way they talked, read, and told stories. Teachers who incorporated the communities' "ways with words" in their classes helped students expand their repertoires dramatically.

While Heath studied communities in the southern United States, the seminal work of Ochs and Schieffelin (1984) and of Schieffelin and Ochs (1986, 1989) in Samoa and New Guinea, respectively, cemented language socialization as a respected field of study. Their dual emphasis on socialization *to* language, [i.e., how children become speakers of the language(s) of their community] and socialization *through* language (i.e., how children learn to become culturally competent members of their community via language) resulted in powerful cross-cultural insights (details in Chapter 1, this volume). The patterns of language socialization that distinguished the Samoans and the Kaluli of New Guinea on the one hand from middle-class Anglo Americans on the other were rooted in contrasting ideologies about individual achievement and autonomy. Mainstream American families address the child as an individual more than as a member of the group. Accordingly, caretakers in these communities adapt their speech and their children's speech in keeping with contrasting models of child development.

LANGUAGE SOCIALIZATION IN LATINO COMMUNITIES

Researchers who tried to apply the Ochs and Schieffelin findings to Latino families found similarities as well as internal diversity, changes over time, and crossover patterns (Bayley & Schecter, 2003; González, 2001; Schechter & Bayley, 2002; Zentella, 1997a). Some Latino caregivers do not adapt the situation to the child, and prefer directives instead of indirect ways of orienting the child to the group's norms. But the assumption that there is a general lack of fit between home and school practices in regard to directives contradicts the evidence from numerous Latino families (Chapters 3 and 4, this volume). As Garrett and Baquedano-López (2002) point out, language socialization models and methods must be expanded and applied to multilingual situations. This volume helps fill the void by introducing readers to language and literacy in Latino homes, churches, and schools across the country.

To date, most language socialization studies of bilingual populations in the United States have focused on one community and/or ethnic background. There are significant book-length ethnographies by Vásquez, Pease-Alvarez, and Shannon (1994) on Mexicans in the California Bay area, Zentella (1997a) on Puerto Ricans in New York City, González (2001) on Mexicans in Phoenix, Schecter and Bayley (2002) on Mexicans in northern California and San Antonio, and Farr (in press) on Mexicans in Chicago. Our book is the first to focus on language socialization practices among a diverse group of Latinos in diverse settings: Mexicans, Central Americans, Puerto Ricans, Dominicans, and Cubans in Los Angeles, San Diego, San Antonio, Tucson, Chicago, New York, and Miami.

Readers will learn that different Latino caregivers take different approaches with children at different times, and some of it is a very good fit with what is expected in the classroom. Even when cultural differences seem to explain why some Latino children do not elaborate extensively or do not speak up in class, it is counterproductive to view the problem as lodged in the home, and ultimately the mothers' fault, especially when so little is known about the funds of knowledge of the home (Chapter 9, this volume). At issue is the interplay of some overlapping and some distinct cultural traditions, assimilatory forces, individual agency, and institutional expectations, as well as the difficulty of assessing the relative importance of each.

"DOING BEING" BILINGUAL AND LATINO IN SPANISH, ENGLISH, AND SPANGLISH

Subjected to the pushes and pulls of transnational networks, religious and secular models, and conflicting Black/White/Mestizo/Indio/Latino racialized identities, Latino children often communicate their complex reality in bilingual and multidialectal speech patterns that are misunderstood and devalued. Auer (1984) speaks of "doing being bilingual" to underscore the dynamic process involved in being bilingual and the context-dependent ways in which individuals and communities are bilingual in different ways at different times; the same can be said of "doing being" Latina or Latino.

Bilingual and Latino identities in the United States are constructed in Spanish and English ethnic dialects that serve as badges of membership in specific communities. Spanish dialects in the United States repeat the sounds and structures of the homeland variety, as set forth in Lipski (1994). The inevitable contribution of English borrowings and frequent language alternation is sometimes labeled Spanglish, Tex-Mex, or *pocho*, and mistakenly considered a linguistic mishmash (Zentella, 1990, 1997b). The extent to which a group is proud of its variety of Spanish can determine whether or not group members teach Spanish to their children, and language attitudes are an indelible part of language socialization. Prescriptive attitudes against southwestern Spanish made one mother decide not to teach her child Spanish because her husband was a non-standard speaker (Chapter 2, this volume), and a New York–born Puerto Rican mother spoke Spanish to Rodríguez (Chapter 8, this volume), but not to her children, because she thought the researcher's Castilian Spanish dialect was *bonito* (pretty), unlike hers.

Negative attitudes toward the ways that Latinos speak English can prove equally damaging. A stereotypical Spanish accent is the butt of jokes in the popular media, even though most Latinos were born in the United States and many do not speak English with a Spanish accent. Children can be misidentified as English-language learners when in fact they are native speakers of an ethnic dialect of English, such as Chicano English or Puerto Rican English. Although the linguistic details remain to be studied, these varieties borrow some features from immigrant Spanish and others from local working-class White and Black dialects, contributing to their low status (Bayley & Santa Ana, 2004; Fought, 2003; Santa Ana & Bayley, 2004; Urciuoli, 1996).

Dialect dissing and Spanglish bashing amplify the powerless status of Latinos (Zentella, 2002). Parents may try hard to encourage English and pass on Spanish along with their moral views about language, but they are not immune to attacks voiced in national debates about bilingual education and English-only laws, feelings of guilt about their lack of English, or blows delivered by their own children (Chapter 10, this volume). Fortunately, some youngsters manage to resist Hispanophobic attitudes and policies by fashioning alternative conceptualizations of the linkages among language, nation, race, and ethnicity; they embrace hybrid linguistic and cultural creations that contest the oppressive policies that buttress dominant discourses (Chapter 11, this volume).

THE ANTHROPOLITICAL PERSPECTIVE

The contributors to this volume approach their communities from a perspective linked to what Zentella (1997a, 2002) has termed "anthropolitical linguistics," that is, research that sees through the language smokescreen that obscures ideological, structural, and political impediments to equity. Highlighting an anthropolitical perspective makes clear our opposition to the scientific experimental approach to education that is increasingly favored by governmental agencies, because it drowns out the multiple voices of our communities and hides the impact of powerful external forces, particularly the dominant language ideology. Instead, we stress how Latinos—and all of us—are enmeshed in socioeconomic and political realities as well as some-times conflicting cultural frameworks that shape our ways of speaking and our ideas about life. The choices Latinos make about how to raise their children in the United States depend on the information and opportunities they are given and their ability to counteract the damaging language ideologies shaped by the market value of English, English-only campaigns, and a legacy of linguistic purism and linguistic insecurity that is erasing Spanish. Most worrisome, as Urciuoli (2001) points out, is that as overt racism has become less acceptable in public discourse, "race has been remapped from biology onto language" (p. 201), allowing notions of inherent inferiority to be transferred to the languages of racialized minorities with impunity. As a consequence, the anthropolitical perspective shares a concern with "language as an instrument for gaining access to complex social processes," which Duranti (2003, p. 332) places in the vanguard of the study of language as culture.

We aim to introduce the lay reader to basic concepts of language socialization, the diversity of practices within Latino communities, and their educational implications. Most of the chapters are based on months or years of ethnographic observations and analysis of audio recordings, but we have omitted the linguistic details on discourse that are characteristic of traditional language socialization studies in order to leave room for practical applications. Accordingly, the transcription conventions that appear in the excerpts of recorded speech are basic.[2] Specifically, we tackle mainstream views of childhood and of the role and nature of language socialization, urging readers to consider "socialization from what to what?" (Chapter 11, this volume). We note the tension between group culture and individual agency, particularly as it refers to conventional stereotypes of Latinos as family-oriented, Catholic, devoted to Spanish, and male dominated (Johnson, 2000). The cleavages within each Latino group along generational, regional, class, and racial lines are as important as distinctions based on national origin. Each chapter is a testimony to the fact that no group stands outside a tradition of meaning and value, to its benefit, and together they suggest some universal practices that facilitate language socialization in multilingual communities, to the benefit of all.

THE BOOK'S CHAPTERS

Every contributor to this volume encourages readers to question essentialist links between cultural groups and behaviors, which assume that all Latinos, or working-class Puerto Ricans, or middle-class Cubans, and so on are the same. We underscore, instead, the situated nature of particular family or community orientations to speaking and reading, and the resulting inter- and intra-group divisions.

In Chapter 1, Zentella describes the premises of the language socialization framework that has provided seminal models of contrasting childrearing patterns in monolingual cultures and alerts readers to the challenges that bilingual communities represent. Examples include her own childhood and contemporary observations of Colombians and Puerto Ricans in New York City. Caregivers experience bilingualism differently in response to personal and group migration histories, state and local policies, and the depth of transnational networks. As a result, their children are exposed to changing and sometimes conflicting orientations to language at home and in the schools, even within communities of the same ethnic background. Chapters 2, 3, and 4 analyze family patterns in four Mexican communities: the San Francisco Bay Area of California, San Antonio, Chicago, and Los Angeles.

Bayley and Schecter (Chapter 2) explain why some families in California and Texas adopt the school language at home while others do not, albeit in the pursuit of similar goals. *Mexicanos* also differ in the ways they speak to children depending on their regional origin, as Farr and Domínguez Barajas (Chapter 3) document in their analysis of the frank and playful speech of *rancheros* in Chicago. Bhimji (Chapter 4) found similar speech in Los Angeles, as well as directives and other forms of persuasion usually not attributed to working-class families. These analyses are applicable to the language styles that teachers employ and those they expect students to master. In Chapter 5, Ek reminds educators that religious institutions play a critical role regarding language and literacy. The church she studied links Spanish literacy to staying on God's path and expects the youth to do well in public school, but it also conveys contradictory messages about the outside world, including the schools.

The children described in these chapters include the most visible and invisible, the most fortunate and unfortunate. Lavadenz (Chapter 6) points out that Central Americans are plagued by memories of the violent turmoil in their homelands that forced them to flee to Los Angeles where they feel invisible and struggle against being culturally and linguistically swamped by the local Mexican population. Roca (Chapter 7) offers a personal account of raising a privileged bilingual and biliterate toddler in Miami with the help of the city's Latinos, despite the lack of commitment of its educational system. Rodríguez (Chapter 8) takes us into Dominican homes in New York City, where parents of children with language disabilities support homework tasks despite their limited English and difficulties with the special education bureaucracy. She underscores the need for educators who are sensitive to the painful burdens of the caregivers of students with special needs and who can explain alternative programs and student evaluations clearly. Mercado (Chapter 9) reports on her efforts to help teachers "see what's there" in the homes of their underachieving New York Puerto Rican students, with particular attention to language as one of the families' many funds of knowledge that can be an effective resource in the classroom.

In the final chapters, socialization outside the home is a central focus. Relaño Pastor (Chapter 10) analyzes Latina mothers' encounters with teachers, priests, and their own children that shape their moral views about language. They demand respect for Spanish and for their attempts to speak English and want to pass on those values to their children, but they wrestle with conflicting feelings. Finally, González (Chapter 11) demonstrates how the children in a successful dual-language program challenged the narrow and disempowering discourse promoted during a statewide effort to crush bilingual education in Arizona. Those children, with a polyphony of voices that celebrated leprechauns and mariachis, and all the families in the book reflect the new approaches to education and language that Latinos are advancing, awaiting our committed cooperation. The Afterword highlights the common ground in the chapters that we hope will encourage educators and parents to join forces and build on the strength in Latino families *con educación, respeto, y confianza* (with education, respect, and confidence).

NOTES

1. In this book, the term *Hispanic* appears when official policies or census data are cited. Elsewhere, we prefer *Latino*, shorthand for the more explicitly gender-inclusive but cumbersome *Latina(s) and Latino(s)*, because it is a Spanish term that acknowledges the Latin American origin of immigrants.

2. **Transcription conventions:**

.	indicates falling intonation.
—	indicates a cut-off word or false start.
<u>word</u>	indicates emphasis on underlined item.
WOrd	uppercase indicates loudness.
(1.2)	numbers in parenthesis indicate silence in tenths of a second.
. . .	indicates missing part of a sentence.
. . . .	indicates complete sentence omitted.
HHH	indicates laughter.
xxx	indicates unitelligible word(s)
* * * *	indicates change of topic, omitted.
/werd/	phonemic transcription
<o>	spelling

Premises, Promises, and Pitfalls of Language Socialization Research in Latino Families and Communities

Ana Celia Zentella

Latino parents are often blamed for the educational failures of their children, including the fact that almost half of U.S. Hispanics (44%) have less than a high school education, compared to 13% of the rest of the nation (Suárez-Orozco & Páez, 2002). Parents are accused of not helping with homework or the learning of English, not attending school parent–teacher meetings, and not reading to children or providing books. Even the first Hispanic secretary of education (Lauro Cavazos, under President George H.W. Bush) charged that Hispanic parents did not care enough about their children's education.

Those who know how much Latino parents want their children to succeed could mount a more convincing defense if they understood how different groups of Latinos view their role in the development of children's oral and literate abilities, and how they go about implementing those views. But the complexity of Latino communities is daunting, and descriptions of parental practices are not enough to connect teachers with caregivers as effective partners. The ideology that sustains the practices that sustain the families—and how what parents do at home with language and literacy is perceived by the dominant society—must form the core of educators' understanding. Immigrant parents are misunderstood not only because of the infamous language barrier but also because parental efforts are evaluated with reference to a foreign and conflicting model of what it takes to be a competent parent. Language socialization researchers go beyond "the problem is they don't speak English" to investigate which immigrant traditions are functional or dysfunctional in mainstream schools and other institutions that determine whether children flourish or fail. They ask: Which language and literacy practices do immigrant families keep and pass on to the next generations and why, which do they leave by the wayside or transform, and which new practices do they adopt? They seek answers within the context of the worldview that makes sense to the families and guides their practices, and they seek to highlight "the recursive, mutually constitutive nature of the relationship between social structure and individual agency" (Garrett & Baquendano-López, 2002, p. 344). Without these insights, gatekeepers in schools, health facilities, and social service offices may impede Latino children's access to a solid education, decent jobs, and good medical care because they misconstrue the values and practices of the home. When I recall my childhood in the South Bronx in New York City with my Puerto Rican mother and Mexican father, I shudder to think how Secretary of Education Cavazos and those who agree with him would have judged my parents.

My sister and I never saw our parents read a full-length book in English or Spanish, although they read letters from Puerto Rico and Mexico, the *New York Daily News* and *El Diario*, and *mami* had prayer books. But there were no novels, no bookshelves, no magazines on coffee tables, and least of all cookbooks. I did not get books as gifts, nor did I consider a book a desirable present, and I was not read to. The library books I brought home were never the topic of family discussions, and I did my homework alone. *Mami* used to yell at me to stop reading late into the night. She said that so much reading was bad for me; it could *volverme loca*, that is, drive me crazy. I continued to read, to my peril. I remember vividly the day I read, almost 20 years after I left home, the following line in a classic study of Puerto Rican families in East Harlem in the 1950s: "It is held that too much studying or reading is detrimental to the child's health, because too much weakens the brain and a person may go crazy from overstudying" (Padilla, 1958, p. 209). I was impressed, not having expected a book to enlighten me about my mother's attitude to my study habits. So the fact that she thought too much reading would *volverme loca* was not an idiosyncrasy of my mother's or an ignorant effort to stifle my education or keep me from reading the world, but a cultural folk belief. I wanted to know more, but Padilla's study stopped short of explaining how that Puerto Rican view was related to the culture's ideas of what is important in life. Also, I wondered why my mother prized "common sense," her favorite words in the English language, much more than a high IQ. Whenever teachers told *mami* I had a high IQ, she would rephrase that concept in her inimitable way: "Yes," she would say, "she has plenty ICE CUBES, but they are melting in her brain because she has no common sense." *Mami* distrusted IQ scores and book learning and favored common sense and creativity, especially being, as she pronounced it, "oriyinal" (original). All her life, if I happened to say something she considered on target or insightful, she would demand: "*¿Eso es tuyo, o te lo leíste en algún libro?*" (Is that your own [idea], or did you read it in a book?) It just didn't count as much if it wasn't "oriyinal."

Mami's attitudes led me to wonder about the ways in which Puerto Rican and other Latino families in the United States orient their children to speaking, reading, writing, and learning—in their home language or in English. What similarities or differences within and across cultures are there in how children are expected to learn how to talk, to produce and interpret written texts, and to demonstrate what they know? What counts as being smart in different groups? How are those patterns linked to overarching ideologies? Most important, do differences at home make a difference in school; that is, how do children who follow language-related rules unlike those of the dominant society fare in U.S. classrooms? Bilingual kindergarten teachers like my sister wonder why so many 5-year-olds from immigrant families seem unable to answer simple questions, in English or Spanish. And all teachers want to know whether they can count on immigrant parents to be co-teachers in the home. Language socialization research *promises* to answer these questions, but its *premises* can obscure certain *pitfalls* when it is not carried out properly, and the end result may reinforce the blame laid at the feet of Latino parents, especially mothers. This chapter addresses those promises, premises, and pitfalls, as a step toward reversing the frustration and failure that distress parents and teachers alike.

PREMISES OF LANGUAGE SOCIALIZATION RESEARCH

The basic premise of language socialization research is that "language learning is cultural learning" (Heath, 1986, p. 145). Even before children learn to speak, they begin to learn the rules for becoming a competent member of their society through the language(s) of their caregivers. Hymes's (1972) pivotal notion of "communicative competence" stressed that knowledge of the rules for the conduct and interpretation of speech is more crucial than grammatical competence, that is, knowledge of phonology, semantics, and grammar. Schieffelin and Ochs (1986, 1989) underscored the tandem role of language in socialization by pointing out that children are socialized *through* language and *to* language at the same time. Put another way, language is the vehicle via which a group's ways of "being" and "doing" are learned, while children also learn to use the linguistic codes of their communities in culturally specific ways in order to be communicatively competent, not just grammatically proficient. Latino children frequently acquire two or more codes, because many are raised in communities that are bilingual and multidialectal. For example, Puerto Rican children in New York's El Barrio are raised as Puerto Ricans in the popular and standard Puerto Rican varieties of Spanish and/or English that are spoken to them. They also learn to speak one or more of those varieties of Spanish and English and to use them in Puerto Rican ways. In addition, they may pick up the African American Vernacular English of close friends and neighbors and the Dominican dialect of co-workers and in-laws, as well as other dialects of Spanish or English spoken in their primary networks (Zentella, 1997a). Multidialectalism also charac-terizes many Mexican American communities, although the verbal repertoire is different (Fought, 2003).

All cultural groups orient their children to language in keeping with their particular worldview, including "local theories of mind and emotion, local concepts of paths to knowledge, local modes of legal and political decision making, language ideologies and the like" (Ochs, 2001, p. 228). Views about the nature of language and the role of parenting in its acquisition may differ from one group to another, and not all groups offer explicit training in lan-guage or recognize the same developmental stages. Different orientations result in different norms for the social conduct of speech, such as to whom children should speak, about what, and how, when, where, and why they should speak. In the real world, these orientations and the linguistic codes via and to which children are socialized are never evaluated dispassionately, but many of our prejudices remain unchallenged. Bourdieu (1991, p. 43) denounced "the illusion of linguistic communism"—that is, the idea that everyone has equal and unfettered access to the code that enjoys the greatest linguistic capital—while the processes that ensure the inferiority of popula-tions that speak minority languages and dialects remain invisible. In main-stream institutions like public schools, children are subjected to methods and attitudes steeped in prejudices, and they receive little help with juggling the competing linguistic and cultural demands of the home and outside world. Fairclough insists, correctly, that no substantive and lasting educational change can take place without "critical language study," which "highlights how language conventions and language practices are invested with power relations and ideological processes which people are often unaware of" (quoted in Valdés, 1998, p. 16). My version of a similar approach, wedded to a commitment to seek redress for unequal language and power relation-ships, is "anthropolitical linguistics" (Zentella, 1997a). From an anthro-political linguistic perspective, language socialization research must unmask the ways in which one or more group's ways of speaking or raising children are constructed as inferior to the benefit of the continued domination of a powerful class, and it must challenge the policies that encourage and enforce subjugation. Of particular concern is the construction of the most burdened and vulnerable members of an oppressed community—mothers in poverty—as unfit parents and, consequently, unworthy citizens. Monolingual and bi-lingual communities are both affected because different languages and dialects of the same language are invested with contrasting amounts of cultural capital, reflecting the socioeconomic and racial status of their speakers. The study of African American Vernacular English in the United States has advanced the most on this front (Baugh, 2000; Labov, 1972a, 1972b; Lanehart, 2002; Morgan, 2002; Rickford & Rickford, 2000; Smitherman, 1999).

Language socialization research in bilingual immigrant populations is in its infancy, but the field itself is solidly rooted in the groundbreaking cross-cultural work of Bambi Schieffelin and Elinor Ochs (1986), who contrasted the interactions between (monolingual) caregivers and young children in traditional Samoan and Papua New Guinea cultures with those of (monolingual English-speaking) Anglo American White middle-class families. They found the traditional cultures to be situation-centered (s-c) in their socialization of children, in contrast to the child-centered (c-c) Anglo American middle class, and they linked each pattern to distinct ideologies about individual achievement and autonomy. Figure 1.1, based on Ochs and Schieffelin (1984), reveals that the two approaches are polar opposites, distinguished primarily by how much adults adjust their speech when talking with children and how much they adjust the children's speech. As the pluses and minuses in the figure indicate, adults in s-c families do not simplify their speech to children or expand their children's speech, unlike adults in c-c families, who do both.

In general, social groups that are more situation-centered, like the Kaluli of Papua New Guinea and Western Samoans, adapt children to the situation at hand, whereas child-centered groups, like the Anglo American middle class, adapt the situation to the child. The specific areas in which the s-c and c-c caregivers differ in levels of adaptation are the following:

1. *Caregivers' register*: Do caregivers use simplified speech when they talk to children (c-c) or unsimplified speech (s-c)?
2. *Meaning*: Do caregivers negotiate what the child means by expanding and paraphrasing what the child says (c-c), or do they interpret the child's meaning according to local norms (s-c)?
3. *Participant status*: Are caregiver and child considered equal cooperative partners in proposition building (c-c), or are children more likely to be directed to address or take into account other people (s-c)?
4. *Topic*: Do child-initiated topics take precedence (c-c) over the caregiver's wishes for the child to respond to the situation at hand (s-c)?
5. *Typical communicative situation*: Is communication normally two-party, limited to caregiver and child (c-c), or are others usually present (s-c)?

Groups that do not simplify language, treat infants as conversational equals, and convert children's speech into an adult model strive "to socialize chil-

FiGURE 1.1. Situation-Centered and Child-Centered Socialization

Adult Speech	Type of Family	
	Situation-centered	Child-centered
Simplification by caregivers of speech to child	−	+
Expansion by caregivers of speech by child	−	+

Child-centered	Areas	Situation-centered
Simplified baby talk, short utterances, focused on here-and-now	Register	Unsimplified modeling: child directed to repeat to third party in wide range of speech acts and situationally appropriate registers
Negotiated via expansion and paraphrase	Meaning	Interpreted via local expectations of child language and behavior
Cooperative proposition building between caregiver and child	Participant Status	Child directed to notice others
Child-initiated verbal or nonverbal acts	Topic	Arises from caregiver wishes for child to respond to range of situational circumstances
Two-party	Typical Communicative Situation	Multiparty

dren into culturally appropriate persons and this goal may override any goal relating to drawing out and validating the child as author of a unique personal message" (Ochs & Schieffelin, 1995, p. 78). In contrast, caregivers in c-c families often try to meet an infant at its own level by employing baby talk, for example, "Baby do wee-wee or poo-poo?" English speakers are not the only speakers of baby talk; many cultures have a word for it. In Puerto Rico it is known as *chiquiteo*, and in the Dominican Republic as *hablar chiquito* (to speak small). The baby-talk register, described by Charles Ferguson in 1964, consists of "consonant cluster reduction, reduplication, exaggerated prosodic contours, slowed pace, shorter sentences, syntactically less complex sentences, temporal orientation to the here and now, and repetition and paraphrasing of sentences" (Ochs & Schieffelin, 1995, p. 74). With or without baby talk,

> the child centered caregiver helps adapt the situation to the child by conversing with the child as a conversational partner, seeking out child appropriate topics and tailoring the talk to the child's level, simplifying and repeating, engaging the child in regular routines, eliciting clarifications and elaborations, and expanding and extending the child's speech—all the while communicating in a very sympathetic tone of voice—an "affect laden register." (Pease-Alvarez & Vásquez, 1994, p. 84)

This description could be the voice-over of a video of my niece's interactions with her 3-year-old. The style is so prevalent in mainstream Western societies that it comes as a surprise to many members of the middle class that not all children are raised in this way. The c-c model is as powerful a part of the dominant norm as Standard English, and its status is such that we tend to evaluate parents favorably if they raise their children in this way and negatively if they do not.

PROMISES OF LANGUAGE SOCIALIZATION RESEARCH

U.S. schools are unprepared for the increasing linguistic and cultural challenges they face. Latino enrollment alone in public schools grew by more than 4 million, or 291%, between 1968 and 1998, and it continues unabated (Orfield, 2002). The promise of language socialization research is that informed educators should be able to communicate more successfully with diverse groups of students by reducing the potential conflicts between the schools' ways of teaching and learning and those of the cultures of their students. Researchers inspired by Shirley Heath's seminal book *Ways with Words* (1983) have corroborated the validity of this promise. Heath documented the language genres and literacy events in three monolingual English-speaking populations in the Carolinas (Black and/or White, working and middle classes) and the ways in which each community's "ways with words" affected the academic success of their children. Most important, she proved that teachers could tap into each community's ways with words to help failing students learn to read and write at or above grade level, once they understood that what they thought was the right and only way for parents to teach children was in fact only *one* way.

Heath (1986) identified six verbal genres that mainstream school-oriented homes and classrooms shared, all of which are linked to the adaptations of child-centered families in the Ochs and Schieffelin model:

1. *Label quests*: Naming items or their attributes, or asking "What's/who's this/that?" type questions.
2. *Meaning quests*: Inferring the child's meaning; for example, the baby says, "Up mommy," and the mother says, "You want to get up on my lap."
3. *Recounts*: Asking for retelling of incidents or information known to listener and child; for example, "Tell Grandpa what we did this morning."
4. *Accounts*: Giving new information or interpretation; for example, "How did you get around in the zoo?"
5. *Event casts*: Providing running narratives of present events or forecasts; for example, "First we'll get dressed, then we'll go to visit Grandma, and then we'll go to the park."
6. *Stories*: Fictional accounts of characters involved in a series of events.

Children who get years of practice with these language genres at home can be expected to perform better, when they enter kindergarten or first grade, than those who have had little exposure to them. Success in school is facilitated in part because teachers interpret children's familiarity with the ways language is used in the classroom as evidence that those children are ready and willing to learn and that their parents care about their education. The mainstream family practice of the "bedtime story" serves as an effective introduction to the schools' approach to print, the alphabet, narrative structure, the organization of texts, and books as sources of pleasure and facts (Heath, 1982). In the lower-working-class African American homes that Heath observed, reading was often a group practice in which children and adults responded to texts in personally involved ways and interpretations were shared verbally. The success of the teachers who incorporated Heath's findings led to a call for modifying the culture of the classroom to accommodate the cultures of the students. On the other hand, local schools and nationwide public service announcements continually urge parents to adopt the schools' literate behaviors, as if that would guarantee success.

PITFALLS OF LANGUAGE SOCIALIZATION RESEARCH

Relying on home-versus-school conflict models can obscure the more powerful role played by institutional inequalities and racism. Moreover, my lan-

guage socialization research among Latino families in New York City con-
curs with that of others who advise caution in bilingual situations (González,
2001; Schecter & Bayley, 2002), because of three possible pitfalls:

- The danger of *essentializing*; that is, the tendency to posit certain
  behaviors and/or ideologies as essential characteristics of a group,
  thereby ignoring or obscuring inter- and intragroup diversity, particularly as related to national origin, class, and race
- The validation and *privileging of parents who act as teachers of literate behaviors* and otherwise follow a child-centered model, at the
  expense of parents who adopt a different role
- The *implied determinacy* of the research; that is, the view that if parents teach X, then their children only learn X and cannot do Y and Z
  (Schecter & Bayley, 2002)

Failure to avoid these pitfalls results in an analysis that blames the cultures
and the parents, and encourages facile solutions.

Essentializing Groups

Popular labels such as "Spanish speakers," "Latinos," and "Hispanics" suggest a monolithic group, although the members may have little in common
beyond Spain's colonization of their homelands in the 15th and 16th centuries. The more than 35 million people in the United States with roots in 21
Spanish-speaking nations defy *essentialization*, particularly in view of their
increasing numbers and diversity. Between 1990 and 2000 there was a 57%
increase in Latinos in the United States. Mexicans continue to constitute the
majority (58.5%) and Puerto Ricans are still the second-largest group (9.6%),
but their proportions are declining as the numbers of Dominicans, Salvadorans, and Central and South American immigrants grow at a faster pace.
The variety of Spanish that each group speaks serves as a national flag, and
there is a hierarchy of dialects whose status can be traced in part to the varieties spoken by the original settlers and to the impact of indigenous and
African languages. For example, the Spanish of southern Spain that was trans-
ported to the Caribbean and other coastal areas where slaves were later concentrated is less valued than that of Castile, the capital province, which
traveled to the highlands of Latin America (Zentella, 1990). In addition to
national origin and linguistic distinctions, class and race account for telling
intragroup differences that ease the accommodation of some groups and impede that of others (Zentella, 1997b). Not only is there no homogeneous U.S.
Latino community, there is no one Puerto Rican or Mexican or Colombian
community, and even within the same families it is crucial to distinguish

the immigrant members from those born and raised in the United States. Of particular importance are the language proficiencies that range along a bilingual continuum (Silva-Corvalán, 1994), because they determine which linguistic codes children are socialized "to" and "through." At one end of the continuum, less than 10% of all Latinos in the United States are mono-lingual in one or more dialects of Spanish, and at the other, 20% are mono-lingual in one or more dialects of English. All the gradations of Spanish- or English-dominant bilingualism exist in between those poles, with the region-ally/ethnically linked dialects of Spanish (e.g., southwest Mexican, Nuyorican) and English (e.g., Chicano English, Puerto Rican English) suffering the great-est stigma. Nevertheless, the linguistic variables and discourse markers that distinguish the varieties of Latino Spanish and English, most of which re-main undocumented, affirm ethnic solidarity among their speakers (Fought, 2003; Santa Ana & Bayley, 2004; Urciuoli, 1996).

The bilingual and multidialectal complexities of Latino life are not as well known as they should be, even to teachers in daily contact with many Latino students. In southern California's schools, near Mexico's border, "teachers and school administrators across all sites [middle and high schools] underestimated the number of immigrant students in their classrooms and schools by 300%, and simply did not differentiate immigrant students from American-born limited English proficient students" (Ramírez, 2001, pp. 2–3). One major difference between Mexicans and Puerto Ricans, on the one hand, and all other Latino groups, on the other, is that most of the latter were born in Latin America, whereas the majority of Mexicans and Puerto Ricans were born in the United States and tend to be English-dominant. Linguistic and cultural conflicts between immigrant children and those born in the United States surface in every group and are at the root of political differences among the adults (García Bedolla, 2003), but most teachers are not prepared for such conflicts and teach both groups with the same methods and objectives.

Children with distinct proficiency skills in Spanish and English and contrasting orientations to literacy and books can be found in the same classroom, community, or family. *Growing up Bilingual* (Zentella, 1997a) compared five New York Puerto Rican elementary school girls who were raised in the same tenement in a poor community in *El Barrio*, or East Harlem. (In the following descriptions, all the names are pseudonyms.) Isabel, the only child of a loving but alcoholic mother with limited education and income, had little experience with books in English or Spanish and was in special education classes for the language impaired. Her best friend, Lolita, who benefited from her older sister's success in Catholic schools outside of *El Barrio* as well as the guidance of her high school–educated father and work-ing mother, attended the same school as Isabel but was enrolled in the bilin-gual class for intellectually gifted children. As a child, Lolita often read and wrote for Isabel and others, in Spanish and English, with ease. She later went on to community college, whereas Isabel dropped out of tenth grade and had two children before her 19th birthday. Despite Isabel's determined efforts to give her children a better life than she had had, she stated matter-of-factly and unselfconsciously that she never sat down with them to read in English or Spanish.

Quite the opposite situation exists in the home of two sisters, 3 and 6 years old, who live in an eight-room apartment in an exclusive neighborhood. Class differences introduce new variables, including the greater availability of teachers and literacy materials in and outside the home. These upper-class girls have been read to in both languages since they were 1 month old. Their highly educated South American mother and their Central American nanny are available to read to them in Spanish throughout the day, while their wealthy Anglo father reads to them in English every morning and at night. After their day in private schools, the girls return home to their huge double bedroom, with floor to ceiling bookshelves housing more than 150 books in both languages. The 6-year-old has a personal subscription to children's catalogs and magazines, a datebook for keeping track of play dates, and it is her voice that greets callers bilingually on the family's telephone answering machine.

In a much more modest neighborhood not far away, the 5-year-old daughter of parents with degrees from the University of Puerto Rico is also a confident bilingual and is bicultural. The child speaks, reads, and writes Spanish (acquired at home) and English (learned in school) fluently, and she draws on both cultures when she plays music, selects books, draws, and dances. Guitars, *cuatros* (Puerto Rican four-string guitars), *salsa* (contemporary dance rhythms including the mambo), and *bomba* (a traditional Afro Puerto Rican dance) are part of her discourse. In contrast, two U.S.-born college graduates in a lower-middle-class household—a New York–born Puerto Rican mother and an African American father—are raising 6-year-old Crystal in English only, with little reference to Puerto Rican or African American cultures. Crystal's aunt was my undergraduate assistant. She tried to write her field notes on her sister's child in a detached observer's voice, but she could not refrain from comparing her niece unfavorably to the upper-class South American/Anglo and middle-class Puerto Rican children we observed. About Crystal's home, she wrote:

There is little emphasis on daily reading outside of homework. She is read to at the convenience of the parents. She draws and writes—in English only—constantly, but on her own initiative. She also watches TV (or videos) for at least 1½ hours daily, often in her own room while her parents watch TV by themselves in their bedroom. She is engaged in partner conversation occasionally but not constantly. *As a result* [emphasis mine], the child isn't as talkative and has a smaller vocabulary than the other children I observed. When I was present most of the verbal exchange consisted of commands. For example, "Come here so we can go over your homework" or "Sit down" or "Stop jumping", etc. . . . The mother feels that children learn more from observation than explanation.

My student's notes make no mention of the fact that Crystal had suffered a serious ear infection and operation as a toddler, which may have contributed to the differences between her verbal abilities and those of the comparison children. Nor did she mention that the pressures of Crystal's parents' jobs depleted their time and energy during the week, but on the weekends they involved Crystal in visits to family, trips, and other activities that nurtured her oral and literacy skills. Like my student, too many observers are selective about what they focus on in family visits and quick to blame the parents. As Ochs (2002) and all anthropologists insist, it takes long-term ethnography to achieve a holistic portrait. Based on short and incomplete synopses such as the ones I have included here, many teachers might not hesitate to judge which parents are doing a better job and to predict which children will do better in school "as a result," but they could be mistaken.

Privileging a Teacher Model of Caregiving

This brings us to the second pitfall we must be wary of: *the privileging of literate behaviors* and the greater respect given to parents who follow a teacher model of parenting. Even school reform movements can be based on this prejudice. In northern Californian and San Antonio schools, Schecter and Bayley (2002) found that "curricular reform efforts link parental performance of activities that support and extend the school's agenda to children's educability" (pp. 164–165). In other words, the more the child has a caregiver who acts like a teacher, the more the child is considered educable. In one poignant example, Schecter observed a Mexican mother in northern California who did not know what to do with the 3 × 5 vocabulary flashcards that her child brought from school, thus exemplifying the distance between what schools expect parents to do and what parents actually know how to do. Usually, it is the mother who gets blamed for not bridging that gap, not the father or the teacher, adding to the burdens placed on the shoulders of immigrant women.

Educators might prefer to teach the sisters from the well-to-do family described above because of the emphasis on biliteracy in that home, but they might think twice if they had seen and heard the girls carrying on. My student's notes convey her shock at the lack of restrictions on their behavior:

> These children definitely appeared to have the run of the place. They were allowed to jump, scream, stomp, run, and anything else they wanted to do. . . . They were given no behavioral restrictions: shouting, pushing, tripping over tape-recorder wires. The few times she [their mother] did mumble to them to stop doing something, she was blatantly ignored. . . . They were allowed to raise their voices to us. . . . They are obviously very accustomed to having everything their way.

My notes register the same dismay, but what upset me most was that I had brought the family a box of expensive Italian cookies and the girls crumbled every one, as mountain-building materials. Also, I was angered to see them act dismissively toward their nanny, not responding to her *Good-byes* until told to do repeatedly. My notes end bluntly: "Spoiled brats—do whatever they want, whenever they want." Clearly, despite the generational, class, and educational distance between us, my New York Puerto Rican student and I share a similar set of prejudices. Those of us who were raised in more situation-centered families often find child-centered children disrespectful, demanding, selfish, and insufferable, and those attitudes may persist despite years of exposure to child-centered norms. Others who were raised in child-centered families or who later become part of the mainstream find the children of situation-centered families slow, unresponsive, lacking initiative and independence, and unprepared for school-like tasks and routines. In the working- and lower-middle-class families that I observed, there was less emphasis on books and reading than on knowing right from wrong, respectful and cooperative behavior, cleanliness, and observation before participation. For example, the 18-month-old daughter of lower-working-class Dominican immigrants was praised for taking her dirty diapers to the garbage and for bringing the telephone receiver whenever requested. No books appeared during our visits, and literacy was not mentioned when her development was discussed. For many working-class Latinos, the best indication of *educación*, more accurately translated as good breeding or manners than formal education (Reese, Balzano, Gallimore, & Goldenberg, 1994), is in children's behavior and speech rather than in their book learning. *Un niño educado/una niña educada* (a well behaved boy/girl) is identified by his or her respectful tone of voice, avoidance of taboo words, and appropriate terms of address, such as *abuelo/a* (grandpa/ma), *tío/a* (uncle/aunt), *madrina/padrino* (godmother/-father). Traditional ways of greeting and leave-taking (*pedir la bendición* and *besar la mano*) are often required of children in Puerto Rican and Dominican homes. "To ask for a blessing" (Puerto Rican) and "to kiss the hand" (Dominican) both involve saying *"Bendición"* (with the title of elder) on greeting or leaving an elder. Even adults conform to this behavior. The loss of Spanish includes the loss of these traditional blessings. These behaviors, along with the ability to respond appropriately or keep quiet as requested, are linked to cultural notions of *respeto* (respect) and *relajo* (disorderly behavior) (Lauria, 1964), which maintain their pivotal role. Their acquisition reflects directly on the parents' ability to raise children well. For example, I may be impressed by my 3-year-old grandniece's skills at the computer, but I am more concerned about what she says and does when I tell her it is time to turn it off.

Assuming That Parental Reading Is Essential to School Success

Observers who focus on literacy activities do an injustice to families who stress behavior more than books. Charges of parental neglect are based on the fallacious view that children whose parents do not read to them will not learn to read and write well. This is the final pitfall, what Schecter & Bayley refer to as "implied determinacy," the assumption that what parents do not practice at home cannot be learned by children in school. Also implied is the view that children of parents who adopt a teacherlike role and stress literacy inevitably succeed. Yet we know that schools have a long history of teaching children many skills and subjects that are foreign to the home, and that not every teacher's child becomes an advanced or avid reader. All too often, however, parental reading is portrayed as a magic bullet, a way to guarantee academic success.

We should indeed encourage parents to read to their children, but homes without books are not endangering a child and parents who do not read to their children are not bad parents. We may agree with the view that "for children whose lives are bound by deprivation, [books] offer not only escapism but also the possibility of escape" (Klass, 1995, p. 72), but how much damage is done to parents by constructing them as incompetent because they do not read to their children? One pediatrician equates the lack of books in a home with serious deprivation:

> When I think about children growing up in homes without books, I have the same visceral reaction as I have when I think of children in homes without milk or food or heat: It cannot be, it must not be. It stunts them and deprives them before they've had a fair chance. (Klass, 1995, p. 71)

This pediatrician and others who share her view should know that in many homes where there are few books, adults and older children foster literacy in other ways. Rodríguez (Chapter 8, this volume) observed a Dominican family that created its own stories and preschoolers who imitated older siblings doing their homework. Similarly, Schecter and Bayley (2002) found the school academic agenda dominated home literacy activity in the Mexican families they studied.

Some of the most productive literacy events are linked to religious activities (Chapter 5, this volume) and/or games. In *El Barrio*, Isabel, who never sat down with her children to read, joined a Spanish Bible study group where texts were read and discussed aloud, and she took her children twice a week. Also, everyone in that family was a Scrabble fanatic, playing with English words for hours on end. When I was a child, I thought my mother invented Scrabble because she cut paper bags into squares and wrote a letter of the alphabet on each; we sat on the floor and put words together. *Mami* also had me copy and memorize long poems in Spanish and English, which I recited to visitors and at my father's Mexican society's *veladas* (cultural soirées), where I learned formal Spanish by imitating the guest speakers. My teachers never knew that I had those abilities, and I doubt they would have judged me college material if they had heard *mami*'s rants against too much reading and reliance on books.

What neither my teachers nor I understood was the connection between the centrality of the family in working-class Puerto Rican culture and parental fears of book-related illness. Padilla (1958, p. 209) noted that despite the fact that East Harlem parents believed too much studying could drive children mad, they wanted their children to read and do homework assignments, "since they keep the children busy and quiet in the home and are considered evidence that they are learning." Those parents and my mother may have feared that a child who continually immerses herself in the solitary act of reading distances herself from the shared activities of the family and shirks her duties toward its members. Anyone who becomes severed from the core support group risks mental illness, as psychotherapists would agree. Parents who favor "common sense" and view too much reading negatively may be carving out space for oral traditions and keeping children in the protected bosom of the family. In my case, my writing skills were developed as an extension of *respeto* norms and to maintain family ties. As a young child I printed my name and the appropriate kinship title in Spanish on all birthday, Easter, Mother's Day, Father's Day, and Christmas cards. Later, I was required to write an "oriyinal" thank-you note for every present in the appropriate language *before mami* would let me keep the gift. Reading and writing appropriately for bilingual and bicultural contexts, with an emphasis on originality and with the intention of fostering meaningful connections with others, continue to guide me to this day.

COMPARING ANGLO AND LATINO STANCES
REGARDING LITERACY

There was no contradiction between my mother's prohibitions against reliance on book learning and her insistence on speaking, reading, and writing well, and on getting A's in school. She valued excellent oral and literate abilities but did not view reading books as the best way to acquire them or as a measure of good parenting. Nor did those abilities define *una niña educada* the way they do in some Anglo middle-class families. Ochs's (2002) recently elaborated framework for understanding the socialization of cultural competence can be applied to a comparative analysis of Anglo and Latino approaches to literacy training with great profit. She considers four dimensions of the social context most relevant for getting at the ways in which children are socialized to be culturally competent: actions, stances, identities, and activities. An action is "goal-directed behavior," an activity is "two coordinated actions," and identities refer to social personae including statuses of the child and the parent. Stances can be both "affective" and "epistemic"; the former include "a person's mood, attitude, feeling or disposition, emotional intensity," and the latter "a person's knowledge or . . . sources of knowledge and degrees of commitment to truth and certainty of propositions" (Ochs, 2002, p. 109).

Anglos and Latinos may share some aspects of these dimensions but differ in others or in the emphasis they place on one or the other. The action of reading on the part of a child and the activity of reading to a child are evaluated positively by both groups, but they do not define the identities of the child and the parent in Latino families with the same emotional intensity (stance) that mainstream Anglos invest in them. A telling example of the ways that activities and identities can be linked inextricably appears in Ochs's study of an autistic Anglo American child. Because he has trouble with math, the child declares, "I am not good at being a kid" (Ochs, 2002, p. 112). Clearly, this middle-class boy has internalized a link between the ability to do math well and what it takes to be "good at being a kid." Because he cannot perform well in math activities, his identity as a kid is challenged. Similarly, the Anglo mainstream emphasis on literacy forges an inextricable link between literacy activities and positive child and adult identities: Parents who read to their children are good at being a parent, and children who learn to read well are good at being a child. Latino parents may emphasize different activities, those that maintain the norms of *respeto* and strengthen family bonds. Their psychological stance, in Ochs's terms, is what distinguishes both groups the most.

The Latino caregivers I have observed view reading and writing as indispensable for school, work, church, and personal communication, but they do not define the good child based on his or her literacy activities. And the emotional intensity with which some upper middle-class caregivers stress literacy for the purpose of getting the best scores in order to get into the best schools is foreign to many working-class people. As Ochs (2002) points out, there are "considerable differences in how communities use actions and stances to realize particular activities and identities," particularly in their "frequency, elaboration, and sequential positioning" (p. 114). Until long-term ethnography in a variety of Latino homes allows us to specify precisely how their actions, activities, identities, and stances differ from those of dominant Anglo families, we must suspend negative judgments that construct parents as unfit or their children as unteachable on the basis of literacy activities. In any case, there is enough research on literacy to confirm that being read to is not sufficient.

Home literacy practices must involve actual engagement with reading and writing in order to translate into academic success (Schecter & Bayley, 2002). Moreover, Schecter and Bayley maintain that oral and literate skills in the first and/or second language are not as linked or similar as popularly believed and that reading and writing must be learned. One piece of good news is their finding that children who read and write in Spanish, and even do English homework in Spanish, can do as well or better in school, and in English, than those who speak and read and write in English only. Educators tend to blame Spanish in the home when a student does poorly in school, even when other children in the same Spanish-speaking family may be doing very well in the same school. Contrary to the view of misinformed educators and others like the Texan judge who accused a mother of abusing her 5-year-old because she was raising the little girl in Spanish (Verhovek, 1995), parents who raise their children in Spanish are not thwarting the efforts of educators or hurting their children's chances in life. They are not the enemy.

CONCLUSION: SEEKING COMMON GROUND

To be successful, alliances between educators and Latino families must be based on mutual respect for our cultural differences, without exaggerating them to the point that they obscure our shared humanity and dreams. Richard Shweder (2000), a cultural psychologist, reminds us that no group "stands outside some tradition of meaning and value" and that "membership in some particular tradition of meanings and values is an essential condition for personal identity and happiness" (p. 8). Increasing globalization requires that everyone cross cultural boundaries, not just immigrants. We encourage teachers to embrace the opportunities for their own personal growth and to become better teachers. For Latino children, border crossings can be particularly

painful if their culture is considered inferior to the dominant one (García &
Hurtado, 1995). Because the abilities and attitudes that can ease transitions
and reduce the psychic costs of adaptation may be part of a Latino student's
cultural repertoire, we must avoid stereotyping and limiting that repertoire.
It behooves us, instead, to seek out and capitalize on the "over-arching, pos-
sibly universal, communicative and socializing practices that may facilitate
socialization into multiple communities and transnational life worlds," and
to be sensitive to distinct "psychological stances of certainty, uncertainty,
emotional intensity and politeness" (Ochs, 2001, p. 228). Everyone is
equipped to grow and change, especially the young; but only if we recognize
our common ground and communicate our belief in their ability to learn new
skills and ways, and honor their parents' concerns, will our schoolchildren
grow into their full capacities.

CHAPTER 2

Family Decisions About Schooling and Spanish Maintenance: *Mexicanos* in California and Texas

Robert Bayley & Sandra R. Schecter

In this chapter we illustrate the diversity of language-use practices of Mexican-background families in the two states where the greatest number of people of Mexican- origin live, California and Texas. Given the numbers as well as the diversity of Mexican-origin communities in these states, we cannot cover their full scope. We therefore limit our focus to the San Francisco Bay Area in California and San Antonio in Texas. Specifically, we describe the ways that *Mexicano* parents, particularly mothers, negotiate the sometimes conflicting tasks of helping their children to succeed in school while attempting to preserve cultural and linguistic continuity.

MEXICANOS IN SAN FRANCISCO AND SAN ANTONIO

The Mexican-origin communities in the San Francisco Bay Area and San Antonio differ in ways that are crucial for minority-language maintenance and cultural continuity (Allard & Landry, 1992; Giles, Bourhis, & Taylor, 1977; Landry & Allard, 1994). The most important of these differences are the following:

1. *Concentration*: San Antonio has a Latino majority while Latinos constitute a minority in the San Francisco Bay Area.
2. *Composition of the Latino community*: The San Antonio Latino community overwhelmingly consists of people of Mexican descent; the Latino community around San Francisco is more diverse in terms

of national origin and includes many immigrants from Central America as well as other Spanish-speaking countries.

3. *Ethnic mix*: Latinos and European Americans are the two main ethnicities in the San Antonio area. The San Francisco Bay Area is much more heterogeneous ethnically and racially.

4. *Length of residence in the United States*: The San Antonio Latino community has fewer recent immigrants than the San Francisco Bay Area community.

5. *Distance from Mexico*: San Antonio is much closer to Mexico than San Francisco, and residents of San Antonio have the possibility of visiting Mexico more often.

6. *Language policy*: Unlike California, Texas has not adopted official language legislation, and bilingual education is often (although not always) available to immigrant children entering primary school.

All of these differences have consequences for "ethnolinguistic vitality" (Allard & Landry, 1992) and for patterns of language use. Indeed, all except length of residence in the United States would suggest greater Spanish maintenance in San Antonio than in the San Francisco Bay Area. Here, we briefly discuss these large-scale societal factors. We shall see later, however, that general societal factors cannot fully explain the day-to-day and moment-to-moment language choices that result in children's maintenance or loss of Spanish.

The San Francisco Bay Area is one of the most ethnically and linguistically diverse areas in the United States. Indeed, in California as a whole, no single ethnic group constitutes a majority of the population. And, even among Latinos, people of Mexican background are one group, albeit by far the largest group, among many. San Antonio, with a majority Mexican-origin population and many almost exclusively Latino neighborhoods, has a very different population profile. Moreover, in contrast to northern California, which tends to draw immigrants from central Mexico, most people of Mexican background in San Antonio trace their origins to the northern Mexican border states of Coahuila, Nuevo León, and Tamaulipas, while others are descendents of people who settled in Texas when the area was still under Spanish or Mexican rule.

The communities differ in other ways. Although San Francisco, like San Antonio, was founded before the U.S. annexation of California and the Southwest, the Mexican-origin community in many northern California towns is of fairly recent origin. For example, Lincoln City (a pseudonym), one of the San Francisco Bay Area towns where we worked, had almost no residents of Mexican origin in 1960. However, by 1990, Mexican-origin children made up the largest group in the school system. In California as a whole, one study

(Solé, 1995) reported that approximately 70% of Mexican-background adults were born in Mexico.

The picture in south Texas differs from that in northern California. San Antonio was a well-established town when Texas gained independence in 1836 and continued to have close ties to Mexico. Throughout the 20th century the Mexican-origin population grew rapidly, concentrated in the west and south sides of the city. Although in recent decades the Latino population has expanded into new housing developments as well as established neighborhoods in the northwest and northeast sections, people of Mexican origin have continued to constitute the overwhelming majority of the city's west and south sides. In Texas as a whole, in sharp contrast to California, less than one-third (30%) of Mexican-background adults were born in Mexico (Solé, 1995).

Geography would seem to favor Spanish maintenance in San Antonio to a greater extent than in the San Francisco Bay Area. Most San Antonians with relatives in Mexico can return for visits in less than a day's drive. Mexican immigrants who live in northern California face a far more arduous and expensive journey if they wish to visit Mexico.

Finally, the two areas differ in their language policies. In 1986 Californians passed Proposition 163 declaring English the official language of the state, and after 1992, voters approved a succession of ballot measures aimed at various segments of the Latino community, culminating in 1998 in Proposition 227, a measure effectively banning bilingual education. The overall effect of these measures has been to create an atmosphere in which Spanish is threatened and Mexican cultural identity is devalued. Texas, in contrast, has never had an official language, and both bilingual and English as a Second Language (ESL) programs are common throughout the state. Moreover, there have been no serious attempts to limit services to non-English-speaking children to the extent that has characterized California.

STUDYING FAMILY LANGUAGE USE

The families profiled in this chapter participated in a multifaceted study of the relationship between home language socialization and the development of bilingual and biliterate abilities by Mexican-descent children (Bayley, Schecter, & Torres-Ayala, 1996; Schecter & Bayley, 1997, 1998, 2002). Schecter and Bayley (2002) discuss the methods and data sources for the larger study. We examined family language practices in a broadly representative sample of 40 families in two distinct communities. The 40 families had at least one parent or primary caregiver of Mexican origin and at least one fourth-, fifth-, or sixth-grade child who served as the focal child. We selected children in the fourth to sixth grades because that is when students in bilingual education programs are normally transitioned to all-English classrooms. Support for Spanish must then come from sources outside the school, primarily the home. The intent of the larger study was to provide educators and policy makers with a deeper understanding of the adaptive and interpretive learning strategies that children from bilingual families bring to the classroom.

In this chapter, we attend closely to caregivers' responses to the following questions, asked in Spanish or English according to their preferences:

- Have your wishes about the languages you want your child to know affected your decisions about schooling?
- What decisions have you made about your child's schooling?
- How involved do you get with your child's school activities? Do you help him or her with homework assignments, for example? Are you involved with any school organizations? Do you have many contacts with your child's teachers?
- Would you say the schools have been supportive of what you're trying to do? If so, in what ways? If not, what could they be doing that they're not doing?

Parents and children volunteered information about school experiences at many other points during our meetings. In particular, the topic of the role of schooling surfaced in parents' discussions of the relationship they saw between language and cultural identity, and in their representations of the obligations and prerogatives of parents and other stakeholders in matters of children's education. Also, we captured many interactions around school-related topics during the course of the extensive home observations that we conducted as part of the larger study (Schecter & Bayley, 2002).

In this chapter, we focus on six families, three from California and three from Texas, selected from the larger sample. The six families represent a range of decisions regarding home language socialization practices and schooling, as well as immigrant generation, socioeconomic class, and life modes. Their social and demographic characteristics are shown in Table 2.1.

COMMITMENT TO EDUCATIONAL ACHIEVEMENT AND CULTURAL MAINTENANCE

All the parents profiled here were committed to their children's educational achievement in English. In addition, all defined themselves in terms of allegiance to their Mexican heritage, and most indicated that Spanish was important to their sense of cultural identity. In both California and Texas,

TABLE 2.1. Social and Demographic Characteristics of Families

Family	Caregiver's birthplace	Caregiver's occupation	Focal child's gender and age	Focal child's birthplace (age of arrival in U.S.)
		California		
Castillo	M (single parent), Nayarit	M, Factory worker (unemployed)	f, 9	San Francisco Bay Area
Galán	M, Jalisco F, Baja California	M, homemaker F, cleaning company worker	m, 11	San Francisco Bay Area
Lozano	M, Sinaloa F, Sonora	M, factory worker F, construction worker	f, 10	Sinaloa (3 yrs.)
		Texas		
Sierra	M & F, southwest Texas	M, service representative F, teacher	m, 10	San Antonio
Saldivar	M, southern California F, Texas (border area)	M & F, owners of small construction business	f, 12	San Antonio
Torres	M & F, San Antonio	M, cafeteria worker F, factory worker	f, 11	San Antonio

Key: M, mother; F, father; m, male; f, female.
Note: All names are pseudonyms.

parents viewed Spanish as an important social resource in maintaining cultural traditions and ethnic identity, and many, even among the U.S.-born parents, insisted on the use of at least some Spanish in parent–child interactions. However, parents differed on how they saw the idealized roles of home and school in relation to Spanish maintenance and the promotion of cultural awareness. Parents also differed in the priority they assigned to language maintenance and cultural awareness, on one hand, and to academic success in mainstream schools, on the other. Some parents opted for a strategy of home language use that matched the language practices of their children's schools, whether the school practices favored language maintenance or shift. Parents in other families opted for a strategy of home language use that complemented the language practices of their children's schools.

Spanish Language Maintenance at Home and at School

Among the California participants, nearly half of the caregivers who used Spanish with their children in family interactions elected to enroll the children in bilingual programs where Spanish, in varying degrees, was a language of instruction. For many families who chose such programs, the pragmatic consideration that one or both parents spoke little or no English was the deciding factor. Many of these parents believed that a school program where their children were encouraged to develop Spanish would both assist and validate their parenting actions, because some spoke only Spanish.

Antonia and Luís Lozano (all the names in this chapter are pseudonyms), who immigrated to the northern California community of San Ignacio when their daughter Lupita was 3, illustrate one strategy of concurrent home and school language maintenance. Offered a choice within their local school district, the Lozanos chose to enroll Lupita in a bilingual program, a move they hoped would support her use of Spanish in everyday interactions. (The choice to enroll a child in a bilingual program in California has become much more difficult since Proposition 227 passed in 1998.) Luís, who spoke threshold English, worked seasonally in manual labor. At the time of our study, Antonia did not have an income, her day and evening hours being consumed largely with caring for Juanito, Lupita's young brother. Prior to Juanito's birth, Antonia had worked in a clothing factory where the other employees spoke Spanish. For both mother and father, but especially the monolingual Antonia, use of Spanish in family interactions was crucial to the maintenance of parental authority, and both insisted on Lupita's speaking Spanish in the home. Luís recounted feeling the need to emphasize the point to his daughter on more than one occasion: "*Yo le había dicho a ella . . . cuando está su mama enfrente, que no hable inglés porque no la entiende.*" (I'd told her . . . when her mother is present, not to speak English because she doesn't understand.)

The Lozanos relied on Lupita's teachers to cultivate in their daughter *una actitud positiva* (a positive attitude) toward the use of Spanish outside the classroom, and in this expectation they were not disappointed: "*Las maestras dicen que es bueno que ellos hablen los— los dos idiomas.*" (The teachers say that it's good that they speak both languages.) Although the Lozanos were not entirely satisfied with Lupita's progress in English reading and spelling, they attributed this outcome to a general laxness on the part of the U.S. educational system rather than to problems associated with her bilingual program.

Similar concerns about home language use and her role as a mother were voiced by Berta Castillo. A single mother who immigrated from Nayarit state to northern California when she was 15, Berta explained her decision to use only Spanish in home interactions with her two school-aged children, Emma and Rodrigo, aged 9 and 8, respectively:

Es más fácil porque yo tengo la amplitud de utilizar todas mis ideas y ponerlas en— en voz verdad. Y en inglés tengo que limitarme, estoy marginada.... Pero en español puedo decirles uh cuando juegas, brincas, y esto, tú no puedes aprender bien como debe de ser, no puedes enfocar.	It's easier because I can use all my ideas and put them in— and verbalize them, right? And in English I have to limit myself, I'm limited.... But in Spanish I can tell them um when you play, jump, and so on, you don't learn well like you should, you can't focus.

For Berta Castillo, as for most caregivers who chose to pursue an aggressive Spanish-maintenance strategy, related decisions involved an important ideological component. Berta, whose family has subsisted on welfare checks, associated mastery of both English and Spanish with the better life that she was determined her children would enjoy. Conversely, she associated loss of Spanish with their low social status and poverty. The association of mother-tongue loss with impoverishment emerges clearly in her account of the vision that led to her conversion, as it were, to a stance that sought to maximize her children's exposure to and use of Spanish:

Anteriormente yo les hablaba en inglés y me respondían en inglés, y en una ocasión ... miré un programa en la televisión ... un jovencito Mexicano, que trató de hablar en español y lo habló TAN mal, verdad.... Entonces me— me— hice en mi imaginación que eso sería el reflejo que-que- van tomando mis hijos en el futuro, verdad? ... Entonces sentí una gran necesidad de que tenían que ser bilingües. Y allí comenzamos a— hablar español todos los días y prohibirles completamente el idioma inglés en mi casa.	Before I used to speak to them in English and they answered me in English, and one time, I saw a television program ... a Mexican youth, who tried to speak Spanish and who spoke it SO badly, you know.... Then I conjured up in my imagination an image of my children in the future, you know? Then, I felt a real need that they had to be bilingual. From then on we began to speak Spanish every day and to ban English completely from the house.

Berta Castillo's awakening occurred before Emma, her older child, started school, well in time for her mother to identify a local public school that offered a "primary language" program where Spanish–English bilingual teachers provided instruction simultaneously in both languages. As Emma described the program, "*Allí se mezclan— mezclan el idioma en inglés y español* so *todos pueden entender y pueden escribir en el idioma que quieren.*" (There they mix— mix the language in English and Spanish so everyone can understand and can write in the language that they want.) Asked which language she prefers, Emma responded, "*español*" (Spanish). "*Se me hace más fácil*" (It's easier for me), Emma volunteered, a condition she attributes to the exclusive use of Spanish in her home.

Language Shift at Home and at School

A number of families in both California and Texas opted to use English at home with their children and to enroll the children in all-English classes. Despite these decisions, however, none of the parents opposed the idea of speaking Spanish. Most, in fact, thought that the ability to speak, read, and write more than one language was a good thing and hoped that at some point their children would develop such abilities if they did not have them already. The decision to favor the use of English in the household coupled with the selection of an English instructional program was often negatively motivated, that is, a precautionary action to ensure that one's child's opportunities for success would surpass those of children with less access to the linguistic resources of mainstream society. Indeed, several second- and third-generation U.S. citizens explained their desire to shield their children from the prejudice and shame that they experienced growing up in the United States. Some reported experiencing discrimination simply for being of "Spanish" background; others spoke of being punished for using Spanish on or near school premises. Such narratives of punishment or humiliation for speaking Spanish at school were particularly common among the Texas mothers, more than half of whom had been born in the United States or immigrated here as young children and did not speak English when they entered school. For example, Alicia Sierra related the following experience from her own first year of school in southwest Texas:

> Well, first of all, we were not allowed to speak Spanish. And when you're starting school in first grade or kindergarten . . . you don't know English. I mean—going to the bathroom—how can you tell her [the teacher] you have to go to the bathroom? So of course that happened to me—I had an accident right there. . . . I felt humiliated because it was in front of the whole class . . .

Partially in response to her experiences as a child, Alicia determined that her own children would acquire English as their first language, although she and her husband frequently used Spanish between themselves. This decision was reinforced by the strong urgings of her parents and in-laws, beginning even before the birth of her first child:

> . . . my mom used to say: "Don't talk . . . in Spanish. Speak English, because that's the way of today." You know. So it was all like, "Hey, they have been telling me all along," you know, plus my mother-in-law, you know, would also come along and say: "It's better that they learn English first and then Spanish." So it was like all these relatives, all these people telling me, so it was an automatic thing.

The results for minority-language maintenance have been predicable. Ten-year-old Larry Sierra, who has lived all his life in the predominantly Anglo San Antonio neighborhood where the Sierras moved after their marriage, speaks no Spanish and has only minimal understanding. Indeed, when asked what he did when his mother spoke to him in Spanish, Larry answered, "I just say 'What?', and she tells me in English."

Our second example of concurrent home and school language shift illustrates the consequences of negative attitudes toward the varieties of Spanish spoken in many Latino communities. Like the Sierras, Veronica and Alfonso Saldivar and their three children live on the north side of San Antonio. Veronica grew up bilingually, acquiring English from her parents and Spanish from her grandparents, with whom she spent summers as a child. Alfonso acquired Spanish as his first language and English after entering school.

The Saldivars' bilingualism proved advantageous. In fact, for a number of years, Veronica Saldivar worked for a Spanish-language media outlet, a position where fluency and literacy in both Spanish and English were essential. However, despite the value that bilingualism had in her own life, Veronica elected to raise her children in English. In part, her decision was motivated by the circumstances in which she lived. Her neighbors included few Spanish speakers, and she reasoned that most of her children's playmates would be monolingual in English. And, like Alicia Sierra, she felt that her children would be better prepared to succeed in English-medium schools if they used English at home. However, her decision, which was a source of some tension in the family, was also motivated by her fear that her children would acquire what she believed was a debased form of Spanish. Veronica commented:

> It kinda— it kinda puts me on the spot you know because I don't want to teach them wrong. We've had arguments about it and I— I— I, you know, he [Alfonso] wants the kids to learn Spanish and I didn't teach 'em. I want them to learn the proper way of

speaking Spanish and what concerns me A LOT is this Tex-Mex
Spanish. It concerns me a lot because my husband speaks Spanish,
but he has a lot of Tex-Mex in it and uh I don't want the kids to
learn that way. I want them to learn the proper Spanish only because
I know that's the right way.

Veronica's adherence to prescriptive norms, combined with the other influences mentioned, led to her decision to raise her children with English. This
decision was influenced by her experience as a high school student of Spanish in south Texas. Although she was a fluent bilingual, she struggled in her
very traditional Spanish classes. She commented,

You go to school and . . . , you know, right away they start teaching
you the past tense and the present tense and it just really threw me, it
really threw me, once I started, you know, taking Spanish in school. I
never even thought about anything like that when I was speaking
Spanish, and then when I started taking it in school, it just threw me
a whopper right there, you know.

Veronica determined that her children would be spared the difficulties she
had experienced and learn what she regarded as proper Spanish in school.
As in the case of Larry Sierra, the result was predictable. Twelve-year-old
Lisa, the focal child in our study, had virtually no productive ability in Spanish
and only minimal receptive ability.

Complementary Home and School Language Practices

Slightly more than half of the parents whose home language practices were
oriented to Spanish maintenance elected to enroll their children in mainstream
English programs. In some cases this decision was explained as an outcome
of the fact that a bilingual program was not available. In other cases, particularly among the children of U.S.-born parents, children were ineligible
for bilingual programs because their parents spoke English, regardless of the
language they spoke most at home, or because children had acquired sufficient English to pass the tests for placement in mainstream classes. In other
cases, however, decisions to opt for complementary home and school language choices were grounded in beliefs about the roles and obligations of
the family versus the school in the socialization of children, as well as in
pedagogic rationales about the conditions under which the development of
bilingual and biliterate abilities in children most beneficially occur. Moreover, for some parents, a perceived lack of quality of language instruction in
the local bilingual programs was a major factor in their choice.

Some parents who supported Spanish maintenance and yet chose to enroll their children in regular English programs believed that the presence of two languages in the curriculum would impede their children's academic progress. For example, in explaining their strong commitment to Spanish maintenance through home practice, Sonia and Pedro Galán, residents of a working-class community in the San Francisco Bay Area, expressed the view that the responsibility for maintaining the primary language—a goal they linked to cultural maintenance—belonged to parents. In outlining the dire implications of linguistic loss, they revealed sentiments similar to those of Berta Castillo reported above. Thus, Mrs. Galán commented:

Nosotros seguimos— seguimos tratando de mantenerlas um, porque como en su familia de él, hay un— hijo de un tío— que los dos hablan español, pero a él no le enseñaron . . . él lo entiende pero no lo puede hablar. Y digo que es feo que uno platique y él lo entiende pero no lo puede hablar.	We keep— keep trying to maintain them um, because like in his family, there's a nephew— the two [parents] speak Spanish, but they didn't teach it to him . . . he understands, but can't speak. And I think it's terrible when someone speaks [to him] and he understands but can't speak.

The Galáns first considered looking into a bilingual program in which to enroll their son, Diego, but decided to place him in a regular English class instead. Pedro explained: " . . . *No iban a poder aprender inglés y español al mismo tiempo . . . porque no puede [hacer] las dos cosas un niño pequeño, pienso yo.*" (" . . . they weren't going to be able to learn English and Spanish at the same time . . . because a young child can't do the two things [at once], I think.")

THE STANCE OF SCHOOLS

Schooling officials with whom families came into contact held differing conceptions about the roles of Spanish and English in the instruction of Latino children. These differences are not surprising, since the educational community remains divided on the issue of bilingual schooling (cf. August & Hakuta, 1997; Rossell & Baker, 1996; San Miguel, 2004; Wong Fillmore, 1991), despite the preponderance of research findings indicating that well-structured bilingual programs facilitate language-minority children's educational progress (see, e.g., Krashen, 1999; Ramirez, Yuen, Ramey, & Pasta, 1991; Thomas & Collier, 2003; Willig, 1985). Interestingly, schools overwhelmingly recommended that parents adopt home language practices to match the language of their child's formal schooling. Teachers would encourage caregivers in the use of Spanish with their children who were enrolled in bilingual programs; conversely, where English was the sole language of instruction, teachers and other school personnel would counsel parents to make English the sole or primary language of home interactions. One Spanish-dominant mother reported that in her first meeting with her daughter's kindergarten teacher, the teacher firmly advised against teaching the child to read Spanish at home, in order not to "create a conflict" that would cause the child to experience problems in school.

Despite this implicit notion concerning the responsibility of parents—particularly mothers—to organize their family work in line with the school's agenda (cf. Griffith, 1995), mothers, and sometimes fathers, commented that most of the teachers were unaware of the discourse practices their students participated in outside of school and failed to recognize the value of input from family members (cf. Chapter 1, this volume). Parents also reported that their children's schools did not express a commitment to specific goals of parental involvement by showing interest in parents' views regarding the role and importance of primary-language maintenance in language acquisition (cf. Delgado-Gaitán, 1990; Valdés, 1996). In fact, in some cases we found evidence of a disregard for parental concerns. Elena Torres, a working-class Texas mother, provides an example of the distance frequently found between the aspirations of mothers and the agenda of the schools. A year before she agreed to participate in our study, Mrs. Torres, concerned by her three English-dominant daughters' lack of Spanish proficiency, began to devote considerable effort to helping the girls revive Spanish. She set aside one day a week when Spanish was to be used in home interactions, Mrs. Torres's Spanish-dominant mother began a program of informal tutoring, and the family started to attend Spanish-language church services. Elena provided active support on a number of dimensions for the school system's agenda for her children, serving as an active member of the PTA and as a volunteer, accompanying children on field trips and overseeing homework assignments. Although she expressed a strong desire to see some Spanish in the curriculum of the schools her daughters attended, "even just 30 minutes a day, where they can go in and speak only Spanish and the correct Spanish," she evidenced no hope that such support would be forthcoming.

Finally, at the California site, we also noted that a significant minority of parents reported some confusion about the nature of the school program in which their children were enrolled. In particular, they found the terminology used in school–home communications—such as "primary-language program" and "mainstream"—confusing. One mother who was informed that her child had been placed in a primary-language program was unclear as to whether the term *primary language* was intended to denote the child's native tongue (in this case, Spanish) or English. In four cases, parents who had believed that their children were enrolled in either a regular English program or a Spanish–English bilingual program later discovered that the children actually had been placed in special ESL classes. In two of these cases, parents did not appreciate the implications of these distinctions for their children's academic development until the children had completed several years of primary school.

THE BASIS FOR CAREGIVERS' DECISIONS

As we have seen, parental views concerning the roles of English and Spanish in their children's education differed. The issue, moreover, was almost always articulated as one of Spanish versus English, with considerations of quantity and quality figuring strongly. In general, caregivers did not appear to have access to the findings from the professional literature that stress the importance of literacy-related activity for academic success. When parents did acknowledge the importance of reading and writing, they were referring to these activities in the context of school-based learning. Parents' differing views, along with the constraints imposed by their own linguistic repertoires, provide some explanation for the divergent decisions about schooling and curricular options described above. Clearly, however, these views cannot fully account for the diverse strategies caregivers followed in pursuit of their stated goals.

What, then, is the basis for these crucial decisions? Surely they are not gratuitous, for almost all caregivers displayed a considered and articulate opinion about how they believed the management of language and culture should proceed in U.S. society, about Spanish maintenance and its relationship to cultural identity, and about the factors they believed fostered language learning. Caregivers also expressed clearly developed beliefs about the respective roles, responsibilities, and prerogatives of different social institutions—primarily schools and families—in matters of child development. These two sets of beliefs intersected at different junctures for different families, leading to different decisions about children's schooling. Despite such differences, however, caregivers' decision-making processes appeared to operate within a coherent ideological whole: Their understanding of the role of schooling connected to their understanding of maturational processes and to how the latter are facilitated or inhibited by environments such as home and society. As members of a linguistic and cultural minority, the families with whom we worked, whether they lived in California or Texas, confronted issues that middle-class Anglo families normally do not have to confront. Chief among these issues, of course, are questions of the respective roles of schools and homes in children's language and academic development. Indeed, the elaborate and carefully reasoned explanations of their decisions about their children's schooling and their own home-language practices provided by the majority of the caregivers give the lie to the mistaken notion that Latino parents are unconcerned about their children's educational achievement.

Finally, we wish to offer some remarks on the orientation of mainstream schooling to the central dilemma. As we have seen, educators as well as parents held differing beliefs concerning the benefits of various curricular options for the social and academic development of language-minority children. Contrary to the experience reported by most second- and third-generation immigrant parents, a good many educators supported strategies and policies that sought to promote minority-language maintenance, a stance some linked to the empowerment of minority families. Educators also held views concerning the division of responsibility between school and home for the child's development and concerning home language use and other child-care practices that they considered to be part of parents' work. In some cases, educators opposed the use of Spanish in the home and urged parents to switch to English whenever possible (and sometimes even when it was not possible because the parents did not speak English), believing that would facilitate children's academic development. In other cases, however, educators supported parental efforts, as in the case of the Castillo family discussed above. And the lack of school support that frustrated Mrs. Torres's efforts to maintain Spanish may be remedied by two-way bilingual programs, where both English and Spanish are used as languages of instruction and the student body is comprised of half English-dominant and half Spanish-dominant children (Chapter 11, this volume). Since 1996, a number of school districts in Texas have established two-way programs.

Although our own sympathies are clearly on the side of language maintenance, we have no problem accepting that professional educators disagree about the effects of instruction in more than one language or the type of bilingual program that is most effective for language-minority children. We are concerned, however, about the increased tendency on the part of mainstream schooling to link parents' performance of activities that support and extend the school's agenda to children's educability. Such expectations, in addition to contributing to the stressful nature of schooling-related decisions, may lead to disillusionment and add to the many conflicting pressures faced by language-minority parents.

CONCLUSION

In keeping with the theme of this volume, we have emphasized the diversity found in Mexican-origin families in the two areas where we worked. Parents adopted a variety of strategies as they sought to negotiate the sometimes conflicting demands of school agendas and their own desires for linguistic and cultural maintenance. This diversity is in part a consequence of the large-scale social and demographic factors that we outlined at the beginning of the chapter as well as of the opportunities for schooling available to children. However, it is also a consequence of individual family decisions concerning the appropriate roles of caregivers and schools in children's overall development. In fact, large-scale social and demographic factors had less effect than we originally anticipated. Parents in both states exhibited a full range of opinions and rationales for their decisions about Spanish maintenance and schooling. Moreover, such decisions are not one-time choices, particularly for families who elect to maintain Spanish. Rather, these decisions must be constantly reaffirmed, often in the face of opposition from relatives and others, even in areas such as San Antonio, where conditions seem to favor Spanish maintenance. As Zentella notes in the Introduction to this volume, language socialization research offers one way to understand the diverse choices with respect to schooling discussed here. We suggest, however, that work in language socialization needs to take greater account of the dynamic nature of language choices in bilingual families and the ways in which those choices change as individual circumstances change. Finally, our own work, as well as the work of others (e.g. Pease-Alvarez, 2003; Valdés, 1996), has shown that Latino parents, including parents who have not had the opportunity for extensive formal education, have well-developed ideologies about the roles of home, school, and community in children's language socialization. We suggest that home–school collaboration may be enhanced to the extent that educators take those ideologies into account and work with families who are trying to maintain linguistic and cultural continuity while ensuring that their children achieve school success.

ACKNOWLEDGMENTS

This research was supported by U.S. Department of Education Field-Initiated Studies Program Grant R117E40326-94 and a Spencer Foundation Grant to both authors and a National Academy of Education Spencer Fellowship to Robert Bayley. Marta Avila, Adriana Boogerman, Elvia Ornelas-García, Martha López-Durkin, Diane Sharken-Taboada, and Buenaventura Torres-Ayala assisted with observations, interviews, and transcription. Special thanks to the families who allowed us to share their lives and trusted us to tell their stories from our perspectives.

CHAPTER 3

Mexicanos in Chicago: Language Ideology and Identity

Marcia Farr & Elías Domínguez Barajas

Mexicans have had a presence in Chicago throughout the 20th century, and in recent decades their numbers have increased exponentially, doubling from 1960 to 1970, quadrupling from 1970 to 1980, and growing more moderately during the 1980s; by 2000 over 1 million people identified as Mexican (Farr & Domínguez Barajas, 2005). Chicago has sustained much of this growth, but counties surrounding the city have also experienced an upsurge in Mexican-origin populations. To better understand the midwestern Mexican community's sense of self and place in U.S. society, particularly in Chicago, this chapter explores the language ideologies articulated and lived by one social network of Mexican immigrant families living in the heart of Chicago's Mexican neighborhoods. We first introduce the network itself and its sense of identity as *rancheros* (small-property rancher-farmers) from western Mexico. After that, we describe two culturally significant ways of speaking into which children are socialized. Next we illustrate their language ideologies regarding Spanish and English, including their rural *ranchero* dialect of Mexican Spanish and bilingual education. We conclude by considering the implications of this research for educators and others who interact with similar populations.

RANCHERO NETWORKS

Mexican emigration to Chicago always stemmed from states in western Mexico, such as Michoacán, Guanajuato, and Jalisco (Kerr, 1976). In recent decades, many immigrants have formed transnational communities that largely maintain western Mexican regional identities, the most salient of which is *ranchero*, visually marked by men with mustaches and cowboy hats, boots, and embroidered belts characteristic of western Mexico. *Ranchero* identity evolved in isolated frontier regions of Mexico after the Conquest (Barragán López, 1997). *Rancheros* emphasize a primarily Spanish heritage, distinguishing themselves from indigenous (Indian) Mexicans and emphasizing individualism (González, 1974) rather than communalism (which they ascribe to Indians), although this individualism is embedded within the context of familism. That is, their emphasis on the uniqueness of the individual *and* the importance of the family undermines the conventional dichotomy between North American individualism and Latin American familism or communalism. *Rancheros* are also distinct from urban elite Mexicans, who view them as uncultured "hillbillies" who don't know how to interact appropriately in polite society. In turn, *rancheros* view city dwellers as effete people who do not really work but only shuffle papers.

These families began migrating to Chicago in 1964, when one man came as a *bracero* (laborer) in the last year of the U.S.–Mexico Bracero Program. After this man came his brothers, and eventually wives and children who had initially waited for them in Mexico. Finally, in the 1980s single women from the *rancho* joined uncles and aunts in Chicago, and currently many young people, with and without families, continue to arrive, leaving the older generation behind in the *rancho*. Because they are disdained by elite Mexican society, migrating to Chicago circumvents their lack of "leverage" (*palancas*) in Mexico and opens opportunity for upward mobility, the *progreso* (progress) so central to *ranchero* identity.

The network is now strong in Chicago, helping new arrivals with housing and jobs. Many network members live, work, and socialize together, forming the fabric of each others' lives. Families save money by living with relatives before buying their own houses in core Mexican neighborhoods in Chicago, moving to "better" neighborhoods farther south in the city as their situations improve economically. Many also build homes in the *rancho*. Moreover, everyone with legal papers returns to Mexico frequently for special celebrations (weddings, baptisms, and fiestas) and to oversee their (entrepreneurial) avocado orchards. Thus the network is markedly transnational, communicating with and talking about those not physically present on a daily basis. Even members of the second and third generations have strong interpersonal ties to the *rancho*, sometimes spending months at a time there as children. They are socialized into *ranchero* ideologies and linguistic practices by their grandparents in Mexico and by their parents and other relatives in Chicago. Moreover, the neighborhoods in which they live in Chicago are often heavily Mexican and heavily *ranchero*, as are the public schools most children attend. Chicago, then, provides a complex mix of Spanish and English for them, with Spanish predominant in the community, since Chicago's segregated ethnic neighborhoods maintain many non-English languages.

Their neighborhoods provide plenty of Mexican food, music, clothing, jewelry, and so on. One can live most daily life in Spanish: at church (which now has an altar to Mexico's *Virgen de Guadalupe*), at home, in the stores, on the streets, in community centers, and even—for some—at work. For example, many adult women work in food preparation and other factories almost entirely with other Mexican women, limiting their exposure to English. Many men, in contrast, have more opportunity to use English with English-speaking bosses and co-workers, although they, too, often work together in small Spanish-speaking groups, for example, in railroad construction. Members of the second and third generations who go to school in Chicago learn English fluently by the end of elementary school, and some have difficulty with Spanish fluency and accuracy after years of schooling in English. Some parents deliberately teach their children Spanish literacy, concerned that this aspect of their heritage will be lost as they acquire the much-needed English language, and some insist on the use of Spanish in the home. The next section explores language use in the network, framing the discussion in terms of language socialization.

LANGUAGE SOCIALIZATION: LEARNING TO TALK *RANCHERO*

This chapter is based on 15 years of participant observation and audiotaping (by the first author) in both Chicago and the *rancho*. During this long-term ethnography, many children in the network have been born and raised, and those who were children at the beginning of the research are beginning to marry and have children themselves. Farr (in press) describes and analyzes three ways of speaking that are culturally significant in this community. In this section we contrast a primary framework for speaking (Goffman, 1974), *franqueza* (frankness, candor, and directness, including earthy, rough talk), in "serious" or regular talk with more playful and poetic uses of language. *Franqueza* has been described elsewhere in detail (Farr, 2000a) as the way in which men, women, and even children construct themselves as self-assertive and individualistic, a way of speaking that presumably developed in the material history of *rancheros* in frontier regions of Mexico. Thus, a *ranchero* sense of personhood includes knowing how to *defenderse* (defend oneself) verbally. The way of speaking that expresses and constructs that sense of personhood, *franqueza*, is characterized by frequent use of directives (usually as syntactic imperatives) and direct questions (sometimes even described with the verb *interrogar* [interrogate]). Directives are used not only toward children, as some research on working-class families suggests (Bhimji [Chapter 4, this volume] includes more counterevidence of this finding), but also by children as they construct their own authority and autonomy with *franqueza*, within appropriate contexts. The following examples illustrate this direct style of speaking:

Direct Questions

> ¿¡*Por qué tú no has venido?!* (Why haven't you come?!) [man in rancho to Marcia]
> ¿¡*Qué pasó?!* (What happened?) [answering telephone, after caller identifies him- or herself]

Directives (Imperatives)

> ¡*Aguántese, si es hombre!* (Handle it, if you're a man!) [younger sister to older brother in *rancho*]
> ¡*Mamita! ¡Córrele!* (Mommy! Hurry up!) [young daughter to mother in *rancho*]

Such direct, unadorned language is common in daily conversation, as *rancheros* are said not to *andar con rodeos* (beat around the bush). As one woman put it, *De lo que tiene uno más miedo de ir [a hacer]— de una vez* (What one is most fearful of [doing]— confront it at once), evoking a well known proverb, *Al mal trago darle prisa* (Bitter drinks should be gulped down). Children are socialized to be strong, self-assertive individuals who frequently speak their minds directly and candidly with what has been called "the arrogance of their Spanish heritage" (González, 1991). This direct, self-assertive way of speaking and behaving is exemplified in Chicago when people, out of pride, quit jobs abruptly when treated badly by employers or take children out of summer programs (suddenly, without discussion) when the teacher has yelled at them and made the children nervous. *Franqueza*, then, is common in ordinary daily speech for "serious" communication. When talk turns playful, however, seriousness is put aside. The primary framework of direct (utilitarian) speech is then complemented by indirect teasing, joking, and punning, often within the verbal activity of *echando relajo* (joking around) (Farr, 1994, in press). People show high regard for those who *tienen gracia* (speak with wit and grace), who add *sabor* (flavor) to their speech (Farr, 1993). Word play is constant, sometimes with *doble sentido* (double meaning, one of which can be sexual), and a rich range of genres fill daily conversations with the delight of verbal artistry; children avidly attend to these speech events so that they, too, can acquire such verbal skills. Adults engage children in dialogues with *bromas de confusión* (joking that confuses the child on purpose) so that they will learn to "handle," interpret, and eventually produce such playful language and teasing (Eisenberg, 1986).

In the transcript below, a young aunt attempts to teach her 3-year-old niece to call her by her "new" name in Chicago (Betty, based on her first name, Beatriz), rather than by her childhood nickname from the *rancho* (Ticha). (Names used in the transcript are pseudonyms.) The mother, also in her 20s, playfully attempts to undermine the aunt's efforts, and the two women engage in a humorous battle of words via the child. (Also present is the senior author, though here she only laughs.) For transcription conventions, see Introduction, footnote 2.

The words in bold in lines 10–11 show the mother teasing the aunt by undermining her efforts to get the child to use her new name. She does this by playfully suggesting inappropriate language for the child to say to her aunt—a sanitized version of "go to the devil." The mother persists in teasing both her child and the aunt by insisting, in lines 26 and 29, that the aunt does not love the child—by either name. The words in bold in lines 30–32 show the aunt's use of playful language that confuses the child. The aunt expresses her frustration about her lack of success in getting the child to use her new name in line 34, when she switches to the formal pronoun *le* (objective form of *usted*) from the informal *te* (objective form of *tú*) that she has been using in addressing the child. This use of the formal pronoun indexes the formality of her role authority over the child and is used when adults reprimand children or direct their behavior.

1 Child:	*En un cuento. Yo no sé de—* [pause] *Ticha.*	In a story. I don't know— [*pause*] Ticha.
2 Aunt:	*Me llamo Beatriz.*	My name is Beatriz.
3 Marcia:	[laugh]	[*laugh*]
4 Child:	*Ticha.*	Ticha.
5 Aunt:	*Beatriz. Soy la Beti. A ver dime Beti. Dime. Dime "Hola*	Beatriz. I am Betty. Let's see, say Betty to me. Say it.
6	*Beti. ¿Qué tal? ¿Cómo estás?"*	Say to me, "Hi Betty. How's it going? How are you?
7 Child:	*Ayy*	Ayy.
8 Aunt:	*Ay pues sí, así me llamo, me llamo Beatriz pero me dicen*	Well yes, that's my name, my name is Beatriz, but they
9	*Beti.*	call me Betty.
10 Mother:	**Dile "¿Veti pa' 'onde tía?"**	**Say to her, "Get yourself where, Auntie?"**

11 Child:	*¿Veti pa' 'onde tía?*	Get yourself where, Auntie?
12 Aunt:	*No, Beti. Beti Beti, a ver dime.*	No, Betty. Betty Betty. Let's see, say it to me.
13 Child:	*Beti.*	Betty.
14	****	****
15 Aunt:	*¡Ay Dios cuánto amor con la tía, ayy!* [laughs]	Oh my God, how much love for your aunt, ayy! [laughs]
16 Mother:	*¡Cuánto amor te ha salido a ti ahora!*	How much love has come out of you now!
17 Child:	*Ay.*	Ay.
18 Aunt:	*Ay por favor, dime "Ay por favor Beti."*	Oh please, say to me, "Oh please Betty."
19 Child:	*Ay mami porque yo me llamo—yo soy la—*	Oh mommy because my name is— I am—
20 Aunt:	*Carmen*	Carmen.
21 Child:	*— la yo yo em— a mí me quiere ella.*	— the I, I— she loves me.
22 Aunt:	*¿Verdad?*	Right?
23 Mother:	*¿Quién?*	Who?
24 Child:	*Ticha.*	Ticha.
25 Aunt:	*¿Quién es ella?*	Who is she?
26 Mother:	*Tu tía Ticha no te quiere.*	Your Aunt Ticha doesn't love you.
27 Aunt:	*Yo no soy Ticha, ¿Quién es ella? Beti, Beatriz.*	I am not Ticha. Who is she? Betty. Beatriz.
28 Marcia:	[chuckle]	[chuckle]
29 Mother:	*Tu tía Beatriz no te quiere.*	Your Aunt Beatriz doesn't love you.
30 Aunt:	**Ohh dile "clarines que sí mami."**	**Ooh, say to her, "darn tootin', Mommy."**
31 Child:	**Clarines que sí mami.**	**Darn tootin', Mommy.**
32 Aunt:	**Dile "hojas de moreno."**	**Say to her, "You betcha."**
33 Child:	*'Ira Ticha xxx*	Look, Ticha xxx
34 Aunt:	*Oh yo no soy Ticha yo le dije.*	Oh, I am not Ticha, I already told you.
35 Marcia:	[Chuckle]	[Chuckle]

In line 10, the mother initiates the play on words by supplanting the intended meaning of the word *Beti*. Whereas the aunt wants the child to recognize the word *Beti* as a proper noun (i.e., as her aunt's new name), the child's mother plays on their rural Mexican dialect's pronunciation of the verb *vete* (pronounced by them as /veti/) (you go/get yourself) to subvert the intended effect. Although it is highly unlikely that the child is aware of the complexity of the verbal play, she is the conduit of the humor, and this places her at the center of the creative verbal experience. By giving her a central role in this instance of subversive humor, the child's mother directly involves her in experiencing the response to such humor. That is *veti* invokes the common phrase *vete al diablo* (go to the devil), expressing resistance to Beatriz' attempt to establish a more "English" nickname for herself. Countless such linguistic routines firmly impress upon the child the power of verbal ability and creativity to elicit similar responses from others, and, in addition, they help in the child's development of metalinguistic awareness by exemplifying the indexical quality of language.

In line 30 Beatriz plays with the usual phrase *claro que sí* (of course— literally, clearly yes) by replacing *claro* (clear) with *clarines* (bugles). The result makes no semantic sense, but the phonological similarity between the two allows Beatriz to make a play on words. The child will have to interpret this nonsense phrase as best she can, eventually learning to enjoy such play and even produce it herself. The aunt follows up her play on words with another common expression of affirmation, this time without changing it—*hojas de moreno* (you betcha) in line 32. This excerpt is interesting for the way in which implicit teaching (the playful transformation of *claro* to *clarines* in a common expression) is embedded within a conversation dedicated to explicit teaching (call me Betty, not Ticha). The aunt explicitly instructs her young niece to call her by her new name, but she implicitly teaches language play by simply doing it and expecting her niece to figure it out (or not). Such a language socialization routine simultaneously imparts both specific language teaching (phonological play with words) and the cultural preference for such speech play.

Thus far we have described two ways of speaking, one serious and one playful, as cultural preferences within this social network of *rancheros*, describing the first as a primary framework for speaking and the second as a marked contrast to such regular communication. We have argued that children, observing and in dialogue with adults (and older siblings and cousins), learn to be members of the group by learning how to talk in these socially approved ways. In what follows we illustrate the network's language ideologies, including some paradoxical ambivalence.

LANGUAGE IDEOLOGIES

All network members stress the need for the mastery of both Spanish and English. Spanish is essential as the language of the home, the extended family, and their homeland. English is necessary because it is the language of public transactions, official matters, and most schooling in the United States. The need for bilingual fluency is considered more important for the children in the network than for their parents. Older members hold on to the idea that their stay in the United States is temporary or contingent on other events, and although they recognize the importance of learning English, it is neither easy for them to learn (at their ages) nor particularly essential to carry out their daily tasks. Nevertheless, most first-generation adults do learn English, at least to a limited degree, and some are fluent.

Those who grow up in Chicago are bilingual and encourage this ability in their own children. Angelica, for example, considers it reprehensible that Mexican families should lose Spanish from one generation to the next. She says:

Y se ve muy mal a veces cuando uno va a visitar a otros familiares y no saben inglés y los niños lo único que saben es este inglés y no pueden deci— hablarles en español.	And it looks bad sometimes when one goes to visit other relatives and they don't know English and the only thing the children know is English, and they can't say— can't speak to them in Spanish.

Ismael, Angelica's brother-in-law, fervently promotes the retention of Spanish among children growing up in the United States. In the earthy and plainspoken style (*franqueza*) characteristic of *rancheros* (expressed in a brief code switch in English), Ismael stresses the importance of roots and a Mexican identity for his children. When he talks about the importance of Spanish maintenance among Latinos in the United States, he also notes that in a multilingual culture knowledge of other languages is an asset instead of a disadvantage:

Para mí es una lástima ver que una— que un— que una persona con cara cien por ciento mexicana o de otro, de otro, otro país latino le hable usted en español y le diga "Oh I'm sorry I don't speak Spanish." I say, "Fuck—" It sounds disgusting . . . *Yo quiero que mis hijos cuando crezcan hablen inglés, hablen español, [y] si ellos tienen oportunidad de estudiar otro, otro idioma, fabuloso.*	It is a shame for me to see that a— that a— that you speak to a person with a 100%-Mexican face, or from another, another, another Latin [American] country, and have that person say to you, "Oh, I'm sorry, I don't speak Spanish." I say, "Fuck—" It sounds disgusting . . . When my children grow up, I want them to speak English, Spanish, and if they have the chance to study another, another language, great.

The passionate appeal for the maintenance of Spanish seems firmly grounded in the idea that identity must be consciously fashioned and pursued in order to preserve the cultural ties that define a group. The importance of language for identity formation is not limited to national-level languages but extends to the nonstandard variety or dialect that characterizes the network members' place of origin. Given that most first-generation network members have limited educational backgrounds (2 to 5 years of formal schooling), only a few of them use standard Mexican Spanish. Most of them are aware of this, and they often make apologetic comments about their own forms of expression and language use. The attitude toward their rural *ranchero* dialect, however, is ambivalent. They recognize that the features that mark their Spanish are not standard features, but this does not always lead to insecurity. Abstractly, they acknowledge that the use of nonstandard forms leaves them open to discrimination and even ridicule, but in practice their linguistic particularities promote social cohesion by recalling and instantiating their place of origin, the place where everyone speaks as they do.

Although members of the younger generations sometimes use dialect features in their speech, they also more frequently articulate the language ideology of purism that pervades modern schooling in both Mexico and the United States. People on both ends of the transnational circuit experience this linguistic ideology, especially in regard to varieties of Spanish. In Chicago, a Spanish teacher at a Mexican public high school denigrated a young (second-generation) student's use of *ranchero* linguistic features as *su españolranchereado* (your *ranchero*-style Spanish), believing it his mission to "improve" his students' Spanish by insisting that they adopt standard features.

An elderly woman in the *rancho* commented on the topic of *ranchero* Spanish: *Dicen que somos mochos, ¡pero nos comunicamos!* (They say that we are *mochos* [uneducated *rancheros* who "cut off their words" inappropriately], but we communicate!) Yet her (Mexican) high school–educated daughter and granddaughter regularly correct their husband's/father's use of *semos* for the standard *somos* (we are) and *venemos* for the standard *venimos* (we come). *Semos* and *venemos* are part of a larger set of archaic Spanish features (called *barbarismos,* or barbarisms, by purists) that survive in rural Mexican Spanish (Cárdenas Negrete, 1967; Sánchez, 1994). Such dialect features function as class markers in discrimination against them, both in the United States and in Mexico.

Network members realize that language-based problems are due not only to a lack of English but to the dialect of Spanish, or English, that one speaks. Their aspirations for their children stem from this awareness. Most repeatedly stress their desire for their children to be fluent in the standard form of both languages, because they recognize that their children's upward social mobility depends in great part on linguistic ability. Thus, the mastery of

English and Spanish is seen as an essential step toward upward social mobility, but given the predominance of English as the language of authority and power, Spanish, by virtue of remaining tied to circles of intimacy, is at risk of not being maintained beyond the third generation.

Paradoxically, the passion for bilingualism that Angélica and Ismael express does not entail a commitment to bilingual schooling. All network members insisted on the importance of children being equally competent in Spanish and English, but some expressed reservations about bilingual education. For example, Liduvina, an older mother of six grown women who have done very well in school (four have gone to college, and one is pursuing a postgraduate degree), expresses this contradiction: She considers bilingual education a right, but she chose to have her daughters in English-only classrooms.

A mí no me preguntaron si quería yo que la Dalia juera [fuera] [a un aula bilingüe], pero cuando yo me di cuenta, hablé con la maestra y le dije que se iba a confundir mucho teniendo los dos [idiomas], que por qué no me hacía favor de ponerla nomás en inglés porque todas han ido a inglés. Porque entonces el español lo iba a aprender aquí en la casa, ¿verda'? Y entonces la maestra me dijo que estaba bien y la cambió porque— a lo mejor lo que digo no está bien pero— muchos niños pierden el tiempo porque los tienen confundidos. Les dan un poquito de inglés y lo demás en español, [y] pues entonces no avanzan ni en uno ni en otro. A lo mejor habrá niños que sí.

I wasn't asked if I wanted Dalia to be in a bilingual classroom, but when I found out, I spoke to the teacher and said that she was going to get very confused having both [languages], so for her to do me the favor of placing her in English-only, because all [my daughters] have gone to English-only [classrooms]. Because she would then learn Spanish here at home, right? And then the teacher told me that it was all right, and she moved her because— maybe what I say is not right but— many children waste their time because they confuse them. They give them a little bit of English and the rest in Spanish, so then they don't make progress in one or the other. [But] perhaps there are children who do.

Liduvina clearly is ambivalent about bilingual education. She thinks it necessary but expresses reservations about the benefits it affords students, concerned that it might hinder the acquisition of English. This may be due to lack of information about the success of bilingual students. Media oversimplification of issues and confusing program labels also contribute to misinterpretation of the aims of bilingual education. Some parents who hear that

Spanish is the default language of instruction in the bilingual classroom perceive this as denial of an essential tool for upward mobility, similar to African American concerns about Ebonics in the schools (cf. Perry & Delpit, 1998). Evidently, parents like Liduvina think English is not given the priority it deserves in bilingual classrooms and that this is a disservice to the children. Ironically, since the acquisition of English is the primary goal in U.S. bilingual classrooms, in contrast to dual-language programs, the maintenance, development, and mastery of Spanish is generally not given the attention many parents suspect it receives (Chapter 11, this volume). Spanish-speaking parents such as Liduvina often delegate home as the designated site for learning and using Spanish, a manifestation of the pressures they themselves often feel in the workplace (i.e., Spanish is reserved for personal domains, and English for public ones).

José expects that bilingual education is more taxing on his children than an English-only program. Nevertheless, he considers it a necessary sacrifice for the sake of the family's heritage and considers bilingual education a good foundation for the children's early education, although not essential at higher grade levels. José, however, makes a concession to English on the grounds of his children's nationality since they are U.S.-born. This leads him to view bilingual education—and the teaching of Spanish—not as a right that should be demanded of the schools but as a responsibility that must be met primarily at home. After taking a deep breath and letting out a slight chuckle, José says:

[*La educación bilingüe*] *es un tratamiento especial porque si nosotros aprendimos el inglés, lo aprendimos por obligación, por necesidad del trabajo. Los hijos que son nacidos aquí, tienen que aprender el inglés con más razón porque ellos son de aquí. Este es su país de ellos, así es que obligatoriamente tienen que saber ellos un inglés perfecto. Eso es obligatorio.*	[Bilingual education] is special treatment because if we learned English, we learned it because we had to, because we needed a job. The children born here have to learn English more so because they are born here. This is their country, so they are required to know English perfectly. That is obligatory.

Although José views bilingual education as "special treatment," which his generation didn't need to learn English (as self-reliant *rancheros*), he reluctantly accepts it for his children. José explicitly recognizes the United States as his children's country and, by extension, feels that his U.S.-born children have a primary responsibility to master English. Yet he also believes that his children have a duty to master Spanish. In this regard, he shares Liduvina's notion of linguistic separation along the lines of public and private domains. Unfortunately, this stance supports the hegemonic status quo: Spanish must defer to Standard English in public domains, marginalizing Spanish—and Spanish speakers—by default.

CONCLUSION

Despite many years of transnational ties between their *rancho* and Chicago, and despite the maintenance of *ranchero* ways of being and speaking, this social network grapples with issues regarding linguistic and cultural identity in response to the realities of school and work in Chicago, especially regarding language and education. Their relegation of Spanish to the private domain of home limits their children's access to literacy in Spanish and to the standard dialect (*norma culta*). Moreover, as their rural dialect was denigrated in Mexico, so it is denigrated in Chicago. Given the close tie between language and identity (González, 2001), the denial of a language is inevitably a denial of identity. The combined effect of restricting Spanish to the private domain and the public denigration of their Spanish dialect may lead to the loss of Spanish over the generations. Yet their strong commitment to the maintenance of Spanish, and the demographics of Chicago (with its large ethnically concentrated neighborhoods), may significantly constrain the pressures toward linguistic assimilation and language loss. Chicago is a different environment for non-English-speakers than is, for example, the U.S. Southwest. It was never part of Mexico, it has been built by immigration, and large numbers of non-English-speaking Poles (Portes & Rumbaut, 1996) mitigate the local English-only fervor, which has been contested by non-English-speakers throughout the history of Illinois (Judd, 2004). The recent (1998) debate over bilingual education in Chicago, for example, considered not whether bilingual education should be available but for how long it should be available (3 years). Most bilingual education in Chicago, however, is oriented toward a transition to English, not the maintenance of Spanish or other languages. Only dual-language programs, which do enjoy some official support (Judd, 2004), at least attempt to maintain non-English languages (but see Potowski, 2005).

Schools, of course, teach standard varieties of languages. What, then, becomes of the particular dialect that is tied so closely to identity? In contrast to this network's voiced desires that their children learn the standard varieties of both English and Spanish, their vernacular Spanish receives little explicit attention in the home, but it is clearly appreciated and dynamic. Children learn to be creative in the ways in which their parents are creative with language, and most of these lessons are carried out implicitly through the experience of conversation itself and in the context of social interaction. Language in the home is vibrant and abundant, as well as complex and sophisticated in its own right. These lessons in linguistic creativity, and in language and identity, are continually reinforced, as are the values that underlie them—by which the children are expected to succeed regardless of geographic context.

The use of both *franqueza* and creative verbal play saturates the lives of the children in this network, whether they find themselves in Chicago or their *rancho* in Mexico. These linguistic practices, embedded in social values that highlight self-reliance, pragmatism, sincerity, and courage, as well as an aesthetic delight in creative and humorous language use, ultimately lead to a paradoxical set of attitudes toward children's language use. On one hand, parents inculcate skillful and creative language use by children and value bilingualism. On the other hand, they are skeptical of bilingual education and often choose English-only instruction for their children. Such ambivalence reveals an unanticipated and still-not-assimilated fact of the transnational experience for this social network. Although Chicago has been the source of tangible gains and personal progress for many families (both for those living in Chicago and those living in the *rancho*), the transnational experience exerts a dual pressure, especially for the second and third generations—that of being bound to two histories, two cultures, two languages, and two nation-states. Such pressure is especially evident in their desire to retain the sociolinguistic traits that define them but that are challenged in the negotiation of a bicultural identity in Chicago.

What implications does this research have for practitioners who deal with similar populations? How can teachers, social workers, health personnel, and representatives of federal, state, and local agencies make use of this sociolinguistic description of *ranchero* Mexicans? First, this research undermines common stereotypes of Mexicans in the United States. The *ranchero* individualistic identity, as expressed and constructed in their speech, disrupts the commonly assumed dichotomy between U.S. individualism and Mexican communalism. Similarly, *ranchero* identity is indexed in their vernacular dialect. Such dialects do not indicate a lack of intelligence or cognitive ability; rather, they represent and construct personally significant regional and/or ethnic identities—and, as such, they should not be denigrated, nor their speakers made to feel marginal or inferior.

Second, the ways of speaking described here, both "regular" *franqueza* and the creatively playful, could be built on to teach various written genres. *Franqueza* shares much with the "plainspoken" style of essayist literacy in English (Farr, 1993), and students' familiarity with verbal art and speech play could facilitate the reading and writing of creative genres such as poetry. To fully utilize what students bring to the classroom, teachers should make explicit connections between instruction and familiar ways of speaking, as Lee (1995, 1997) has shown with African American English "signifying" and literature instruction, and as Domínguez Barajas (2002) has shown with the use of proverbs to teach essayist writing.

Finally, given the influence of teacher expectations on student achievement, research such as this can inform and, perhaps by informing, contribute to a positive disposition on the part of teachers and others who interact with people such as those presented here. A more knowledgeable and respectful attitude can make a world of difference in the concrete interactions that make up intercultural communication. Then differences (and similarities) can be acknowledged and understood rather than used as resources for conflict (Erickson, 1984).

CHAPTER 4

Language Socialization with Directives in Two Mexican Immigrant Families in South Central Los Angeles

Fazila Bhimji

This chapter examines the language experiences of parents, siblings, and other caregivers of young children in two Mexican working-class families at home in Los Angeles. The focus is on the use of directives by caregivers with young children. Research on child-directed discourse in families with lower socio-economic backgrounds suggests that although parents use a variety of linguistic practices when they talk with one another, they tend to reduce the complexity of their language when talking to young children (e.g., Bernstein, 1986; Feagans, 1982; Hoff-Ginsberg, 1991; Newport, Glietman & Glietman 1977; Snow, Arlman-Rupp, Hassing, Jobse, Jooster, & Vorster, 1976). More recently, Hart & Risley (1995) claimed that parents who are economically advantaged provide their children with a more enhanced language experience than parents who are poor. However, Hart and Risley do not attend to the fact that older siblings, cousins, fictive kin, and even neighbors may play a significant role in a child's language socialization, countering some of the indirect effects of poverty. For example, older siblings may assume the role of caregivers when parents are consumed by obligations that limit their time with their children. Moreover, these scholars do not address questions of poor children's limited access to quality education, public libraries, parks, and even health care, which may affect their linguistic development. Although it is beyond the scope of this chapter to discuss the inequities and racism that Mexican immigrant children encounter, some of the challenges they face are addressed briefly. The principal focus is on the diverse types of directives employed by caregivers in lower-working-class Mexican families.

Directives, as defined by the philosopher of language Searle (1976), are "attempts of varying degrees by the speaker to get the hearer to do something with the propositional content that the hearer does some future action" (p. 11). Directives can be expressed in the form of need statements, imperatives, embedded imperatives, permission directives, and question directives (Ervin-Tripp, 1976). Although philosophers of language and anthropologists discuss the complexities of directives, many child language researchers argue that the presence of directives in maternal speech negatively correlates with the child's linguistic development (Clarke-Stewart, 1973; Hoff-Ginsberg, 1991; Kaye & Charney, 1981; Newport et al., 1977; Olsen-Fulero, 1982). There is a binary understanding of children's language socialization that assumes children in poorer families receive imperatives and children in middle-class families are treated as conversational partners. Such scholarship influences commonsense understandings of children growing up in poor, immigrant family settings. Many people, including educators, think that poor children of color are raised in contexts where there is minimum interaction and communication between caregivers and children.

It becomes essential to examine the pragmatics of language use in bilingual homes in order to appreciate the syncretic, or merged, linguistic practices that result as very young children interact with their immigrant parents and grandparents as well as with siblings and cousins raised in the United States. By specifically focusing on the pragmatics of language, specifically directives, we reveal how the meshing of the linguistic practices of the first generation with those of the second generation counters static notions of language socialization.

This work stems from a larger longitudinal (18 months), ethnographic study of low-income Mexican families with school- and preschool-age children. The families resided in one of the poorest neighborhoods in Los Angeles and were headed by hard-pressed first-generation Mexican immigrants. I believe that my own first-generation immigrant identity helped me connect with the families, and the fact that I was an immigrant from a third world country (Pakistan) blurred some of the boundaries between researcher and subjects. My brown skin and dark hair also facilitated access to the community; on many occasions I was mistaken for a Latina. As a former teacher of some of the children, I was accorded special status, but distance diminished over time as I attended family gatherings, parties, weddings, birthdays, *quinceañeras* (coming-of-age parties for 15-year-old girls), and major holiday celebrations, including Christmas, Thanksgiving, and the Fourth of July. At several *quinceañeras* I enjoyed young people's creativity as they refashioned the traditional "waltz" by fusing urban hip-hop dance styles, similar to the ways in which they fused Spanish and English. The neighborhood and the families' living space reflected and contributed to the syncretism that characterized children's language socialization.

THE NEW INNER CITY

According to the 2000 census, Latinos constitute 47% of the population in the city of Los Angeles and 45% in Los Angeles County. Spanish is used 13 times more than the next most common language, Chinese (López, 1996). The three Mexican families who form part of this study live in South Central Los Angeles, which has experienced a significant ethnic shift. In 1965, South Central Los Angeles was 81% African American, but by 1990 only 45.3% were African American, 50.1% were Latinos, 2.7% were White, and 1.9% were Asian. While the rest of California prospered, South Central did not; income gains between 1980 and 1990 were half of the rest of the city (7.2% versus 14.8%). The poverty rate for families in South Central Los Angeles (30.3%) was double the city's rate and triple the national rate, and conditions have not improved significantly since then. Small single-family houses, built in the 1940s, dot the neighborhoods. Despite the poverty, the atmosphere is almost always festive and lively, as sounds of children playing and music can be heard streaming from the houses. On weekends many balloons announce children's birthdays, *bautizos* (baptisms), *quinceañeras*, and baby showers. Festivities may go on until late at night. Teenagers told me that they liked to live in the "ghetto" because "at other places, you can't have parties until late." They have experienced the fact that in many L.A. neighborhoods, noise ordinances, like curfews, have become a form of racial profiling where Heavy Metal is cool but *banda* (Mexican band) is a misdeamonor (Davis, 2000). Although the face of the inner city has changed and is being revitalized through microlevel entrepreneurship, evidenced by images of *La Virgen de Guadalupe* on many storefronts, these efforts are unrecognized or persecuted. South Central continues to be represented in monolithic, stereotypical ways as a gang-infested and high-crime area. There is gang activity, but there is little critique of structural factors that lead to gang activity or appreciation of the many hardworking families. Hence, South Central Los Angeles remains segregated in many respects. The impact of spatial apartheid became obvious to me when I drove teenagers around other neighborhoods in Los Angeles. I had wanted them to see the South Asian markets, boutiques, and beauty salons that have been on the increase in the Palms area on the Westside; and as we drove past the many ethnic restaurants, one of the teenagers asked me what a Thai restaurant was. I was surprised because Thai restaurants are common in Los Angeles, but the children rarely left their neighborhood. As I continued to drive, they commented about how nice everything looked, although Palms is by no means affluent. It is, however, very ethnically diverse, but Angela only remarked that "a lot of White people live here." The people of color, even though they were not groups she recognized, receded into the background; only Whites, with whom she had little contact, stood out.

The young children who were growing up in families with undocumented parents or siblings experienced further spatial restrictions. Particularly since the terrorist attacks of September 11, 2001, the news had circulated among immigrant families that *la migra* (the immigration police) was everywhere: at the airport, at swap meets, outside the church, at the Laundromat. Even very young children are socialized to the concepts of "legal" versus "illegal." Older children in the families are well aware of where fake Social Security cards are sold at the best prices, where the undocumented can find work in the city with few questions asked, and how much a relative might have paid a *coyote* (smuggler) in order to get to Los Angeles from Mexico.

Given their difficult circumstances, it is small wonder if poor Mexican American children's English vocabulary does not always compare favorably with that of middle-class children. Because they lack supportive social structures and are identified from birth as children of *ilegales* who live in "the ghetto," the early educational experience of young children of poor Mexican immigrant families is left largely to struggling family members. In the homes I observed, the family was a strong source of support despite financial and academic limitations, and despite the adults' limited English. Spanish is the glue that binds families together as they go about living their everyday lives. Parents teach children to tease and talk in traditional Mexican Spanish styles. Fictive kin also tease young children, challenging them to defend themselves. Older children go to schools where they learn to be bicultural and bilingual; in turn, they socialize their younger siblings in bilingual and bicultural ways, and teach their parents English. But each family had special circumstances that were destined to leave distinct imprints on its children.

TWO FAMILIES IN SOUTH CENTRAL LOS ANGELES

The following paragraphs will highlight ethnographic profiles of two families of Mexican origin, both living in one of the most disenfranchised areas in California. One family suffers chronic unemployment while the other is self-employed. These profiles provide the macro context in which the micro verbal interactions of caregivers and children are situated.

The Rodríguez Family

Of all the families that I met during my fieldwork, the Rodríguez family (all names are pseudonyms) was the most economically disadvantaged—but the liveliest. The parents, the oldest child, and her boyfriend were undocumented. The parents had unstable employment and depended largely on state monies for their subsistence. This family began migrating to the United States from a *rancho* (small village) in México in 1989. Both parents arrived with little formal education; Jesús, the father of the family, completed first grade, and Carmen, the mother, finished fourth grade. Jesús came alone; a year after finding a job, he arranged for Carmen and their 1-year-old daughter to join him. Jesús has held several manual jobs since his arrival, and Carmen occasionally works at home for sweatshops. For hours spent trimming pants and shirts, she earns $5 at the end of the day; the family could not survive without assistance from WIC, AFDC, and Medi-Cal for the children. Because the adults are undocumented, Carmen often laments, with much chagrin, "*Somos mojados*" (We are wetbacks). She has internalised the negative attitude of mainstream society toward undocumented immigrants to such an extent that the denigrating term *mojados* forms an integral part of her identity (cf. Solís, 2002).

The Rodríguez family now has seven children. Esmeralda, 2 years old at the time of the fieldwork, is the youngest. She is exposed to Spanish and English because her youngest siblings and her parents speak to her in Spanish and her teenage sisters and godmother's teenage daughters take an active role in teaching and speaking to her in English. I once observed her sister Angela teaching Esmeralda the English words for items around the house because Angela thought that other children of Esmeralda's age spoke much more English and that, in comparison, Esmeralda knew "nothing." All three of her teenage siblings agreed that Esmeralda should have a good knowledge of both Spanish and English, but when they taught her new vocabulary it was always in English.

Esmeralda has two older brothers—Carlos, age 4, and Ricky, age 3—and four older sisters. One sister, Veronica (age 5), has a special talent for spontaneously enacting pretend games. She can transform almost any household object into a play object: An old mattress turns into a queen's castle, a shopping cart with laundry is transformed into an airplane, an exercise machine is overturned to function as a spinning wheel for "macaroni," and duct tape is used to tie up her younger siblings. Before attending school, Veronica spoke only Spanish, with the exception of some very short English phrases such as "gimme gimme," but when she started first grade she began to code-switch between English and Spanish much more frequently. And she began to give English lessons to her mother.

The syncretic practices in this particular family were well evident. Younger children who spoke English socializad their parents into English, whereas older members of the family engaged in traditional linguistic practices such as teasing and the use of irony and humor in their speech. This family was among the poorest I met and yet the children, who owned few toys, demonstrated their creativity through invention and verbal games in English and Spanish, which are rarely acknowledged in mainstream discourses about the children of the poor.

The Fernández Family

Only the Fernández family was self-employed. The parents sold tacos and meat parts each weekend from a truck parked in front of their house. The children were also quite involved in the running of this business and assisted the parents in a variety of ways. Thus, the family business served as a significant site for the children's socialization.

The whole family of María and Mario Fernández, from Guanajuato and Mexicali, has been in the United States since 1986. Seven years after arriving alone in 1979, Mario, a legal resident, returned to Mexico and brought his wife and two children to the United States. The oldest child, Carolina, determined to obtain a higher education, did much of the paperwork on her own to obtain her work permit. The process was by no means easy, and she learned about the bureaucratic hassles of the immigration bureau at an early age. After finally receiving her work permit and becoming eligible to pay nonresident fees for college, she was denied financial aid on the grounds that she still had to complete her legal residency. Carolina remained determined and, paying her own way, continued to take science courses in hope of transferring from her community college to UCLA; she aspires to become an astronomer. I observed Carolina (over several years) spend hours pouring over the Immigration and Naturalization Service's (INS) website, writing letters, talking to various community lawyers, and keeping in close touch with her college counselor. Tensions of the sort that Carolina endured, a common occurence in poor immigrant communities, rarely enter public discourse, although they frustrate many academic dreams. In 2003, Carolina, her siblings, and her mother finally obtained work permits, legalizing their status. Now with a 3-year-old son, Carolina remains undaunted in her ambitions and has learned to question all authorities, even her mother. On one occasion she argued against one of her mother's heroes: "When we were young, you told us that Columbus discovered America and that he was such a hero, when in reality it was the Indians that suffered because of him." Her willingness to challenge standard views and break with gender and age roles in the process may help make her dreams come true.

Unlike Carolina, her parents did not have much formal education. Her father attended first grade and her mother, María, finished elementary school. María initally worked in sweatshops in the United States, until she invested her meager savings in a small *lonchera* (food vending truck), which allowed her to sell tacos and cooked meat parts on weekends in front of her home. María starts the day early, serving breakfast at 6:00 A.M. and ending her day after 7:00 P.M. She is constantly working at many tasks, including nursing her aging parents, who live with the family, and taking care of her four children's needs. Despite her hard life, she is lively and cheerful. A devout Catholic, María attributes much of her success and happiness to the Virgin (of Guadalupe) and the angels, and she often tells vivid stories to her children and customers about the miracles wrought by the angels.

The entire family assists María in the business, which helps develop their linguistic and entrepreneurial skills. Her husband does the grocery shopping and cooks. Carolina warms the tortillas and handles the cash, and the older boys, Edgar and Enrique, ages 10 and 12, run small errands such as getting *cilantro* (coriander) from the store. The youngest child, Vicente, age 3, greets the clients at 6:00 in the morning. As the children grow older, they increasingly manage their mother's business in an independent fashion. When María was in the house nursing her parents, I saw Carolina handling the cash and Enrique warming the tortillas, while Edgar pushed a shopping cart full of prepared meats from the backyard where Mario was cooking.

Three-year-old Vicente is also known as *Vicentito*, Jimmy, *Papi* (little father), and *Gordito* (Fatso). Although Vicente has more Spanish names, which his parents and grandparents use, his older siblings favor the English one, Jimmy. Vicente's multiple names index his bicultural/bilingual socialization, and his daily contacts in the neighborhood immerse him in both Spanish and English, strengthening his developing bilingual and bicultural identities. The ice-cream vendor knows that he can count on Vicente as a regular customer, in Spanish, and Vicente has a strong friendship with the family's *compadre* (ritual kin), who works next door. When Vicente's mother sells food on weekends from her front yard, Vicente walks over to visit *Bigote* (Moustache), as the *compadre* is called, to chat in Spanish. Carolina and Enrique talk to each other mainly in English, occasionally switching to Spanish. However, they and their parents talk to Vicente mainly in Spanish. Vicente uses both Spanish and English in his speech; his English is a source of much amusement within the family.

TYPES OF DIRECTIVES WITHIN THE FAMILIES

Contrary to the commonsense understanding concerning verbal interactions between parents and children, parents did not give overt commands to their children simply for the purpose of social control. I counted 650 directives in 35 hours of videorecordings. For the purpose of this study, I employed Mulder's (1998) classification of directives into three categories:

1. Explicit or bald, where the action to be realized is specified in its literal form and the directives are unmitigated
2. Implicit, when the action to be realized is primarily determined from the context
3. Interplicit, when the directives cannot be considered explicit or implicit and thus fall into an intermediate category

The families did not limit themselves to bald imperatives or use only directives to socially control their children, and the directives were embedded in a variety of sentence structures. The following paragraphs and the accompanying tables illustrate this point. Table 4.1 shows the total number of directives as well as the breakdown of the three types of directives.

Of the total number of directives (n = 650) employed by the caregivers I observed, 63% of them were explicit imperatives, such as *Dile,* "Bye" *(*Tell her, "Bye"); 21% were interplicit, such as when a toddler who is trying to climb into a shopping cart full of laundry is advised, *"Un pie en el frente"* (One foot in front); and the rest (16%) were implicit types of directives, such as *Se dice "gracias"* (One says "thank you"). Even the bald imperatives were often mitigated, as caregivers softened their voices and/or accompanied them with justifications that expanded on the request. And directives served other purposes beyond simple compliance. For example, caregivers gave young children directives to teach small tasks as well as social and verbal skills, such as saying "thank you." The directives appeared in varied sentence types, which are illustrated in Table 4.2, with examples.

Imperatives were employed for the majority (65%) of the directives, but all the caregivers employed other sentence-type directives including declaratives (12%), such as *Vas a jugar con carritos (*You are going to play with cars), and interrogatives (7%), such as *¿Por qué te quitaste la camisa* (Why did you take off your shirt?). Directives were sometimes modified with the use of modals, such as *Y puedes comprar esto también (*And you can buy this as well). In addition, caregivers frequently used subordinate constructions to explain why and how children should comply, in an attempt to convince them. Not all caregivers gave directives to all their children for the same purpose or in the same manner. The child's age and birth order as well as the size of the child's family each played a role in how directives were delivered and the extent to which overt commands were softened by tone of voice, justifications, and teasing; the youngest were favored with more such practices. In sum, young children were exposed to complex language structures and uses of language via directives.

Table 4.1. Principal Types of Directives Addressed to Children

Types of Directives	English Translation	Number of Each Type of Directive	Percentage of All Directives
Explicit (e.g., *Dile,* "Bye")	Tell her "Bye"	409	63
Interplicit (e.g., *Un pie en el frente*)	One foot before the other [to child climbing onto a shopping cart]	137	21
Implicit (e.g., *Se dice "gracias"*)	One says "thank you"	104	16
Total		650	100

Table 4.2. Directives Addressed to the Children According to Sentence Type

Types of Directives	English Translation	Number of Each Type of Directive	Percentage of All Directives
Imperatives (e.g., *Junta chile*)	Gather chile.	423	65
Declaratives (e.g., *Vas a jugar con carritos*)	You are going to play with little cars.	78	12
Interrogatives (e.g., *¿Por qué te quitaste la camisa?*)	Why did you take off your shirt?	45	7
OTHER		104	16
Elliptic (e.g., *[Dile]* Apple)	(Say) apple		
Modified Directives (e.g., [with que] *¡Que te calles!*)	(I demand) you keep quiet!		
Total		650	100

The use of directives with young children also indexed significant socio-cultural meanings. As Farr and Domínguez Barajas (Chapter 3, this volume) point out, in *ranchero* families bald on record imperatives indicate a *franqueza* (frank and direct) style, which socializes children to be strong and self-assertive individuals. The caregivers in the Mexican families I observed did not, however, adhere to a monocultural style of speaking with their children because some, particularly older siblings, use politer forms, employing linguistic devices such as *quieres?* (Would you like to?) that soften a directive politely. This is not surprising, as older siblings have been exposed to non-*ranchero* styles in their networks at school and in the neighborhood. In the four excerpts below, interactions between first- and second-generation caregivers and Vicente and Esmeralda illustrate several ways in which directives were employed.

BICULTURAL/BILINGUAL WAYS WITH DIRECTIVES

The Fernández family was the only one in the sample with a computer, which their mother purchased (used) from a friend. On one of my visits, Carolina proudly told me that her 3-year-old brother "Jimmy" could successfully use software that allowed him to make snowflakes. "I would like to see that," I answered. What followed was a 20-minute computer-mediated conversation between Vicente and his older sister. Vicente was not interested in making snowflakes on this particular day; instead he wanted to play with a software that allowed him to look at dogs. Carolina repeatedly asked him to make snowflakes using indirect forms of directives (for transcription conventions, see Introduction, footnote 2):

I. Teen sister Carolina and 3-year-old Vicente

1	Vicente:	*No quiero.*	I don't want to.
2	Carolina:	*¿No quieres hacer* snow-flakes?	You don't want to make snowflakes?
3	Vicente:	*No.*	No.
4	Carolina:	*¿Este?*	This one?
5		*Espérate.*	Wait.
6		*Mira ¿quién es?*	Look, who is this?
7		*Santa Clos.*	Santa Claus.
8	Vicente:	*No.*	No.
9		*Bow-wow.*	Bow-wow. [*dog*]

[*Vicente points at the computer. A dog appears on the screen.*]

| 10 | Carolina: | *¿Dónde ésta su bow-wow?* | Where is your bow-wow? |

| 11 Vicente: | *Sí.* | Yes. |
| 12 Carolina: | *Aquí ésta bow-wow.* | Here is bow-wow. |

[*Vicente points at the computer.*]

| 13 Vicente : | *Meow. Meow.* | Meow. Meow. |

[*Long pause. Vicente and Carolina watch the computer screen for 40 seconds.*]

14 Vicente:	*Ya horita. Voy a cambiar.*	That's it. I'm going to change.
15 Carolina:	*¿No quieres hacer el este?*	Don't you want to do this?
16	*El que le tienes que ponerle cual quieras.*	The one where you have to put the one that you want.
17 Vicente:	*Sí.*	Yes.
18 Carolina:	*Horita. Te voy a poner éste.*	Now. I will put this one on for you.
19	*¿No quieres hacer el otro?*	You don't want to do the other one?
20 Vicente:	*No ésta y ésta y ésta.*	No this one and this one and this one.

**** [*Points at the computer screen.*]
[*Vicente continues to point at the computer screen and occasionally talk to the screen for 2 to 3 minutes. Carolina allows him to interact with the screen on his own.*]

50 Carolina:	*Por eso.*	That's why.
51	*Es el que te estoy buscando.*	That's the one I'm trying to find for you.
52	*Espérate.*	Wait.
53 Vicente:	*No.*	No.
54	*No.*	No.
55	*Aquí. Aquí. Aquí.*	Here. Here. Here.

[*Points to the corner of the computer.*]

| 56 Carolina: | *¿No quieres jugar esto?* | Don't you want to play this? |
| 57 Vicente: | *No.* | No. |

As Carolina urged Vicente to use the software that would enable him to make snowflakes, she mitigated her directives by employing what Mulder describes as the "volitive modal" *querer* (lines 15, 19, and 56) and four other questions that sought to find out what Vicente wanted to do. Only three directives are explicit (lines 5, 6, 52), and she took the perspective of the child by softening her voice, asking about his preferences, and allowing Vicente a lot of time between interactions to make independent decisions in selecting and playing with the software program.

Child-language researchers have found that dyadic forms of verbal actions characterize mainstream Anglo families (Schieffelin & Ochs, 1986), and many assume that they are infrequent in working-class Mexican households, especially among first-generation parents, given the large families and situation-centered patterns (Chapter 1, this volume). But Carolina and Vincente were often engaged in such one-on-one conversations, and in the following dyadic conversation, Vicente's mother, María, is teaching the boy to sort beans. After a bald on record imperative (No, No, not from there), she demonstrates and makes clear why you must look through the beans carefully and remove the stones.

II. Mother María and 3-year-old Vicente

1 María:	*No. No. De allí no.*	No. No. From there no.
2	*Primero los tenemos que ver así.*	First we have to look at them like this.
3	*Mira.*	Look.
4	*Es una piedra.*	This is a stone.
5	*Mira.*	Look.

[*María picks up a little stone and shows it to Vicente.*]

6	*Ves. Ese tumba los dientes.*	See. This will knock out your teeth.
7	*Sí. Mira.*	Yes. Look.
8 Vicente:	*Tumba eshta?*	Does thish knock out?

[*Continues to give her handfuls of beans.*]

| 9 María: | *No.* | No. |
| 10 | *Por eso tenemos que escoger los que no lleven piedras.* | That is why we have to pick the ones that don't have stones. |

[*Continues to sort the beans.*]

María provides Vicente with detailed explanations about why he should not give her the beans without having sorted through them. In line 2 she illustrates what needs to be done prior to picking up the beans: *Primero los tenemos que ver así* (First we have to look at them like this). In her following turn, María illustrates what Vicente should be looking for: "This is a stone. Look." In line 6, María elaborates by telling Vicente the painful reason why the stones must be removed from the beans: "See. This will knock out your teeth." Note that in line 8, Vicente treats María's earlier utterance as an explanation, because he recycles it as an interrogative: "Does thish knock out?" However, he continues to give María handfuls of beans without sorting through them and she continues to provide explanations: "No. That's why we have to pick the ones that don't have stones." In this illustration, the mother offers justifications and explanations in conjunction with her imperatives, to teach the child in a way that accommodates his age and skill.

The next interaction captures teenaged older siblings, cousins, and neighbors teaching 2-year-old Esmeralda some English vocabulary.

III. Group interaction with 2-year-old Esmeralda

1	Monica:	*Dile apple.*	Tell her. Apple.
2	Esmeralda:	*Apple.*	
3	Betty:	*Apple.*	
4	Monica:	[*to Betty*] *Déjala solita.*	Let her do it alone.
5	Esmeralda:	Appppp	
6	Monica:	*Dile* apple.	Tell her "apple."
7	Esmeralda:	Apple.	
8	Monica:	*Dile* pear.	Tell her "pear."
9	Esmeralda:	Apple.	
10	Monica:	Pear. *Dile* pear. Pear.	Pear. Tell her "pear. Pear."
11	Esmeralda:	Apple.	
12	Betty:	Pear, *Esmeralda*. Pear. Pear.	
13	Monica:	*Dile* TV.	Tell her "TV."
14		Hey, I'm talking to you.	
15		Don't get shy.	

[*Pats Esmeralda's hair down with much affection.*]

16		*Dile* dog.	Tell her "dog."
17		*Dile* cat.	Tell her "cat."
18		[*to the others*] She's hiding her face already.	
19		[*to Esmeralda*] ¿*Quieres chicle?*	Do you want a gum?
20		¿*Chicle?*	Gum?

[*Esmeralda nods her head.*]

21		Well, say "cat. CAT."	
22	Betty:	*Gato dile.*	Cat tell her.
23	Monica:	*Di* cat.	Say "cat."

24 Esmeralda: *Antoni.*
25 Monica: [*to others*] Anthony. That's
                all she knows how to say.
26   My little cousin Anthony.
27 Monica: [*to E*] I'm not telling you
                to say "Anthony."
28   Say cat.
29 Betty: *Di* cat, Esmeralda.   Say "cat," Esmeralda.
30   Esmeralda. *Di* cat.   Esmeralda. Say "cat."
31   *Dile*   Tell her.
32 Monica: *Dile*, "Anthony is a cat."   Tell her, "Anthony is a cat."
33   *Dile* cat.   Tell her "cat."

[*Esmeralda begins to climb on the stoop.*]

34   I'm talking to you.
35   No. You're gonna fall
                down.
36   *Esmeralda (m)ira.*   Esmeralda look.

[*Betty brings a piece of gum to Esmeralda.*]
[*Esmeralda reaches out for it.*]

37 Betty: No. *Di* cat.   [*refusing her*   No. Say "cat."
                                the gum]
38   *Pues. Sí.*   Well. Yes.
39 Esmeralda: CAT.
40 Monica: *Di* dog.   Say "dog."
41 Esmeralda: Dog.
42 Betty: *Dile* family.   Tell her "family."
43   Family.
44 Esmeralda: Family.

In this English lesson, Esmeralda is directed to say common nouns for animals and fruits—Cat, Dog, Apple, Pear—then *TV*; and finally *family* by teens who switch back and forth between Spanish and English. Both her sister, Betty, and cousin, Monica, give her 16 explicit directives employing the imperative prompts *"Di," "Dile,"* and *"Say."* Usually, Esmeralda repeats the words after some coaxing and bribing. For example, in lines 2,5, 7, 9, and 11 Esmeralda repeats the word *apple.* She does not respond to *pear* or *TV* at all, but after 10 prompts she says cat loudly on line 39, after she is promised gum. The bribe is effective because in line 41 she repeats the word *dog* immediately and follows up with an immediate repetition of the word *family.* These directives to repeat nouns out of context contribute to Esmeralda's acquisition of English common nouns, but she contributes her own personal noun to the conversation, *Antoni*, although it is not clear why she brings it up. In line 25, Monica acknowledges Esmeralda's contribution indirectly by repeating it and expanding for the benefit of the others. She explains who Antoni is, in English: "Anthony. My little cousin Anthony." In line 32 she attempts to teach Esmeralda to build on her utterance, by pronouncing the English version of *Antoni* and combining it with one of the words they have been trying to teach her: "*Dile*, Anthony is a cat." Expanding a child's utterances in this manner is another feature of mainstream caregiver talk, as is explicit instruction, but it is usually one on one. Esmeralda's siblings use bald imperatives in a multiparty session, but they also soften them by modifying their voices as well as displaying physical affection (smoothing E's hair), creating playful and teasing instructions ("Say 'Anthony is a cat'"), patiently waiting for the child to utter the correct words, and collaborating in bribing the child with gum. Esmeralda was learning English via unmitigated imperatives accompanied by treats. But the most effective language lesson she learned in this interaction is the fluid way in which young bilinguals switch back and forth from English to Spanish, alternating pronunciation, vocabulary, and grammar seamlessly in the pursuit of the same goal.

The final example is of a practice that has been described as typical in Mexican and Puerto Rican families, the use of young children as messengers in teasing routines (cf. Eisenberg, 1986; Farr, Chapter 3; Zentella, 1997a). This kind of teasing serves as an effective way for one adult to challenge or criticize another indirectly, by having an innocent child make the challenge. It also introduces the child to the culture's playful use of language. The topic that Esmeralda's mother chose to tease about is usually quite a serious one in immigrant families, *la migra* (immigration police):

IV. Madrina (Esmeralda's godmother), mother Carmen, and Esmeralda.

1 Madrina:	[*to Esmeralda*] *Mocosa.*	Snot nose.
2 Carmen:	[*to Esmeralda*] *Cálmate.*	Calm down.
	Dile.	Tell her.
3	*La migra. Dile.*	Immigration police. Tell her.
4 Esmeralda:	*La miga.*	Migation.
5 Carmen:	*Dile.*	Tell her.
6	*Te lleva la migra.*	The immigration police will take you.
7	*Van a venir.*	They are going to come.

[*The Madrina stops teasing Esmeralda and begins another topic with Carmen.*]

When Esmeralda's godmother teased her by calling her a snotnose, Esmeralda's mother directed her 2-year-old to challenge the tease by telling her godmother to calm down and to threaten her godmother by telling her that the INS will come after her (line 3): *La migra. Dile* (Immigration police. Tell her). As if acknowledging the powerful nemesis, Esmeralda did as her mother said, producing a childlike approximation, *La miga* (line 4). Carmen continued to direct Esmeralda to threaten her godmother with deportation until the godmother changed the topic. Apparently, the immigration police have replaced the traditional Mexican *cucuy* (boogey man) for Esmeralda's undocumented mother, revealing the way in which illegal status has become such a critical part of everday life. This is not an isolated incident; the use of *la migra* as a threat to make children behave is common (Zentella, personal communication). In this case, the playfulness of the threat is clear to the adults because the *madrina* has legal status. As Solís (2002) aptly argues and Carmen's teasing demonstrates, even children who are born in the United States learn to fear the consequences of illegality. From an anthropolitical perspective (Introduction, this volume), this fear is of greater concern than whether the child is being teased or directed with bald imperatives.

CONCLUSION

In low-income Mexican immigrant families there is rich and varied verbal interaction in Spanish and English between caregivers and young children. Children growing up in a multilingual and multicultural society such as that of Los Angeles are not socialized in monolithic ways. My data showed that though caregivers' speech to the children consists largely of directives, there is variation in the forms and focus of directives to young children in the families. Caregivers may direct children in explicit or implicit ways, and they vary their directives with respect to the sentence structure. For example, imperative forms as well as declaratives and interrogatives can teach young children social rules and practices. Caregivers may also modify directives in a range of ways. When they wish to convey a sense of urgency and immediacy to their young children, they employ specific imperatives or modals, like *you have to*, and/or raise their voice. When caregivers want to mitigate their requests they may ask "*quieres*" (would you like) or use a cajoling tone of voice or bribes to soften the directive. Additionally, caregivers frequently justify their commands, conveying to the children that their directives are rational and purposeful. Some directives teach young children household tasks, social norms, nominal words, new skills, or how to tease and challenge members of the family. In sum, the children in the two Mexican families I observed in South Central Los Angeles were involved in complex verbal practices.

Furthermore, young children's socialization is an ongoing process; as children grow older and move into higher grades they are exposed to new ways of learning and teaching and in turn socialize their younger siblings in varied ways.

The family practices described in this chapter contest the cultural-deficit or home–school mismatch views that influence some educational reforms and argue for more inclusive and equitable policies that address the poverty, isolation, and uncertain status of hardworking families that are root explanations for their lack of educational success. Some analysts continue to attribute the educational failure of minority children to deficiencies in culture, arguing against better school financing as a fruitless effort. In a *New York Times* op-ed piece, Traub (2000) claimed:

> The success of those Russian and Italian and Irish immigrants three-quarters of a century ago, and many Asian and Hispanic immigrants today, make it plain that the issue has less to do with poverty as such than with culture—with conscious as well as unconscious behaviors. (p. 57)

But how much do we know about the conscious and unconscious behaviors of those who are not succeeding? It is circular reasoning to argue that those who are failing must not be doing what the successful are doing, and that view allows the differential impact of unemployment or below-minimum-wage earnings on populations that are racially, nationally, linguistically, and culturally stigmatized to be ignored. Problems that children of undocumented and poor Mexicans encounter in school settings are blamed on the families' lack of appropriate cultural values and on particular parental practices, such as the use of directives, with no research evidence, which impedes the formulation of appropriate educational initiatives.

Happily, individual teachers can make a difference. Educators can be alert to the range of practices that exist in their students' homes and rework their curriculum to take advantage of the resources of minority students, such as their bilingual and bicultural forms of socialization. At the same time, educators need to mount a stronger critique of structural constraints such as urban apartheid and of attitudes that construct children as unworthy "illegal aliens" because they or their parents are undocumented. By advocating federal programs that challenge systemic inequities—including child care, medical insurance, preschool programs, after-school services, summer classes and jobs, and bilingual education—and by strengthening the languages and literacies that children bring to the classroom, educators can transform their students' lives and ultimately influence policy decisions that can benefit the entire nation.

CHAPTER 5

Staying on God's Path:
Socializing Latino Immigrant Youth
to a Christian Pentecostal Identity
in Southern California

Lucila D. Ek

The majority of U.S. Latinos are Catholic, but an unprecedented number are converting to Protestantism. According to Levitt (2002), "An estimated one out of every seven Latinos left the Catholic Church in the last twenty-five years" (p. 150). There are "7,000 Hispanic/Latino Protestant congregations, most of them Pentecostal or evangelical in theology" (Warner & Wittner, 1998, p. 5). Despite this surge, scholarly attention to the significance of immigrant religious institutions, including their role in socialization, is lacking (Ebaugh & Chafetz, 2000; Warner & Wittner, 1998). One exception is Baquedano-López's (1998) seminal study of the language socialization of Mexican immigrant children to a Mexican identity in Catholic *doctrina* (catechism) classes. However, we know little about how Protestant churches influence language, socialization, and identity for Latino immigrants. Thus, investigating socialization in religious settings is crucial for understanding not only the selves immigrant bilingual Latino students bring into the classroom but also how those identities may affect their learning and achievement.

This chapter examines the language socialization of immigrant Central American and Mexican youth in *La Iglesia* (the church), a Spanish-language Pentecostal church in southern California (names of people and places are pseudonyms). Linguistic interactions at their Sunday school and services during the week socialize the adolescents to a Christian Pentecostal identity that seeks to position them on *el camino* (the path), or God's path, and away from *el mundo* (the world) or the larger society. Adult authorities wish to protect the youth from *perdición* (perdition), that is, falling prey to dangerous practices, including drinking, drugs, and premarital sex. Simultaneously, the youth are being apprenticed to use language in Christian Pentecostal ways that signal church membership and minimize national differences. In this Sunday school, however, socialization to *el camino* is never a simple or neutral process but is a site of conflict, tension, and contradiction. The public schools the youth attend are a locus of the tension between *el camino and el mundo* in that church authorities want the youth to obtain a higher education, but they are suspicious of the mainstream values found there. Inevitably, worldly values seep into the church despite the adults' efforts to insulate the youth.

Children and youth are socialized into social identities that they learn to express by using the linguistic codes of their communities in social interaction (Schieffelin & Ochs, 1986). Viewed as fluid and dynamic, identity is defined as the range of social personae—including social statuses, roles, positions, relationships, institutional, and other community identities—people attempt to claim or assign (Ochs, 1993). This study explores how youth are socialized to a Christian identity as they participate in the language practices of their Sunday school, which include class lecture-sermons, prayers, hymns, and collective Bible readings. I have been a participant observer at the church since October 2000. The primary data set includes approximately 60 hours of audio- and videotapes of the *clase para jóvenes* (youth class).

THE COMMUNITY CONTEXT

The political climate in California, hostile to immigrant populations, complicates bilingual children's learning and development. In 1986, California passed Proposition 163 making English the official language. In the 1990s, the state passed Proposition 187 (1994), which attempted to eliminate health and educational services for undocumented immigrants (declared unconstitutional by the courts); Proposition 209 (1996), which eliminated affirmative action; and Proposition 227 (1998), which virtually ended bilingual education. Among the repercussions: Home and school language practices are changing in ways that limit the use of bilingual students' full linguistic repertoire, especially their primary language (Gutiérrez, Asato, Santos, & Gotanda, 2002).

Despite these policies, the Latino population in California continues to grow and diversify as immigrants arrive daily, many from Mexico and Central America. Mexicans are still the largest group of Latinos in Los Angeles, but Central Americans constitute about 14% of the 1,719,073 Latinos in the city. Together Salvadorans and Guatemalans represent 80% of the city's Central American population (U.S. Bureau of the Census, 2000c).

The community where *La Iglesia* is located has experienced dramatic changes in the last 20 years. Once predominantly Mexican, it witnessed a large influx of Salvadorans and Guatemalans in the 1980s. Nicaraguans and Hondurans followed. These migrations were motivated largely by the desire to escape political and economic upheavals in Central America (Hamilton & Chinchilla, 2001; Orellana, 2001). The number of Koreans who live in the bordering area also grew in the mid-1980s, then dwindled. This community loses many residents as they move to other cities and states or return to their homelands. The Latinos who stay have gained a foothold in the political and commercial life of the city and actively strive to build their community. I grew up very near this area; when I was a child, my parents would often bring my sisters and me to the stores and parks. Now my work brings me back to the community. My interest in one young girl's language socialization led me *to La Iglesia* and facilitated my entry. Although I am not Pentecostal, my working-class Mexican immigrant background and Baptist upbringing help me to identify with *La Iglesia*'s members.

La Iglesia is part of a larger religious movement that promotes evangelism and Christian service. Accordingly, this storefront church emphasizes literacy, especially the interpretation of biblical texts. The larger church has more than 6 million members worldwide, including Latin America. The surge in Protestant conversion in Latin America (Stoll, 1990) has strengthened the transnational aspect of immigrant Latinos' religious lives. One Guatemalan family, for example, often travels back and forth between the United States and Guatemala, attending Pentecostal churches in both countries. When their relatives from Guatemala visit, they attend services at *La Iglesia*. Thus, the church is an important link for the construction of transnational identities that strengthen the Spanish of U.S.-born children.

La Iglesia is open every day, offering different activities to about 80 working-class members, approximately 70% of whom are Central American (Guatemalan, Salvadoran, Honduran, and Nicaraguan) and 30% are Mexican. The majority of the adults obtained an elementary or middle school education in their home countries; they work as dry cleaners, painters, restaurant workers, and housekeepers. Most of their children were born in the United States, and the few born in Latin America came to the States as very young children. The church leaders, most of whom are Central American, include the pastor, his assistants, and six Sunday school teachers. The leaders tend to have a higher level of education than the rest of the congregation. Two of the teachers are in college and work as teaching assistants in public schools.

Five girls and four boys attend the *clase para jóvenes* (youth class) consistently; seven are now in high school and two are in middle school. Three students are U.S.-born: a brother and sister whose parents are from Guatemala, and another girl whose two older sisters, also in the class, were born in El Salvador. Another boy was born in Guatemala, and three teens (two boys and a girl) were born in Mexico. The teachers who have taught the youth class include 20-year-old Tommy, from Guatemala; 25-year-old Alberto, from Honduras; and the pastor, age 30, who is from El Salvador.

At the beginning of my study Tommy taught the only Sunday school class, but when the church moved to a larger space Tommy taught the younger children and Alberto became the youth instructor. With the change in teachers came a change in the tone of the youth class and student participation. Tommy tended to be laid-back, accessible, and funny in his lectures to the students, which included his younger brother and two cousins. In contrast, the students did not know Alberto, who had recently arrived from Honduras. He had a more serious demeanor and the students did not speak up as much or joke with him. Alberto taught most of the youth classes that I taped. Tommy taught the class when Alberto was absent, and sometimes the pastor taught. The language of worship at *La Iglesia* is Spanish; sermons, prayers, hymns, and readings are in Spanish. Sunday school class lectures are conducted in Spanish, although the pastor and Tommy sometimes spoke some English. The youth participated primarily in their first language, Spanish, but spoke a little more English when the pastor or Tommy taught. The class schedule was:

10:15 Opening prayer and song
10:30 Lecture based on multiple written texts, including the Bible and youth lesson book
11:45 Closing prayer and song

Recently, the church began to integrate the youth into the adult sermon by having them participate in the opening prayers and songs with the entire congregation. Then the children and youth go to their separate classrooms, after which they rejoin the congregation for closing songs and prayers.

Almost all class sessions opened with the teacher presenting the *tema* (theme) and a *texto* (text—verses from the Bible or lesson book that students memorize and that guide the lesson. The lesson books are Christian publications in Spanish with titles like *La senda juvenil* (The Youthful Path). Teachers have gone through three lesson books as they struggle to find more enjoyable and relevant material.

The teacher follows the *tema* and *texto* with an original opening prayer of gratitude and petition during which the students, who usually sit in rows, are expected to stand. A few students recite their own prayers, but the majority simply stand, eyes closed. Then the teacher leads the singing of hymns unaccompanied by a hymnal. Most of the songs were hymns that I had heard many times during my visits and during my own church days.

After the prayer, the teacher reviews the previous week's lesson by eliciting the recitation of *tema* and *texto*. Then the teacher begins the day's lesson, which usually focuses on a Bible story. The youth are expected to sit, take notes with pen and paper that the teacher provides, and follow along in their Bibles and/or youth books. The majority of student–teacher interactions occur when the teacher calls on individuals or expects everyone to respond to his questions in a round-robin fashion. The teacher lectures and periodically checks for understanding by saying *"Amén"* (Amen) and students reply *"Amén,"* which guarantees the students' verbal involvement throughout the lecture. During the lesson, students read verses aloud from the Bible either individually or collectively. The teacher makes few corrections save to help them pronounce difficult words. After the lecture, the teacher or a student leads the closing prayer and songs.

Students are constantly reading, interpreting, and discussing written texts, particularly the Bible. Such text-centered activities attest to the central place occupied by literacy in religious education (cf. Farr, 2000b; Heath, 1983; Moss, 1988). As I elaborate in other work (Ek, 2004), literacy is a primary tool for socializing the youth to a Christian Pentecostal identity and to the importance of religious texts, the Bible above all.

CONSTRUCTING *EL CAMINO*

A strict fundamentalism, which calls for a separation from the secular world's values, marks *La Iglesia*. Seeking to protect youth from mainstream influences, the teachers and the pastor repeatedly make a distinction between *el camino* and *el mundo*. *El camino* encompasses such Christian norms and moral values as attending church, reading the Bible, and following God's teachings. Often the path is constructed in opposition to the beliefs and practices of the secular world, such as engaging in premarital sex, attending dance parties, or listening to secular music. Church teachings and, in particular, the lessons for adolescents make explicit the conflicting ideologies of these positions. In constructing this binary, the adult authorities hope to socialize the youth to a Christian Pentecostal identity that remains on *el camino*, so as to gain the strength to ward off *el mundo*'s dangers.

The teachers retell Biblical stories in order to teach religious principles and to convey moral messages. Prior to the excerpt below, the pastor introduced the Biblical character José (Joseph), who was his father's favorite and beloved by God yet still had problems. José's story helps to construct the importance of *el camino* as well as the students' own identities as pious, beloved people of God:[1]

1 Pastor:	*Pero fíjense la clave está en—*	But pay attention the key is in—
2	*realmente en orientar el camino*	really in turning your path
3	*en orientar el camino a la verdad de Dios (.2)*	in turning your path to God's truth

. . . . [*Pastor continues about José.*]

12	*Jóvenes, Dios— escuchen bien lo que voy a*	Youth, God— listen carefully to what I am going to
13	*decir y esto no los van—no quiero que se*	say and this will not go— I do not want you to
14	*creen una conciencia egocéntrica o egoísta*	develop an egocentric or selfish conscience
15	*Dios los ama más a ustedes que al que está en el*	God loves you more than he/she who is in the
16	*mundo y ustedes dirán "¿por qué?"*	world and you may say, "why"?
17	*Porque ustedes están en Su camino*	Because you are on His path
18	*Ustedes son parte— (.2)*	You are part—
19	*aunque Dios ama a todos los hombres es s—*	even though God loves all people s—
20	*la relación que Dios tiene con ustedes es mejor*	the relationship that God has with you is
21	*que la que tiene con un impío.*	better than the one He has with an impious person.

The pastor conveys, first, what it means to be on *el camino* and, second, the benefits of being on the path. His main message, demonstrated by his emphasis on and repetition of "turning your path" (lines 2–3), is that the "key" (line 1) for the youth is to turn their path to God's "truth" (line 3), which will shield them from *el mundo*'s temptations. The second part outlines a benefit of being on *el camino*, that is, a loving father for the youth. This relationship signals an important way in which the community of Christian Pentecostals is constituted. The adolescents have a special role in the community hierarchy, and their acceptance of it is part of being on *el camino*. Moreover, they have a unique status because they are God's favorites; He loves them more than He loves the impious, and thus they are distinguished from the rest of the world (lines 15, 20–21). However, the pastor does not want the youth to think that they are better than others, telling them not to have "an egocentric or selfish conscience" (line 14). By reminding the youth that they "are on His path" (line 17) and by stressing the present tense verb *"están"* (line 17), he highlights their present location on *el camino* as well as the goal of remaining there.

Camino also connotes movement, progress, and dynamism. It invokes the importance of movement in the students' lives as well as their personal growth, including their families' migration. Their status as the children of immigrants is tied to a moral responsibility to God and their continued movement on the path. The pastor explains why God brought them to the United States:

1 Pastor:	*Porque en nuestros países*	Because in our countries
	hay una crisis terrible	there is a terrible crisis
2	*en todos los aspectos*	in all aspects

.... [*Pastor continues lecture.*]

7	*que Dios nos ha traído acá,*	that God has brought us here,
8	*que no fue que nuestros padres nos trajeron*	that it was not that our parents brought us
9	*Dios movió a nuestros padres para que nos*	God moved our parents so that
10	*hiciesen llegar hasta acá*	they would make us come here
11	*y AHORA que estamos acá*	and NOW that we are here
12	*y tenemos todas las oportunidades al frente* (.2)	and we have all the opportunities before us
13	*aprendan a utilizarlas* (1.4)	learn to use them
14	*lo que Dios puede hacer con tu vida.*	what God can do with your life.
15	*Tú eres el cambio.*	You are the change.
16	*Tú representas* (.8) *el, el, el la esperanza de esta*	You represent the, the, the the hope
17	*nación* (.2) *de esta ciudad* (1.6)	of this nation, of this city.

In line 1, the pastor cites the "terrible crisis" that plagues their home countries, which leads to God's protective intervention. It is God, not their parents, who brings them to the United States (line 7), a land of unlimited opportunity (line 12). Here they must continue to live on God's path, for the benefit of their new city and nation. The repetition of *"acá"* (here) (line 7,

10, 11) and the increased loudness in "AHORA" (NOW) (line 11) communicate that the past was left behind and that now the youth must look to their future in the United States. The pastor stresses the word *"utilizarlas"* (use them) (line 13) to convey a sense of urgency about the students' moral agency. He positions the students individually in a transformative future-oriented life with a dramatic plea, repeating the informal singular *"tú"* (you) (lines 14, 15, 16). By telling the students "you are the change," the pastor implies that they are the fulfillment of immigration, the move from *"nuestros países"* (our countries) to *"acá"* (here), the change from the past to the present, and the change from a terrible crisis to *"la esperanza"* (the hope) (line 16). The youth are valuable not only to their parents and their church but also to this nation if they take advantage of the opportunities and fulfill their future promise as agents of God. It is both a lofty expectation and an enormous moral responsibility.

INDEXING MEMBERSHIP THROUGH LANGUAGE

Membership in the community of people on *el camino* is signaled through the language used in the church, most obviously in the use of Spanish but also through other linguistic markers. Youth are socialized to the familylike nature of the Christian community through certain salutations and terms of address. Church members refer to each other by the familial *"hermano/a"* (brother/sister), while the head of the church is called *pastor* (pastor) by both adults and children. The proper way for adults to greet each other and for youth to greet adults is with a handshake accompanied by the phrase, *"Dios le bendiga, hermano/a"* (God bless you, brother/sister), to which the appropriate reply is *"Dios le bendiga"* (God bless you). One morning, the pastor greeted me with *"Dios le bendiga, hermana"* (God bless you, sister), and I mistakenly replied *"Gracias"* (Thank you), thus marking my outsider status. The same salutation is used as a goodbye when the church members leave for home. The verb clause *le bendiga* (bless you) corresponds to the pronoun *usted* (you—singular formal); in this way, the students are learning forms of respect for their elders and church authorities.

Church membership also entails an erasure of national identity, which occurred in four ways. First, the nationalities of the members were not foregrounded. Elders rarely made reference to their home countries; for example, once the pastor alluded to El Salvador when speaking about his father. When Alberto referred to his home country, he would say *"Allí en mi país"* (There in my country) without naming the nation. Elders do not mention what countries they or the children are from in formal classroom and church services. I did not know the youth's nationalities until I asked Tommy a year after I began to visit. Second, with respect to language, the pronouns *usted* (you—singular formal) and *tú* (you—singular informal) predominate at the church to the near exclusion of the second-person singular (informal) *vos* and its verb forms, despite the fact that *voseo* patterns are common in Central America. Lipski (1994) claims they are "the rule in Guatemalan Spanish" (p. 266), but Tommy, who is Guatemalan, used the *vos* form only when speaking to his little brother, Ryan. The following example is from one of the classes (*vos* verb forms are in bold):

Quiero, Ryan que **vayás** *a traer la escalera, te* **subás**, *y me* **bajés** *aquel* [*unclear speech*] . . . *¿vos* **serías** *capaz de levantar la escalera?*	Ryan, I want you to go and bring the ladder, to climb up, and to bring me down that [unclear speech] . . . would you be able to lift the ladder?

Save for this instance, Tommy used the *tú* form with everyone, even with Guatemalan students, some of whom are his cousins. Yet Tommy and his brothers use the *vos* form extensively at home. The two other teachers also use the *tú* and *usted* forms with the students even though they are from El Salvador and Honduras. In addition, a Guatemalan teen explained that she uses *vos* in Guatemala but not at *La Iglesia*. Third, the blurring of national origin is also reflected in the lexicon of the church leaders and students, because standard Spanish or Mexican terms outnumber Central Americanisms. The Salvadoran pastor calls the youth "*muchachos/muchachas*" (boys/girls) instead of the Salvadoran *cipotes* or *bichos* (Chapter 6, this volume). The girl from Guatemala tells me that she knows the word for *pajilla* is *popote* here, referring to the Mexican word for *straw*, so she represses *popote*. The fourth way in which the blurring of nationality occurs is through the common theme that God is a universal God who sees no distinctions among people. Alberto explained:

Dios nos ama a todos. ¿Amén? Al negrito, al blanquito, al trigueño, al mulato, a todos nos ama Dios. A todos nos ama el Señor.	God loves us all. Amen? Black, white, brown, mulatto, God loves us all. The Lord loves us all.

The principal message is that God does not privilege a certain race or ethnicity; such differences do not matter to the Lord. Alberto did not say, "*Dios ama al Guatemalteco, al Salvadoreño, al Mexicano, etc.*" (God loves Guatemalans, Salvadorans, Mexicans, etc.); he focused on racial categories—U.S. racial distinctions—instead of national origins. Alberto's observation, coupled with the forms of Spanish used at the church, suggest the thrust of socialization is not to nationality as in Baquedano-López's (1998) study of Mexican Catholics, but to a universal Christian Pentecostal identity of all the races on *el camino*.

CONSTRUCTING *EL MUNDO*

Despite the teachings of "the path's" values, *La Iglesia* is confronted by the challenge of keeping "the world" at bay. The church elders worried that the youth would engage in sinful activities such as taking drugs, smoking, drinking, gangs, tagging, theft, and lying. Many of their worries centered on sex; they warned about premarital sex, adultery, homosexuality, abortion, and pornography. Adults also preached against celebrating Halloween, attending parties, listening to nonchurch music, and dancing. The pastor preached against tattoos, jewelry, makeup, short skirts, dressing *a la moda* (fashionably), and radical hairstyles, which he labeled *vanidades* (vanities). Accordingly, dress and hair constitute a way of discerning who is on *el camino* and who is in *el mundo*. When visiting the church, I take care to dress modestly and wear long skirts, with my hair pulled back, no jewelry, and no makeup.

Adult authorities stressed that all activities from *el mundo*, no matter how inconsequential they might seem to outsiders, are equally bad and considered sins. Alberto articulated this rigid stance towards all things from *el mundo*:

No hay pecado chiquito, no hay pecado grande, no hay pecado negro, ni tampoco blanco sino el pecado es el pecado.	There is no small sin, there is no big sin, there's no black sin, nor white rather sin is sin.

Echoing Alberto's sentiment, the pastor warned the youth that if they gave in to the world's pleasures they would lose their *identidad espiritual* (spiritual identity).

The warnings about dancing, especially, came up often during Alberto's teachings. In this next example of talk-in-interaction, Alberto constructs a hypothetical scenario meant to warn students about dancing and the seduction of parties:

1 Alberto:	*Alguien dice, "Okay quiero invitarte a un*	Someone says, "O.K. I want to invite you to a
2	*"pari." Pari le dicen aquí ¿no?*	party." Party, you say here, no?
3 Youth:	*Sí*	Yes.

4 Alberto:	*Quiero invitarte a un pari*	I want to invite you to a party

.... [*Alberto continues.*]

7	*Sabe que definitivamente todavía*	you know that definitely you still
8	*le gusta escuchar la música ¿verdad?*	like to listen to music right?
9	*Entonces de hecho se sabe que va a ir a ese lugar*	Then in fact you know you will go to that place
10	*sabe que va a ir a bailar*	you know you will go to dance
11	*Usted puede decir, "¿Pero— pero no:*	You can say, "But— but, no:
12	*quién sabe, hermano?*	who knows, brother?
13	*Yo tengo la autoridad de Dios."*	I have the authority of God."

.... [*Alberto continues.*]

19	*Pero hay una cosa muy importante que entender,*	But there is a very important thing to understand,
20	*en el momento que usted cede terreno al enemigo*	the moment that you yield ground to the enemy
21	*usted será una persona más una víctima más*	you will be one more person, one more victim
22	*para el enemigo*	for the enemy
23	*porque se encontrará en el lugar tentado,*	because you will find yourself in temptation,
24	*hermano ¿Amén?*	brother. Amen?
25 Youth:	*Amén. Sí, mhm.*	Amen. Yes, mhm.

Alberto reaches out to the students through his choice of topic (dancing, music, parties), his use of the Spanglish word *pari* (line 2) instead of *fiesta* (party), and his use of *tú* (you—singular informal) between friends (lines 1, 4). The latter contrasts with his own choice of *usted* (you—singular formal) for addressing the youth (lines 7, 10, 11, 20, 21, 23) to establish the cause-and-effect sequence of events. If the youth know that they like music, then 'if you go to the party, you will dance' (lines 9–10). Students might try to fool themselves into thinking that they will be strong and not dance (lines 11–13), but depending on God's authority will not protect them if they begin by ceding territory to the enemy—their friends who value music, dancing, and partying. According to Alberto, the initial friendly invitation is actually quite sinister and can lead, as he later explains, to "*perdición o una buena caída*" (perdition, or a great fall). Despite the teachers' warnings, it is difficult to insulate the youth from the values of *el mundo*.

EL MUNDO SEEPS IN

The complexity of views related to *el camino* and *el mundo* becomes most apparent in relation to schooling. On the one hand, the church views the secular public school as an important locus of *el mundo*'s values, with fellow students and teachers as the vehicles through which the youth acquire those values. They denounce the schools as godless and responsible for society's problems, as exemplified by the pastor's statement during a sermon:

En las escuelas . . . ustedes saben que no se puede hablar ni mencionar el nombre de Dios. . . . Por ende, tenemos una sociedad perdida, desorganizada, sin sentido, sin fundamentos.	In the schools . . . you know that one cannot talk about nor even mention the name of God. . . . As a result, we have a society that is lost, disorganized, senseless, and without foundation.

On the other hand, church elders and the youths' parents recognize the importance of formal schooling and urge the students to remain in school and to pursue worldly careers—for the good of the church. During a lesson, the pastor explained how the church would benefit:

Si necesitamos un abogado por un caso que tenemos en la iglesia, en la iglesia hay un abogado; tenemos una enfermedad, un médico. . . . Ustedes representan el futuro profesional de la iglesia, de la obra del Señor.	If we need a lawyer for a case that we have in the church, in the church there's a lawyer; we have an illness, a doctor. . . . You represent the professional future of the church, of the work of the Lord.

There seems to be no contradiction here: *La Iglesia* needs professional members in order for the church to thrive; the world offers careers that can help those on the path.

Strict socialization on the path is further complicated by the church's indirect acceptance of some of the practices of *el mundo*. For example, the pastor specifically spoke out against cosmetics, but during one girl's *quinceañera* (15th birthday party) celebration in the church, she wore lots of makeup and a full-length gown. The *quinceañera* itself is not just a birthday celebration but also a coming-of-age party that tends to be very worldly, almost like a beauty pageant, involving elaborate makeup, clothes, and jewelry—the very *vanidades* (vanities) that the pastor preached against. The *quinceañera* was very well attended by the girls' relatives, members of the church, and nonmembers. It was videotaped from beginning (home preparations) to end (elaborate dinner).

The world's beauty and fashion standards emerge in other, unexpected ways. On one occasion, the pastor's wife complimented a girl who was wearing her hair down by saying, *"Te ves muy sexy,"* (You look very sexy). On other visits, I have noticed girls applying makeup in the church and boys wearing their hair spiked despite the pastor's disapproval. These are but some of the many ways in which influences from *el mundo* are seeping into the church. They demonstrate how the very authorities that seek to steer the youth from *el mundo* allow these influences to enter, and the children follow suit. The girl who celebrated her *quinceañera* in full regalia disagrees with the church's stance against dancing and attends school dances, paid for by her parents. Another girl went so far as to leave the church after she challenged the pastor's views on premarital sex. Adding insult to injury, she questioned the pastor in English even though he spoke to her in Spanish, the moral language (Ek, 2003). Although a discussion of gender dynamics warrants greater attention than the limited space here provides, it is important to note that the burden of fighting off worldly temptations falls largely on the girls.

The changing roles of Spanish and English also complicate the process of socialization at *La Iglesia*. As stated earlier, the students are socialized *to* Spanish as well as *through* Spanish, the church's official language. However, Tommy is now the youth class instructor; his increased use of English has the students responding favorably and participating more, asking important questions. During one lesson, an exchange between Tommy and his little brother Ryan shed light on how the students are trying to make sense of the role language plays in salvation. Tommy explained that one day God will talk with everyone about his or her sins to determine whether he or she will go to heaven or hell. With the refreshing naivete of a 10-year-old, Ryan expressed his concern about God's ability to speak with someone who speaks neither English nor Spanish: "But, Tommy, 'cause see, if there's somebody, like, *Koreano, verdad, que no sabe español o el inglés* (Korean, right, who does not know Spanish or English), and like, he goes, can God talk with him?" As the code-switching indicates, Ryan is bilingual in English and Spanish, and he assumes God is similarly bilingual. He worries about Koreans, who speak a language that is foreign to him but that he has heard in the Korean immigrant community that borders the church. In response, Tommy references the biblical story of the Tower of Babel and explains that God can understand all languages because he is the one who "confused" them in the first place. Still, issues of language status and ideologies both inside and outside the church may not be put to rest so easily.

Is Spanish really the moral code of *el camino*? At first, I thought so, and there are examples from my observations that bolster that notion. But the church sees other Latinos and other Spanish-speakers as part of the larger *mundo*, not the *camino*. For example, the pastor stopped the children from watching a Central American parade and warned the youth not to watch *telenovelas* (Latino soap operas) because they are destructive. It seems that Spanish does not necessarily lead to *el camino*.

I never heard any outright statement by church authorities that English is the language of *el mundo*, responsible for taking the young from God's path, but there was much criticism of schools and teachers who function in English. On the other hand, the church itself may be condoning undesirable mainstream values and ideologies unwittingly through the increased use of English in the explication of biblical texts. Proposition 227 increased the emphasis on English and the status of English-speakers in the state's schools. By incorporating English to retain the youth, the church, unwittingly, may be supporting mainstream values and ideologies that attack Spanish and the values attached to it. Will the increased use of English at the church adversely affect the youth's spiritual values and identities, or will the youth embrace bilingualism as an effective tool for staying on God's path?

DISCUSSION

Youth's socialization to religious identity can be a complex, contested, and contradictory process. In *La Iglesia*, adolescents are socialized to a Christian Pentecostal identity through Spanish and simultaneously socialized to use Spanish in religious ways, including greetings and terms of address to signal this identity. Still, the youth speak more English every year, and *La Iglesia* socializes not into national identities but into a universal Christian Pentecostal identity. Moreover, the language used at the church points to a linguistic "Mexicanization" or "Chicanoization" of Central Americans, obscuring and replacing their national identity (Guerra Vásquez, 2003; Chapter 6, this volume). But families travel to their homelands and revert to *voseo* and the national lexicon at home.

The process of socialization for the students is not neutral or straightforward but is complicated by conflicting messages and values, with unforeseeable results. The church establishes a dichotomy between *el camino* and *el mundo*, but it may come to be perceived as a false binary by youth who move back and forth between these worlds and must survive in both. Moreover, church members value education and encourage their youth to become professionals, and they cannot keep them insulated from some of the mainstream values found at school. Fortunately, the youth and their parents, too, consider education to be important for their success, and they believe their faith will help ward off temptation. Embracing the best of both worlds, the youth are not passively socialized; they reject the lumping of all sins together as equally dangerous, and they dress, speak, and behave in ways contrary to some of the church's teachings while still embracing the basic tenets.

Despite its seeming rigidity, the church offers much to the youth in terms of support, caring, and guidance. Tommy, in particular, makes himself accessible, even writing personal letters to let students know he is thinking of them. The teachers set high goals for the youth, both spiritual and professional, and repeatedly remind them of how special they are to both church and God. Additionally, the teens participate in enjoyable activities such as the church band, which performs during the Sunday services, as well as youth groups and camps. To show their concern, church leaders and teachers are constantly changing their curriculum and activities in an effort to make the classes more enjoyable.

THE LESSONS OF *LA IGLESIA*

Questions of language and identity are central to the experiences that determine the future of bilingual Latino immigrant youth. By focusing on language socialization and church identity, this chapter highlights the importance of examining out-of-school contexts to obtain a fuller picture of the complexity of Latino students' lives. We need to bridge home, school, and community spaces for Latino youth and use their identities as resources for learning in the classroom.

The lessons of *La Iglesia* include the following: (1) Not all Latinos are Mexican and not all Mexicans or Latinos are Catholic; (2) contrary to cultural-deficit views, bilingual immigrant Latino students engage in demanding language and literacy practices in their communities; (3) the skills that students develop in churches—which include reading, memorizing, and interpreting high-level texts, such as the Bible—can be leveraged for classroom learning; (4) the value that parents and church elders place on higher education is intertwined with religious responsibility; and (5) the Pentecostal church is an important space for language maintenance and status raising—Spanish is one of God's languages and deserves to be respected and learned well.

How can educators use these lessons to inform their classroom practices? Specific suggestions depend on the grade level, academic discipline, and school policies, but the following are some general recommendations. Teachers should begin by assuming language and literacy abilities instead of deficits for Latino students. They can acknowledge and value Pentecostal Latino students' church language and literacy practices by explicitly letting them know that skills acquired in religious institutions are resources and strengths for learning in school. Given the language shame that Spanish speakers may feel (Chapter 10, this volume), teachers can help by encouraging students to use their Spanish-language abilities in particular classroom activities. In addition, in interacting with parents, teachers must keep in mind that Latino immigrant parents want their children to succeed academically and use this shared goal as a starting point for collaboration. Church lessons play a powerful role in shaping students' identities, morality, and language and literacy skills, as well as in preparing them for the challenges they can encounter in the world. Teachers who understand the church lessons can build bridges between *el camino* and *el mundo*.

NOTE

1. The complete transcript includes more of the students' voices, including "*Amen's*," (Amens), "*Sí's*" (yeses), and answers to direct questions. Space limitations preclude full transcriptions.

CHAPTER 6

Como Hablar en Silencio
(Like Speaking in Silence):
Issues of Language, Culture,
and Identity of Central Americans
in Los Angeles

Magaly Lavadenz

The words of Chabela (pseudonym), a young Guatemalan mother, begin the title of this chapter. The silencing she refers to is learning to pass as Mexican by masking her Central American language and identity, beginning with her trip from Guatemala through Mexico to the United States. The eloquent metaphor, speaking in silence, belies the complex and "expanding repertoires" (Zentella, 1997a) of language, culture, and identity that many Central American immigrants acquire in the United States. Although concealment or hiddenness is part of their experience, so is learning to speak new languages and dialects. Official institutions, including schools, know little of either of these aspects of Central American life in Los Angeles.

This chapter explores the ways in which language and culture affect the identity development of three Central American immigrant families residing in the Los Angeles area, based on focus group data collected at the Central American Resource Center (CARECEN) in Los Angeles and participant observation. Interspersed within the participants' narratives are selections of traditional folklore, as well as writings by local Central American youth.

My interest in Central Americans began more than 15 years ago, when I was a bilingual first-grade teacher in Glendale, California, a Los Angeles suburb. During a meeting for teachers, a colleague who taught in the English segment of our program asked, "And how is Ruth doing, she's such a space cadet?" This derogatory comment about one of my students was a common label for children from El Salvador, Guatemala, and Nicaragua. I was surprised because Ruth was not a poor student; her test scores were in the average range. As I observed her more closely, however, I noticed that she did have difficulty paying attention and completing her work on time; perhaps this was why the teacher referred to her as a "space cadet." I decided to devote my master's thesis and doctoral work to Central American immigrant children (Lavadenz, 1991, 1994) and learned that traumatically violent war-zone experiences increased the likelihood that those children would have difficulty staying on task, concentrating, and not daydreaming. The students who constituted my case studies reported that they were daydreaming about family members left behind—cousins, aunts, uncles, and grandparents who were not as fortunate as they had been. I also learned that Central American immigrant students were more likely to be referred to special education, despite the fact that they were not low-performing students. Suárez-Orozco (1989) attributed the "achievement motivation" of Central American students to an increased sense of responsibility and obligation because of survivor guilt; that is, they had been able to escape the horrors of civil war but their relatives had not. Despite the time that has elapsed since that study, Central American experiences, history, culture, and language continue to be largely ignored in public schools and in teacher preparation programs. Central American students and families do not see themselves represented in the curriculum, nor are their "funds of knowledge" incorporated into classroom practices (Chapter 9, this volume). This study cannot do justice to all Central American immigrant experiences; it is an exploratory examination of the historical context of the language and cultural socialization practices in Salvadoran and Guatemalan families and some implications for practice.

CENTRAL AMERICAN IMMIGRATION TO THE U.S.

Central Americans, from the seven nations shown in Figure 6.1, represent 4.8%, or 1,686,937, of the 38.8 million Hispanics in the nation (U.S. Bureau of the Census, 2000b). Salvadorans and Guatemalans, the two largest groups of Central Americans in Los Angeles and the nation, arrived mainly in the 1980s, at the height of civil wars caused, in part, by decades-long economic, political, and military interventions by the United States (Hamilton & Chinchilla, 2001). Ignoring pleas from international human rights groups, the United States denied Salvadorans and Guatemalans political refugee status, while granting it to Cubans and Vietnamese. Three decades of political and economic turmoil in El Salvador and Guatemala resulted in unprecedented unauthorized immigration to the United States. The following his-

FIGURE 6.1. The Seven Countries in Central America

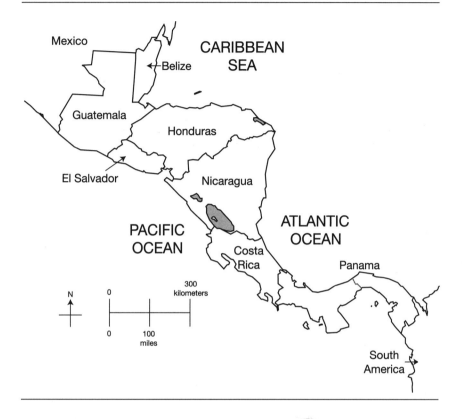

torical and sociopolitical context is necessary to understand the experiences of Salvadoran and Guatemalan immigrants in the United States.

El Salvador

Guanacos, as the people from El Salvador refer to themselves, although the term is used derogatorily in other Spanish-speaking countries to mean "country bumpkin," have a long history of political, social, and economic revolutions. A strong oligarchy of 14 families controlled the land and the governments since independence from Spain in 1821 until recent times, creating a quasi-feudal state composed of rich landowners and indigenous peoples and/or mestizos (Clements, 1984). Uprisings by the poor led to the murder of 30,000 indigenous peoples in 1932, known as *La Matanza* (the Massacre) in the collective consciousness, and resulted in a sharing of power between the 14 families and the military (Menjívar, 2000). In the 1970s and 1980s, the Roman Catholic clergy's political and human rights involvement challenged those in power, who were supported by the economic and military intervention of the United States. The assassination of Archbishop Romero in 1980 triggered civil chaos, and many Salvadorans experienced violence firsthand. Torture, mutilation, and the disappearance of those suspected of siding with the pro-government or guerrilla revolutionaries were everyday occurrences. Death squads massacred entire villages, and migration through Mexico to the United States seemed the only escape. Today, Salvadoran exiles provide the main source of revenue for the country, in the form of remittances sent to family members. But more than a decade of terrorism left an indelible mark on Salvadorans everywhere (Menjívar, 2000).

Guatemala

Guatemala has the largest indigenous population of Central America; 80% to 90% of the U.S. refugee population are Mayan, and 10% to 20% are *Ladino* (European-origin or mixed indigenous/European Guatemalans). More than 10,000 Mayan Guatemalans live in Los Angeles (Loucky & Moors, 2000). Public schools do not request information regarding indigenous languages or origin as part of the enrollment process, ignoring Guatemalan-origin students who may speak one of the four primary Mayan languages and compounding the language-learning problems of this population. For Mayan speakers, Spanish is their second language and English the third. The diversity within the Mayan community is central to their identity. For example, the term *indio* (Indian) is derogatory to Mayans, as it negates their community of origin, listed here in order of predominance: Q'anjob'al (51%), Mam (16%), Chuj (16%), and Jakatek (7%) (Billings, 2000). The shift from being Mayan in Guatemala to being Guatemalan—or *chapines*, as Guatemalans are called—in the United States marks a transformation of language and identity that comes on the heels of years of traumatic deprivation, displacement, and violence.

Conflict in Guatemala was rooted in economic, social, and political imbalances similar to those in El Salvador. Indigenous social networks and organizations were violently suppressed by the U.S.-backed government, causing uprisings that the government blamed on leftists (Menjívar, 2002). In the guerrilla warfare that followed, hundreds of villages were destroyed, between half a million and a million people were displaced, and deaths exceeded hundreds of thousands. Because children were particularly vulnerable to kidnapping and induction into either the government or guerrilla armies during the civil war, many Guatemalan families were separated. Children and adolescents often emigrated alone in order to avoid transcription, as captured in the film *El Norte*. In 1996, following a 36-year period of civil war, a peace agreement was signed.

CENTRAL AMERICANS IN LOS ANGELES

Approximately 190,000 Salvadorans and 100,000 Guatemalans live in Los Angeles County as of 2000 (4.4% and 2.7% of the Latino population, respectively), although organizations such as CARECEN claim the total is closer to 500,000 (see Table 6.1). Research regarding the resiliency, sense of community, and work ethic of Central American immigrant communities is very recent (Hamilton & Chinchilla, 2001; Loucky & Moors, 2000; Menjívar, 2002). Transnational networks link communities in the United States with immigrants' hometowns and provide major economic, social, and political resources (Hamilton & Chinchilla, 2001). These networks are the key to the lived experiences of Guatemalan and Salvadoran immigrants in Los Angeles because they are central to their sense of community and to their adjustment:

> Primary activities and core underlying values relating to work, social interconnectedness and family priorities, as well as prior experience with hardship and even violence, enhance rather than inhibit their adjustment in Los Angeles. (Loucky & Moors, 2000, p. 215)

TABLE **6.1.** Central Americans in Los Angeles County

Country of Origin	Number	Percentage of Total Population N = 9,519,338	Percentage of Hispanic/ Latino Population N = 4,242.213
Belize	34,754	.4	.8
Costa Rica	6,232	.07	1.0
Guatemala	100,341	1.0	2.7
Honduras	20,029	.2	.5
Nicaragua	20, 775	.2	.5
Panama	3,453	.04	.08
Salvador	187,193	2.0	4.4
Total	372,777	4.0	9.0

Source: U.S. Bureau of the Census (2000b).

The historical legacy of activism that infuses Salvadoran and Guatemalan networks in the Los Angeles area led to the establishment of CARECEN and other self-help and social service institutions (Hamilton & Chinchilla, 2001). In addition, political groups were formed to support revolutionary movements in their countries of origin. The networks are both informal (personal contacts) and formal (organizations), including hometown associations— groups of first- and second-generation immigrants from the same towns and villages. Hometown associations provide opportunities to socialize and reminisce, and they raise funds for their hometowns (Menjívar, 2000). The adults in this study participated in formal and informal organizing, and their children attended some meetings and events.

The hub of the recently arrived Central American community is CARECEN, a cultural, legal, and educational center founded in 1983 by Salvadorans, U.S. church leaders, attorneys, and activists. CARECEN is located west of downtown Los Angeles, in an area where 95% of the residents speak Spanish, 35% live at or below the poverty level (as compared to 18.9% for Los Angeles as a whole), and the dropout rate for Latino students at the local Belmont High School is 56% (in contrast to the national Latino dropout rate of approximately 22%). Pico-Union, the location of the focus groups' interviews, remains a central receiving point for Central American immigrants, although Mexican immigration has also increased.

Focus group interviews and ethnographic observations were conducted at CARECEN during 2001, facilitated by the organization's president, Angela Sembrano, and interviews with three immigrant families took place in several locations in Los Angeles in 2002. Amarildo Osvaldo (all names of family members are pseudonyms), one of the Salvadoran fathers, is an employee at CARECEN. His family consists of five children, ranging in age from 5 to 20, and his wife, Betty. He and his wife immigrated 15 years ago. Betty stays home to take care of their youngest, who has Down syndrome, because of his special needs.

Roberto (age 28), Alberto (age 24), and Humberto (age 17) Méndez comprise the second family in this study. As is typical of many Salvadoran families with some resources, their mother remained in El Salvador and the boys were sent to "El Norte" to avoid conscription by either the military or the guerrillas. Dispersal, and subsequent reunification after many years of separation, is common in Central American families. Roberto had attended school only through the sixth grade in El Salvador in order to help support the family. He came to the United States when he was 12 years old and recently completed his General Education Diploma (high school equivalency), working continuously to send money regularly to his mother so that his two brothers could immigrate. While there is no longer a threat of military or *guerrillero* conscription, the brothers fled to escape the paralyzing poverty and economic upheaval caused by almost three decades of war.

The third family, the Grameldas from Guatemala, includes Chabela, the mother whose words provided the title for this chapter. In 1990 she traveled from Guatemala through Mexico without documentation; today she lives with her Guatemalan husband and two young children, ages 9 and 11, in a suburb of Los Angeles. Some of Chabela's family members immigrated to Los Angeles in the late 1960s, reflecting the multilayered experiences of many Central American families.

LANGUAGE DIVERSITY, CHALLENGES, AND CHANGE

The linguistic diversity that exists among Central Americans who immigrate to the United States serves to identify each group with its homeland and links compatriots to each other, but language links are stretched here in new ways. Central America is not uniformly Spanish-speaking, but indigenous languages like Guatemalan Mayan are ignored. Central American Spanish-speakers share some features that distinguish them from Mexicans and other Spanish speakers, but each country in the region also has distinctive vocabulary and pronunciations. In the United States, the Spanish of Central Americans changes under the influence of Mexicans, and every group's language changes as a result of contact with English. The push of language and dialect contact on the one hand and the pull of national or ethnic identity on the other characterize Central Americans' efforts against being silenced and complicate the teaching of English and Spanish to their children.

Regional variations in vocabulary reflect the "pluralistic cultural identity" that characterizes Latin America, which evolved as each country sought to separate itself from Spain's colonial linguistic domination (García, 1999, p. 20). Central Americans identify with their country's lexicon, but maintaining it marks them as non-Mexican during the migratory process through Mexico to the United States, which can cause them to be returned to Central America. For example, the silencing that Chabela Gramelda describes (*hablar en silencio* [speaking in silence]) refers to the monitoring and self-censorship she experienced both during immigration (to avoid deportation from Mexico to Guatemala) and in her interactions with her Mexican-origin friends and co-workers in the United States (as a way to "fit in" and be understood in Mexican-dominant Los Angeles). She recalled having to learn the Mexican national anthem and Mexican words, which she had to substitute for Guatemalan terms (see Table 6.2 for examples).

TABLE **6.2.** Examples of Words/Semantic Differences

Salvadoran Spanish	Guatemalan Spanish	Mexican Spanish	English
		Food	
casamiento	arroz y frijoles	arroz y frijoles	rice and beans
minutas	granizada	raspado	snow cone (shaved ice)
chompipe	chompipe	guajolote	turkey
ayote	guicoy	calabacita	squash
		People	
cachimbona	mamita	mi jefita	mom, ma
chele	canche	güero	blonde
cipote, bicho	patojo, chiris	chamaco, escuintle	child
		School-related	
chaqueta	chumpa	chamarra	jacket
pajilla	pajilla	popote	straw
bolsón	mochila	mochila	backpack
diccionario	amansaburros	diccionario	dictionary

Chabela explains the constant burden of the double consciousness she feels—that is, having to suppress her Central American identity to pass as Mexican:

Siempre estoy conciente de con quién estoy hablando, desde entonces es como que una parte la tengo que silenciar para poder pasar, o que me entiendan.

I'm always conscious of who I'm talking to, since then [crossing the borders] there's a part of me that I've had to silence to get by, or so that I could be understood.

But it is not always easy to remember which words must be avoided or changed lest they give you away and which can serve to align you with the dominant group. (Re)learning common words for foods, people, and utensils (including items used in school) in the Mexican variety of Spanish is a common experience for immigrants from El Salvador and Guatemala. Consequently, Mexican terms are substituted and ultimately replace equivalent words in Salvadoran and Guatemalan varieties of Spanish. The language variety to which Chabela was socialized and raised was suppressed and silenced as a result of immigrating to the United States. For Chabela and others like her, self-monitoring and censorship are primarily an attempt to avoid being marked for possible deportation to Guatemala by Mexican officials. (If they are deported to Mexico, the possibility of returning is greater.) Thus, Chabela's experience reflects many Central Americans' awareness of the dual problem that their national variety of Spanish represents; that is, it identifies them for immigration police and it labels them as outsiders in their Mexican neighborhoods.

Still, it is easier to work on not using particular terms than on changing the way you pronounce vowels and consonants. Several consonants distinguish Salvadorans and Guatemalans from Mexicans, such as the final /n/ that sounds like the velar <ng> of English *sing* instead of the standard alveolar /n/ of Mexicans, and the double <ll>, which is pronounced /y/ but with more palatal friction in Mexican Spanish. Each Central American nation differs from the others in its pronunciation of one or more consonants (Lipski, 1994); for example, Salvadorans aspirate the <s> at the end of syllables, as in /ehpanyol/ for *español*. These few examples suffice to alert teachers of Spanish to expect differences that should be distinguished from errors in reading/ decoding. Teachers of English should also be aware of the potential influence of the way Spanish is spoken in each country on the English of children from those nations.

The most important distinguishing feature of Central American Spanish is at the grammatical level. Salvadorans and Guatemalans use *vos*, an informal second-person subject pronoun (you) and its accompanying verb forms (known as *voseo*), instead of *tú*, which may or may not be maintained by the children of immigrants (Lipski, 1994). The more formal *usted* is used for politeness, consistent with other Spanish-speaking populations that use *tú* informally. Examples of *voseo*, which involves accent and root changes from Standard Spanish (SS), include the following (in bold):

- *¿**Vos sos** Salvadoreño, no?* (You are Salvadoran, no?)
  (SS)*¿Tú eres Salvadoreño, no?*
- *¡**Dejáte** de babosadas y **hacé** lo que te digo!* (Stop your foolishness and do what I say!)
  (SS) *¡Déjate de babosadas y haz lo que te digo!*

Because second-person verb forms are so frequent and occur in common phrases—such as *Vení* (Come) and *Fijáte vos* (Look)—they are a dead giveaway and often avoided in public settings where Latino unity is important (Chapter 5, this volume). All of the Central Americans adopted the formal *usted* with me; when questioned about this, they responded that addressing non–Central Americans (I am Cuban) with *usted* was a sign of politeness.

Contact with English contributes to code-switching among the varieties of Spanish and English that are part of the expanded Central American repertoire. Hector Tobar captures the vitality of this mixing in his novel *The Tattooed Soldier* (1998), in a section about Salvadoran immigrants in Los Angeles:

> *Fíjáte vos, que ese vato* (Imagine [Central American], that dude [Mexican]) from *La Mara* got in a fight with that dude from *La* (the) Eighteenth Street who lives down the block. Yeah, right there in the class. Real *chingazos* (blows [Mexican]). *El de La Salvatrucha estaba* (The one from the [Mara] Salvatrucha gang was) bleeding *y todo* (and everything). (p. 59)

The overall effect of the contact between dialects and languages in Los Angeles is that the features of Central American (e.g., Guatemalan and Salvadoran) varieties of Spanish diminish over time (Parodi, 2003; Silva-Corvalán, 1994).

The most serious threat is not invisibility, however, but language loss. Where contact between languages occurs among more and less socially powerful groups, the result is monolingualism for the weaker language group (Romaine, 1995). Central Americans encounter language contact on a daily basis as a result of their interactions with the regional dominant variety of Mexican Spanish. They are conscious about the monitoring of their own language usage outside the home, and they are also aware of the pitfalls of language loss, as in the case of the Méndez family. Roberto Méndez, the oldest son, head of household, and guardian of his younger brother, reported that he feels that it is his responsibility to maintain language ties to his native Guatemala. He makes a conscious attempt to understand and be understood by non-Guatemalans, but it makes him very uncomfortable:

Cuando estamos oyendo un partido de fútbol, y quizás tengo que ir con los mexicanos . . . quizás lo haga— que tengo que hablar como ellos. Yo siento que no estoy hablando lo correcto. Siento que estoy fingiendo. . . .	When we're listening to a soccer game, maybe I have to go with the Mexicans . . . I may do it—that I have to speak like they do. I feel like I'm not speaking correctly. I feel as if I'm faking.

All three brothers concluded that they preferred their own variety of Spanish to the Mexican variety, which they claim they do not use with each other. However, in an off-tape interaction as the brothers were preparing to leave, they used a typically Mexican expression: *¡Orale vato, vámonos.* (OK dude, Let's go.) Linguistic and cultural assimilation may begin as an adaptation to outside pressures, but it can end up transforming in-group practices.

PRINCIPAL CONCERNS ABOUT EDUCATION, LANGUAGE, CULTURE, AND IDENTITY

Pico-Union/Westlake is known as the most violent section of Los Angeles, where rival gangs, *Mara Salvatrucha* (originally restricted to Salvadorans and Guatemalans, it includes Mexicans now) and 18th Street, reside. It is a bustling area, home to the largest elementary school in Los Angeles Unified School District, Hoover Street School, which many of our families' children attended.

A total of eighteen parents volunteered for the three focus group interviews that took place at CARECEN. Content analysis of the data revealed four main themes that emerged from our conversations: (1) quality schooling and literacy practices, (2) child-rearing practices, (3) Spanish-language usage in the home, and (4) memories of war and immigration. The following sections summarize the key themes that emerged from the focus groups.

Quality Schooling: Supporting Literacy at Home and School

Quality schooling was the overriding concern voiced by Central Americans parents at the CARECEN meetings, corroborating recent research on Central Americans in Los Angeles (Hamilton & Chinchilla, 2001; López, Popkin, & Telles, 1996; Menjívar, 2000). The parents in our focus groups reported creating spaces, both physical and temporal, for their children to do homework, read books, and talk about school. In the Osvaldo household, for example, homework is often "apprenticed" to older children; the responsibilities are shared and distributed across family members so that the burden does not continually fall on the mother, who devotes most of her attention to her youngest son.

Mr. Osvaldo expressed his concern over the need to "re-educate" Central American families about the educational system in the United States:

Necesitamos campañas para re-educar a los padres de familia. No hay comunicación de la escuela. El decir "estamos abierto" no funciona. Tenemos que fortalezer el lazo entre el hogar y la escuela para	We need campaigns to re-educate parents. There is no communication from the school. Saying "our doors are open" doesn't work. We need to strengthen the bond between home and school in order

forcer [*sic*] *una nueva generación*   to forge a new generation of
Salvadoreña.   Salvadorans.

Most of the parents had not completed high school, but they were articulate
about the differences between life in their country of origin and life in Los
Angeles. They employed a "dual frame of reference" (Gibson & Ogbu, 1991),
particularly concerning values, traditions, and schooling. *Educación* (education) versus *escolarización* (schooling) is a key distinction in many Latino
households that differentiates between the values taught in the home as compared to the process of being schooled (Afterword, this volume).

Child-Rearing Principles, Values, and Traditions

Group participants stressed the importance of raising their children *(educar
a nuestros hijos)* to understand the value of being Salvadoran or Guatemalan *and* American, but they expressed concerns about the differences in
schooling in both countries. For example, they commented on the informal
dress of U.S. teachers, interpreting it as a lack of formality or seriousness on
the part of teachers, which resulted in a lack of respect in the classroom (by
students and teachers).

Spanish-Language Use in the Home

Transmitting and maintaining traditions, norms, and values as part of child
rearing were important to the families; Amarildo Osvaldo notes the challenges to maintaining traditional Salvadoran values, especially Spanish:

Es difícil inculcar las tradiciones de   It's difficult to pass on our cultural
nuestra cultura a nuestros hijos   traditions to our children when
cuando no las viven. No es de   they are not living them. It's not
inculcarles de lo que fue, sino de lo   about teaching them what was, but
que viven aquí. Por ejemplo, el   rather about what they live here.
hábito del español se va   For instance, the habit of speaking
desplazando por la preocupación   Spanish is being replaced by the
del inglés.   attention paid to [learning] English.

Roberto Méndez also reflected on his high esteem for English, while maintaining
traditions. He was a devout member of a Christian evangelical church attended
primarily by Guatemalan immigrants, but in his comments about the kind of
wife he was looking for, he stressed English and work skills more than religion: "*que sepa inglés y que pueda trabajar en otro sector, menos el doméstico*"
(who knows English and who can work in another profession, not a domestic

worker). Roberto's dual focus combines the traditional Guatemalan value of finding a hardworking wife with prerequisites for succeeding in the dominant society: She must know English and have marketable skills.

Memories of War and Immigration

Embedded in Central American *educación* is the transmission of feelings about war violence and violence on television. Referring to his experiences and memories of the war in El Salvador, one father of a 9-year-old reported watching the violence of the news on television with his daughter: "*¿Ves eso? ¡Yo viví peor que eso!*" (See that? I lived through worse than that!). This man spoke openly with his daughter, but most parents preferred not to discuss their war experiences too extensively, for fear of reviving painful memories (Lavadenz, 1991, 1994). Often compounding these memories were the memories and realities of immigration, as in Chabela's account of having to "fake" her true Guatemalan identity, and the ambiguity of immigration status.

VISIBLY HIDDEN

Central American immigrant parents/caregivers reported that they want their children to succeed in the United States but also to understand their histories, especially because these are absent from the schooling of their children. However, the narratives of Central American immigrants' children reveal the challenges involved in responding to as simple a question as "Where are you from?" The following autobiographical excerpt by Marlon Morales (2000), an adolescent Salvadoran immigrant, illustrates how children are conflicted between hiding and expressing their true identity in school:

> On my first day in Mr. Bax's fourth grade class, a little boy named Alex came up to me and asked me where I was from. . . . Where are you from? I had learned by the time I was nine that there were many answers to this question. I was searching for the one I'd give Alex. "Here" wouldn't work . . . I learned that the hard way. Saying "here" always made me the fool of someone's joke.
>
> "Mmm," I started. "Mmm," I continued looking him in the eye. I was going to say Mexico, add, "but born here" and leave it at that. My mom said I'm supposed to say this all the time, even at . . . school. Anything Salvadoran like *pupusas* [stuffed corn meal tortillas], *pacaya* [a vegetable], *flor de izote* [a mushroom] and Spanish was always left at home, never in public. Regardless, I looked back into Alex's eyes. "El Salvador," I blurted out. "I'm from El Salvador."
>
> "Cool," said Alex approvingly. "What part of Mexico is that in?" . . . Was I really Mexican after all? Was El Salvador a state of Mexico? I really didn't know. Got to ask our moms. (p. 66)

Marlon Morales's narrative describes the blurring and shifting of identities that occur in part from the fear of being "found out," as Chabela reported. The undocumented status of many Central Americans leads them to try "faking it," "passing as a (documented) Mexican," and becoming invisible to avoid deportation. Countless tales of deportation hearings reiterated the importance of avoiding identification as Central American, if only to increase the chance of being deported to Mexico rather than to El Salvador or Guatemala. This important facet of the socialization of Central American immigrant students is central to their social, cultural, and linguistic identities. It is illustrated with some humor by Raquel Josefina Gutiérrez, a young Salvadoran-Mexican writer who describes the struggle of being a "part-time Salvi." While she's "down with *La Virgen (de Guadalupe)* . . . To be Mexican in public and Salvadoran at home gets a little draining" (Gutiérrez, 2000, p. 29).

The following lyrical text, preserved today orally, is a fitting way to end a discussion of being visibly hidden. Originally passed down by the *Mayas* of western Guatemala, it is the legend of the Man of Lightning, a protector of the people of Jacaltenango. In it, the notion of being hidden as spirits of the ancestors, living and present today as their descendents, echoes a common thread in the accounts of the families in this study. The legend begins as follows:

Pero primero me lavaré la cara y las manos	But first I must wash my face and hands
En la espuma del azul silencio	in the foam of the blue silence
Para luego, con paso firme, penetrar airoso	That I may cross with grace and confidence
A través del pórtico misterioso	The mysterious portico
De mis bravos ancestros, quienes viven hoy	Of my valiant ancestors, who live today
Opacos como el agua en el corazón de la tierra.	Hidden like the water in the heart of the earth.
(Montejo, 2001, p. 33)	(Translation by Magaly Lavadenz)

REVERSING INVISIBILITY:
TRANSFORMING CLASSROOM PRACTICES
THROUGH TEACHER INQUIRY

Educators who use the emerging research on Central Americans to inform their practices can help lessen the psychological discomfort that results from self-censorship and invisibility. While there is no cookie-cutter approach to incorporating Central American language and culture into the classroom, we advocate sociocultural principles to advance culturally responsive teaching. These, in turn, foster classroom and school climates that value the uniqueness of each student, particularly the most vulnerable and ignored. Rather than creating or following a generic classroom/lesson script, educators can conduct their own research about and with students to build a more democratic classroom (Wertsch, Del Rio, & Alvarez, 1995). Sociocultural principles, translated here into a teacher inquiry process, include the following:

- They should transform the role of the teacher to one that (1) facilitates and guides by building on the student's knowledge base while attending to high academic expectations; (2) establishes an inclusive classroom climate where multiple voices/perspectives are valued and shared; and (3) understands that conflict can be used as a learning opportunity through a Freirian model of inquiry, dialogue, and voice (Freire, 1998).
- They should transform a "transmission" model of teaching—that is, one in which only the teacher transmits knowledge—to an additive teaching model which incorporates students' "funds of knowledge" and through which teachers become students of students (Freire, 1998; González et al., 1995). Instructional materials should reflect the communities of the learners, as well as be authentic and relevant to the lived experiences of students (Lavadenz & Martin, 1999).

Concretely, teachers can ask their students to become part of an inquiry whereby teachers and student learn together about key aspects of students' histories, languages, and cultures. I propose a sociocultural/transformative model of teacher inquiry that expands on Alma Flor Ada and Isabel Campoy's (2004) critical literacy phases, elaborating Paulo Freire's model of transformative literacy instruction:

1. *Descriptive phase:* Teachers read, write, and record their observations of and with students and the related literature/resources about, by, and from Central Americans. The question posed here is: What do I want to learn about and with my students?
2. *Personal interpretative phase:* Teachers reflect on what they have written based on their own past experiences, beliefs, and attitudes. This connects the *text* with their own past. The question posed here is: What did I learn about my own history, socialization, and beliefs as a result of what I found in the descriptive phase?
3. *Critical phase:* Teachers engage in a collaborative evaluation with students. This collaboration occurs through dialogue with students. The question posed here is: How can I share what I learned about

my practices and beliefs with my students in order for me to model this and learn from students?

4. *Transformative phase:* Teachers recursively reflect, self-evaluate, negotiate, and engage in dialogue with students. The questions posed here are: What did I learn from the entire process that allows me to make a change in the teaching/learning process for myself and for my students? How can I include more Central American voices in the teaching and learning process?

CONCLUSION

This chapter presented brief narratives and experiences of immigrant families from El Salvador and Guatemala, excerpts from the prose and poetry of Central American authors, and the sociopolitical reasons for immigration to the United States, for the benefit of all those who work with Central American families. The metaphor of silencing has been used to portray the sense of invisibility that characterizes the immigrant experiences of those who participated in this exploratory study, because they must monitor and censor their unique varieties of Spanish and other aspects of their national cultures. In addition, the U.S. government's refusal to grant refugee (legal) status to many Central American refugees (while granting it to immigrants from Communist nations) has caused this immigrant population to be targeted for deportation. Their underclass status and overall instability cast deep shadows of invisibility for Salvadorans and Guatemalans in their neighborhoods and schools. It is fundamental for educators to contribute to the resiliency and survival that their Central American students need to overcome the traumas of war and immigration. We must be sensitive to the psychosocial pain, expressed by Chabela and the Central American youth cited in this chapter, that results from linguistic censorship, cultural monitoring, and language loss. Teachers and educators have a pivotal role to play in avoiding and reversing the pain of invisibility. This can be accomplished by establishing a classroom climate where an additive approach to language learning prevails and where strong Central American and American identities can both flourish. Along with the inclusion of students' and parents' own stories, the addition of Central American images, literature, and languages varieties can be readily incorporated as a result of engaging in the transformative inquiry process.

The transformative inquiry process creates classrooms that are learning sites for democracy. It is through engagement with the lived histories, languages, and cultures of Central American students in our schools that teachers can exercise their power to practice what Paulo Freire termed a "pedagogy of freedom" (1998). This type of engagement leads us to examine, through reflection and action, locally situated policies and practices that maintain and perpetuate invisibility and silence. It calls us to question our individual roles in the perpetuation of oppressive and subtractive schooling as well as to respond in concrete ways by informing and arming ourselves with the knowledge and power of our students' voices. This process transforms traditional teaching methods into a model of teacher professional development that develops a disposition toward change and agency. This disposition is informed by a deepened knowledge of our students and their worlds. Transforming teaching practices from a transmission model to an additive model in this context invites Central American students and their parents to participate in, share, and construct new knowledge within the classroom community. The reversal of invisibility for students will occur, along with the enhancement of teachers' knowledge, skills, and dispositions.

CHAPTER 7

Raising a Bilingual Child in Miami: Reflections on Language and Culture

Ana Roca

How can infants grow into toddlers fluent in English and Spanish? How can a young child's bilingual range be encouraged to develop as much as possible from birth? What roles should parents, friends, neighbors, schools, and the community play as models in order to achieve this goal? This autobiographical essay on raising a child in Miami examines both the pivotal parental role in a child's bilingual development and the role played by Miami's diverse sociolinguistic situation.

Focusing on personal reflections as a Cuban parent on the development of our son, now 3½ years old, I consider the challenges and choices faced by bilingual parents who plan to raise a bilingual child. A key question that bilingual families struggle with is: What can we do as bilingual parents to help create and foster an optimal environment both inside and outside the home that would encourage bilingual development? I reflect here on what we claim to do, our attitudes toward Spanish and English, and the attitudes of others concerning Spanish in our community and in our child's school. Our experience suggests some resources and practical ideas for Spanish-speaking parents who have similar concerns about passing on the heritage language to their children. It also informs some suggestions for educators. We hope this preliminary report on our child's early language development and socialization sheds light on what works and what does not work so well in a family where both parents are bilingual (one is a native speaker of Spanish and the other is a non-native speaker of Spanish with nativelike language abilities). Some of this advice may be helpful to parents who are not bilingual but who seek bilingual support for their offspring.

HOME LANGUAGE USE: MAKING DECISIONS
ABOUT LANGUAGE

The decision to raise a child bilingually in Miami was an easy one for us. What parent wouldn't want their son or daughter to have the advantages of two languages in a city where only one is seldom enough? Unlike other U.S. cities, where speaking Spanish may be frowned upon, here in Miami it comes as naturally as sipping a *café con leche*. Whereas elsewhere Spanish-speakers may practice self-censorship, seeing who's around before slipping into something more comfortable like *el castellano* (Spanish), *aquí* (here), as they say in Cuban, *nadie tiene pelos en la lengua* (nobody is afraid to talk). Spanish is heard, spoken, and written almost everywhere in Miami, including public settings and business environments (car dealerships, drugstores, real estate offices, banks, post offices, shopping centers, department stores, etc.).

The economic advantages of Spanish and English fluency in Miami are well documented: Fluent bilinguals earn on average $7,000 more annually than their monolingual English or Spanish counterparts (Boswell, 2000). Being bilingual also means being eligible for one of the many jobs in south Florida that, officially or unofficially, require Spanish–English proficiency. Besides the economic advantages, my partner and I are aware of many other benefits of bilingualism. As Spanish teachers (Helena, an Anglo American, teaches at a magnet public high school, and I am a professor at Florida International University), both of us know the research in linguistics and cognitive science that points toward the positive cognitive advantages that bilinguals enjoy. From an academic point of view, we did not think twice about bringing up our son, Juan Gabriel, nicknamed Juanchi, bilingually. Our rationale also included the social angle, not just what we know from the fields of psychology, linguistics, and education. We thought of practical everyday living in Miami: Bilinguals are able to experience and enjoy more fully the unique cultural life of the area. "Let's face it," my partner and I agreed, "there's a lot of fun to be had in Miami that happens only in Spanish." Monolingual English speakers, or the monocultural ones at least, tend to miss out on the full Miami experience: the music, media, restaurants, performances, business deals, and jokes—not to mention all those wonderful conversations struck up with complete strangers at cafeteria windows when you stop for a *cafecito* (strong Cuban coffee), this city's fuel of choice for making it through a long, exasperating drive home from work. Spanish is an integral part of these exchanges. And that Spanish is changing every day as the Spanish-speaking population has also become more varied and complex.

To accompany their *café*, Miami residents no longer have to limit themselves to Cuban *pastelitos*. Colombian *arepas*, Venezuelan *pan de bono*, Argentinean *medias lunas*, and a variety of *empanadas* (all breads/pastries/

turnovers) are now widely available here. South Florida's Spanish-speaking community was once almost exclusively Cuban and Cuban American, speaking the varied class and regional dialects of waves of the first exiles in the 1960s and of more recent arrivals. This has not been the case for some time. Dominicans, Puerto Ricans, Hondurans, and even Mexicans lived in Miami before many Salvadorans and Nicaraguans arrived in the 1980s. Then Colombians and Venezuelans came in the 1990s. The newcomers are the Argentines, whose restaurants are popping up all over. Spanish-speakers keep arriving from many countries, including Spain, along with Hispanics from throughout the United States who move here precisely because Spanish can be heard and spoken in comfort in Miami. One of Miami's main attractions for Hispanics is the fact that being bilingual is the norm, with standard literate and professional varieties of Spanish rubbing elbows with many blue-collar versions, including a generous helping of code-switching. Each wave brings an infusion of a new Hispanic culture, with its own vocabulary items, pronunciations, and rhythms that serve as a shot in the arm for our self-maligned Miami Spanish. It's as if the entire Spanish-speaking world awaits Juanchi outside our door.

ADVANTAGES, DISADVANTAGES, ATTITUDES, AND THE "HOW-TO" QUESTIONS

The question facing Miami Latino parents hoping to raise a bilingual child is, then, not "Why?" but "How?" We asked ourselves: What is the best way to rear a fully functional bilingual in a city that suffers a linguistic inferiority complex? Yes, on the one hand Miamians may speak proudly of living in the "northernmost city in Latin America" where Spanish is a lingua franca, but many bilinguals will also claim that they don't speak "proper Spanish" or say with a laugh that they only speak "Spanglish." Having succumbed to damaging notions of linguistic purity, they do not believe they speak the kind of Spanish that Boswell reports will earn them that extra bonus in their paycheck.

As an "expert" on Spanish language and learning, I was confident that we would have no trouble raising our son to be able to read, write, think, and live happily in two worlds. After all, hadn't my mother, María Luisa, been able to do this as a Cuban refugee, with no training, no time, and even less money, when Miami hardly spoke Spanish? Wouldn't my doctorate in Spanish, my training as a linguist, and flexible hours give me advantages my mother never had when we arrived here as political exiles in 1962 with one change of clothes? This was what my partner and I thought when Juan Gabriel was still in the planning stages.

Accomplishing our goal, I should have realized then and certainly know now, is tough—and in some ways harder than it was when my mother and grandmother raised my brother and me in Spanish in an English-speaking Miami. Unlike Juan Gabriel, my brother and I were native speakers of Spanish who had studied in Cuba for several years, and maintaining Spanish was crucial because everyone believed we would be returning to Havana soon, when Castro fell. Most importantly, my grandmother, who always lived with us, was never able to learn English. When nobody else in the community at large was speaking Spanish in public, it was a relief to be able to depend on the warm, comforting feeling of Spanish at home.

Miami is very different now, and we are no longer the outsiders. You might assume that in an area teeming with Spanish-speakers, educating one's child bilingually would be a snap. Or that everyone would be on the same page, in favor of bringing up baby bilingually and emphasizing Spanish at home since English would be learned at school. After all, if your family is going to live in Miami, shouldn't parents be pushing Miami–Dade County public schools to make bilingualism a goal for all its graduates? It's not that easy. The fourth-largest school district in the nation has other priorities, including funding problems and overcrowded schools. This does not mean that bilingual education is unavailable, but parents who want bilingual schooling options have to work for them, live in the right district, and endure long waiting lists. Even language courses for the general population are limited; foreign- or heritage-language study is not a requirement for secondary school graduation in Dade County public schools. This is a shame in a county like Miami–Dade and in a country like the United States, whose Spanish-speaking population is expected to become 25% of the general population in several decades. It is a particularly short-sighted view of education in a post-9/11 era, when schools should be producing bilingual Americans to address security issues, to stimulate international trade, and to foster intercultural communication at home. Only a few of Miami's public schools are up to the challenge.

A handful of well-known bilingual public elementary schools are possibilities for Juanchi when he gets to elementary school age. Coral Way Elementary became nationally recognized for its bilingual curriculum and served as a model for elementary schools across the country in the 1960s; Carver Elementary and Key Biscayne are others we want to investigate. Students who graduate from these programs can continue their studies at Carver Middle School, then go on to the International Baccalaureate Program at Coral Gables High School or at Coral Reef High School. Whether Juanchi ends up in any of the public schools that have a good reputation for language study will depend on available space, school boundaries, and other factors.

Parents who can afford it can find private schools that do a good job of educating students in both Spanish and English. Some, which opened their doors in Miami after having been shut down in 1960s Cuba, emphasize Hispanic cultures and offer Spanish classes while also providing an excellent education in English. Yet most are not real bilingual schools, where Spanish is a medium of instruction; they just offer Spanish as a subject. The latest option is a new charter high school in the Museum of Science building that emphasizes foreign languages and has ties to the Spanish and French consulates; we will see what develops there.

OUR PRE-K OPTIONS

Our son has a long wait until high school, however, and finding a suitable bilingual environment for a 3-year-old is not an easy task, even in Miami. Many private preschools offer Spanish lessons several times a week, but most operate and teach in English. At the Montessori school near our home, we made a "deal" with the teachers in the Toddler House: Speak to Juan Gabriel only in Spanish when you speak to him on a one-to-one basis, and we'll bring *pastelitos* and *croquetas* every time it's our turn for Snack Day. Two of his three teachers were Spanish-speakers who were happy to oblige. It worked out well because, at 3½, Juan Gabriel slips easily from one language to the other. He doesn't miss a beat when we have a group of people over and some speak Spanish and some don't, automatically switching into the appropriate language. When he speaks, he seldom mixes Spanish and English.

We are worried about what will happen to Juanchi's Spanish in the coming year as he moves to a new teacher who is Cuban American and speaks Spanish well but speaks little Spanish with her pre-K students because she feels more comfortable in English. Her students will have Spanish instruction for half an hour several times a week, but other than that we'll be on our own. Although I have cajoled, whined, and begged, this otherwise wonderful school is not willing to experiment with any kind of a bilingual approach in even one of its sections. As a parent and a professor of Spanish, I explained the advantages of having Spanish play a more significant role in the curriculum, particularly since the staff is 98% bilingual and Hispanic. I added that offering a bilingual approach or at least some bilingual activities would live up to the Montessori school philosophy of meeting the needs of individual children. Didn't that include the children's linguistic needs? What was the school's rationale for not offering a bilingual approach? That the Latin American parents want their kids to learn English! Those parents are mostly professionals, middle- or upper-middle-class immigrants who go back and forth between Miami and their home countries. They (unlike me) have no doubts that their children will learn Spanish, because they know that they will spend their summers, and maybe some schoolyears, in Latin America. Those of us who cannot return "home" for long stays—the majority of the Spanish-speakers in Miami—need the kind of bilingual program that professional hemisphere-trotters find unnecessary.

Language attitudes never cease to surprise me. Even at my son's soccer practice, the Mexican coach insists on addressing his charges in English much of the time, even though Spanish is clearly his dominant language. When asked about it, he told me he says everything in both languages, but that has not been what I have observed. He speaks English to the children even when nine out of the ten are heritage Spanish speakers and the tenth is a Brazilian who understands Spanish.

THE BILINGUAL HOME ENVIRONMENT
AND OUR COMMUNITIES: A PLACE FOR SPANISH,
ENGLISH, AND CODE-SWITCHING

Spanish and Cuban cultures are an essential part of our home life. Juan Gabriel was named Juanchi by his Cuban *abuela*—his grandmother, whom he in turn nicknamed Yeya—and he knows that I was born in Cuba. I wish I could say that our household operates fully in Spanish, that Juan Gabriel watches only Spanish videos, and that when he speaks English we ignore him and pretend we don't understand. I would, however, be lying. The truth is that both Helena and I speak to Juan Gabriel almost exclusively in Spanish and he speaks to us also almost exclusively in Spanish (at least 95% of the time would be my estimate), but the two of us very often speak English between ourselves. He watches far too much television (in both languages), although we have spent a small fortune on videos and DVDs in Spanish, searching everywhere on the back of a DVD (since it's never in the same place) to see if it has a Spanish audiotrack. He hears too much English-language news (CNN at home and National Public Radio in the car). When he talks to us in English, we do say *"Dilo en español"* (Say it in Spanish), but we don't pretend not to speak English. How could we? Why would we? It would not be natural or truthful. I believe that one key to success is to use languages in a natural fashion, never forced or in a manner that is uncomfortable. The norm in our daily interactions has been to address him in Spanish. Establishing this pattern early on, I think, has been the most important achievement. It is obvious to me now, after watching our child acquire both languages, how language and cultural identity are quickly and naturally established when there is a rich linguistic and cultural environment in and outside the home.

We have made a conscious effort to teach Juanchi Spanish, but we have not made any effort to teach him English. We believed that his acquisition of English would come by osmosis, as it has, via interactions with the American side of the family, with the English mode of instruction at his Montessori pre-K school, and with monolingual friends. Juanchi listens to us speak to each other in English, and many of our friends sometimes speak to him in English. My partner's mother speaks to him only in English because she does not know Spanish, and *Clifford the Big Red Dog* is not available in Spanish. Thank goodness for *Dragon Tales* on Spanish television on Saturdays and all the DVDs offering Spanish audio.

We read to Juanchi every night in Spanish, selecting from a nice collection of children's books published in Argentina, Colombia, Puerto Rico, Spain, and the United States. Friends who ask us what presents they should buy for his birthday or for the holidays are told that he always enjoys a book. Even though he does not know how to read yet, he loves to have stories read to him and has developed a great love of books and bookstores in our community. Even when a book he picks out is in English, I "read" it to him in Spanish, doing my best at an on-the-spot translation of the story. I have commented on the advantages of being bilingual by pointing out the fact that Grandma Dede can read him some books in English and later *Mami* (me) or Malena (my partner) can read him the version in Spanish; he gets to enjoy the story in two different ways. As a result of hearing the same story in two languages, he is expanding his vocabulary in the same narrative context.

Juan Gabriel doesn't code-switch within the same sentence much, but sometimes his English is a translation from Spanish, for example, "The book of Thomas" instead of "Thomas's book" or "I want that you eat one" instead of "I want you to eat one." He is creative when he is at an impasse; for example, if he doesn't know a word in English, he puts on a big fat gringo accent and says the Spanish word. He will also create an English word from a Spanish one. When we were getting ready for a trip, he tromped up the staircase, announcing "I going to get my mallet"—and returned with his *maleta* (suitcase). When stumped, he might ask for a translation, directly or indirectly. When he said, "*La manzana fue por el camino viejo*," he turned to my partner and asked, *¿Malena, tú puedes decirle eso a Dede?*" (Can you say this for Dede?). Dutifully, Malena translated for Dede, "The apple went down the wrong pipe." It's always the idiomatic expressions that are hardest to get across, even for 3-year-olds who know that "it went down the old road" isn't quite accurate. Juanchi is well aware of the possibilities of using two languages to meet his needs and those of others.

Juanchi usually switches into English when he knows a person cannot speak Spanish (and vice versa), but when he was a bit younger, just under 3, he was still developing his linguistic awareness. We were at a bookstore and he was trying to play with a little boy. Like the cashiers at the supermarket who, to the chagrin of dark-haired gringos, automatically speak Spanish when someone with brown hair crosses their path, he was speaking to the boy in Spanish. The child would not answer. Juanchi came to me and said, "*Mami, ese niño no habla*" (that child doesn't speak). I had heard the child speaking English with his mother, so I told him that maybe he did not speak Spanish. "*Qué pena*" (What a pity), was Juan Gabriel's response.

To practice Spanish outside the home, I take Juanchi to places that are filled with Spanish-speakers, like the Versailles Restaurant Bakery. He has become a "regular," greeting all of the women who dispense caffeine, carbohydrates, and good humor with a loud "*Hola*," and he sits at the counter to converse with them. Hispanic culture being what it is, Juanchi always has a funny and/or meaningful interaction with someone speaking Spanish in such settings. He is not shy in either language, and this has helped his speech development and socialization in both languages and cultures. At 3½, he is quite aware of both Cuban and American cultures. He loves to listen and dance to Celia Cruz's music and to watch her on DVD, and he wears his dressy white Cuban *guayabera* shirt when we visit his *Padrino* (godfather) or attend a formal event. He is as comfortable singing "Lucy in the Sky with Diamonds" or "Puff the Magic Dragon" as he is dancing to or playing my conga drums while we sing along to the Cuban tune of "Guantanamera."

One area that requires further development concerns the appropriate forms of address in Spanish; Juanchi does not yet use the formal *usted* form. He hears us use it, but far less often than *tú*, because most of our contacts are informal. He does, however, hear it in nightly bedtime stories, which should help. I now appreciate why my college students have trouble with standard forms of address in Spanish.

CONCLUSION

The lack of concern for children's Spanish-language maintenance in my community has sometimes taken me aback, like at the Montessori school and at soccer practice. At other times I am pleasantly surprised to find "comrades in arms" in unlikely places. A monolingual African American who works with Helena has had her daughter enrolled in a Little Havana day-care center since she was 6 months old. She wants her little girl to have an opportunity to live life in two languages and to navigate successfully in both worlds. Juanchi is already enjoying his Spanish and English worlds. Some readers may wonder about the impact of having two mothers on Juanchi's linguistic progress, including the attitudes of outsiders and issues of input, but at this point in his language development no significant impact is discernible; we expect the biggest hurdles will involve the educational system. We have to become more involved in our community and schools to make sure that the public at large as well as teachers, school administrators, the new superintendent, business owners, school board members, university professors, and parents support bilingual education, heritage-language development, and Spanish-language instruction. We must demand better language policies and practices in our schools (public or private) because the linguistic rights and future of the Latino communities are at stake and because of what they can contribute to the nation. To demand anything less than quality heritage- and foreign-language education in Spanish is to accept inequality and the marginalization of children who should grow up empowered with literacy in both languages. In sum, we need to be able to "read" more clearly the links among language education policies, funding, and practice in pre-K child-care centers, and we need to intervene on behalf of our children's psychosocial development, their acceptance of Hispanic cultures and language, and the future of Spanish–English bilingualism in the United States. We hope we can count on monolingual English-speaking parents to join our efforts so that all our children can have the opportunity to become bilingual.

CHAPTER 8

Dominican Children with Special Needs in New York City: Language and Literacy Practices

M. Victoria Rodríguez

When I moved from Spain in 1985 to teach in an elementary school in Manhattan, the majority of my first graders were Dominicans. For the following 10 years, I taught at the elementary and college level. Some of my college students, who were in a teacher education program and teaching in the public school system, complained about the lack of preparation of their Dominican students. They explained that they did not even know their proper names, let alone colors, numbers, or the letters of the alphabet. These stories and my complete lack of understanding and knowledge of the Dominican children's language experiences at home led me to study the home learning experiences of three young Dominican children (Rodríguez, 1999). I was later motivated to continue this line of research, focusing this time on young Dominicans with disabilities, a group rarely studied in relation to its educational issues. This chapter briefly introduces relevant historical facts necessary to grasp the racial, cultural, political, and demographic characteristics of Dominicans who immigrated to the United States. It then focuses on the home language and literacy practices of six young Dominican children with disabilities living in New York City.

HISTORICAL, POLITICAL, AND DEMOGRAPHIC PERSPECTIVES

Understanding the socioeconomic, racial, political, and linguistic characteristics of Dominican immigrants requires some familiarity with their country's history and its relationship with the United States. Dominicans come from a

Caribbean island, Hispaniola, which they share with Haiti. Their country, the Dominican Republic, became independent in 1844 after confronting the imperial powers of Spain and France, as well as their neighbor Haiti. Since the Dominican Republic's independence, the country has been under the economic and political domination of the United States.

From 1492 until the early 17th century, Spain had control of the island. Changes in the main economic activities and the extinction of the Taínos, the indigenous workers, led the colonists to import African slaves in great numbers (Moya Pons, 1995). This explains the current racial makeup of the Dominican population, estimated to be 73% mulatto, 16% White, and 11% Black (Sagás, 2000). At the beginning of the 17th century, France established its own colony in the western part of the island, which became the independent country of Haiti in 1804. In 1822 Haiti occupied the whole island, until the Dominican Republic finally became an independent nation in 1844 (Moya Pons, 1995). These historical facts help explain two characteristics that researchers often use to define "Dominican-ness": their strong affirmation of their Hispanic heritage, including the Spanish language (Toribio, 2000), and their everlasting resentment or hatred of Haitians (Sagás, 2000; Torres-Saillant & Hernández, 1998). These attitudes shape the multiple ethnic/racial and linguistic identities that Dominican second-generation students adopt in high school (Bailey, 2001).

After the Dominican Republic's independence, the United States controlled it directly or indirectly, by occupying the country from 1916 to 1924 and again in 1965, and by supporting dictator general Rafael Trujillo and President Joaquín Balaguer for decades (Moya Pons, 1995). Balaguer's support of emigration as a way of controlling the country's population growth, coupled with new laws in the United States that ended quotas favoring European nations, activated a massive Dominican immigration to the United States that continues today (Torres-Saillant & Hernández, 1998). Since the 1960s, Dominicans have been immigrating mainly to the New York City metropolitan area, Florida, Massachusetts, and European cities. Logan (2001) estimated the number of Dominicans in New York City to be about 602,700 in 2000. Despite the growing numbers of Dominicans in New York, research investigating their lives and concerns did not take off until the 1980s, and especially the 1990s, with the creation of the Dominican Studies Institute at the City University of New York. (See Aponte [1999] and James [1998] for an annotated bibliography.)

HOME LITERACY EXPERIENCES OF SIX DOMINICAN CHILDREN WITH DISABILITIES LIVING IN NEW YORK CITY

Researchers have examined the functions and uses of literacy, print, and writing materials available in young children's homes; the ways in which children explore print on their own; and the ways in which adults or mature literates socialize children into language and literacy (Cochran-Smith, 1984; Heath, 1983; Rodríguez, 1999; Taylor, 1983; Taylor & Dorsey-Gaines, 1988). Few studies, however, have focused on home literacy experiences of young children with disabilities (Light & Kelford-Smith, 1993; Marvin, 1994; Marvin & Mirenda, 1993; Marvin & Ogden, 2002; Marvin & Wright, 1997). These studies, which have relied mainly on surveys and interviews, suggest that parents provide fewer types of early literacy experiences at home to children with disabilities than to children without disabilities. Additionally, these parents may not have high expectations for their children's literacy development; consequently, literacy development is not a priority for them (Marvin & Mirenda, 1993; Marvin & Ogden, 2002). Even fewer studies examine the home language and literacy practices of young Latino children with disabilities. Zentella's (1997a) ethnography of a New York Puerto Rican community included the bilingual development of one girl who began special education at 8 years of age. This chapter is a deliberate effort to increase the knowledge base of language socialization of young Latino children with disabilities, as directly observed at home. Qualitative methods helped unearth the literacy artifacts, literacy functions, uses of print, language use in the family, and social interaction around print in the homes of six Dominican children.

This study, which was conducted with the support of a grant from the Professional Staff Congress of the City University of New York, involved six children from four families with the following characteristics: (1) The parents were Dominican, except one mother who was of Puerto Rican descent; (2) two families lived in the northern part of Manhattan and two lived in the Bronx; and (3) in each family there was at least one child between 3 and 7 years of age diagnosed as having a disability (see Table 8.1 for family backgrounds).

The parents' formal education varied but was generally higher than that of many Dominican immigrants. However, because of their limited English they could not get good jobs and lived modestly. All families were headed by a mother and father, except for Tony's (all names used are pseudonyms), whose parents divorced when he was 2 years old. He has continued to live in the apartment of his maternal grandparents, as he did before the divorce. The six focal children were diagnosed as having disabilities that included language impairment, speech impairment, and Down syndrome, and they started receiving special education services early in their lives.

The procedure was the same for each observation. I took notes on what the focal children were doing and audiotaped significant literacy events. In addition, the mothers audiotaped their children when they were participating in literacy activities in my absence, for example, bedtime reading or homework. I also interviewed each mother and Tony's grandmother. The participants were observed for 40 to 80 hours.

TABLE 8.1. Characteristics of the Four Participant Families and Their Children

	The Fernándezes	The Santanas	The Vázquezes	The Duráns
Mother's birthplace	Dominican Republic	New York of Dominican parents	New York of Puerto Rican parents	Dominican Republic
Father's birthplace	Dominican Republic	Dominican Republic	New York of Dominican parents	New York of Dominican parents
Education	M: BA in accounting, in Dominican Republic F: 2 years of accounting in Dominican Republic	M: high school F: N/A	M: 11th grade F: 1 year of college	M: General Equivalency Diploma F: BA in marketing, in Dominican Republic
Participant children's ages	Joel, 7	Tony, 5	Matthew, 4 Andrew, 3	Juan Carlos, 6 Jessica, 5
Children's diagnosed disabilities	Joel diagnosed with severe speech and language delays	Tony diagnosed with Down syndrome	Matthew diagnosed with moderate articulation difficulties Andrew diagnosed with language delays	Juan Carlos diagnosed with a mild receptive language delay and a moderate expressive language delay Jessica diagnosed with mild to moderate delays in language and moderate difficulties in word-finding and articulation skills

Key: M = mother, F = father
Note: All names are pseudonyms

Literacy Materials in the Homes

The amount of literacy materials at home varied according to economic circumstances. Most families had the necessary materials required for school, such as notebooks, pencils, and crayons, but for one family that endured tremendous economic hardship at one point, buying paper and pencils was a luxury. All the families owned some books—more in English than in Spanish. The number of books available was related to both the family budget and the mothers' and fathers' level of education. Where parents had some college education, there were more books in general and more children's books in particular. Usually, the books were not visible. The children's books might be in a drawer or a closet in the living room, or in the parents' room, and occasionally in a playroom or among the toys. Sometimes the books children were using at the moment were in their room. Only one of the families owned a computer, which was connected to the Internet. The rest of the families told me that they wished they had a computer for their children but could not afford one.

Functions and Uses of Literacy in the Home

Reading and writing were embedded in the daily lives of all four families, a phenomenon similarly revealed in other research on home literacy experiences of young children (Cochran-Smith, 1984; Goelman, Oberg & Smith, 1984; Heath, 1983; Rodríguez, 1999; Taylor, 1983). The purposes and types of literacy in these Dominican homes often depended on the practical problems that the families had to solve. Children saw elders read and write to get important information and to get things done. All the families read materials related to their dealings with public agencies and institutions such as Head Start programs, schools, and the university. Head Start programs and schools sent almost daily bilingual letters with information about homework, parent–teacher conference dates, the school calendar, trips, after-school programs, therapy services for children with special needs, and the children's behavior in school. The Committee on Preschool Special Education and the Early Intervention Centers also sent parents the Individualized Education Plan and regular reports on their children's progress, often in English only.

Because the mothers dealt with the economic needs of the family, they read bills, wrote money orders and checks, and filled out mail-order forms. Mrs. Durán worked at home by placing catalogue phone orders. All the mothers scheduled appointments and meetings with their children's teachers. Mrs. Fernández, who attended a community college at one point, read assigned fiction, textbooks, and books on specific topics, and she wrote term papers. Every adult read newspapers, but it was not a regular event. In the Fernández and Vázquez households, older siblings went to the library to borrow books regularly. Mrs. Durán took her children to the library in the summer, when school was not in session.

All family members watched television without consulting TV guides or newspaper listings, but reading and writing were part of daily homework sessions for the mothers, siblings, or friends who helped the children. In the household that included a computer, children played educational games on it and imitated their father using e-mail.

LANGUAGE USE AT HOME AND IN SCHOOL

The patterns of language use in each of the four families ranged from monolingual Spanish to monolingual English to bilingualism, depending on the parents' birthplace. In general, the parents who were born in the Domincan Republic addressed their children and spouses in Spanish and expected their children to answer in that language. The three parents who were born in New York City were bilingual, but only Mr. Durán was also biliterate. Mr. Durán addressed his wife and children in both languages; his wife answered mostly in Spanish, but the children answered mostly in English. Mr. and Mrs. Vázquez talked to each other and to their children in English. Their children understood some Spanish but did not speak it.

All the mothers told the researcher that they wanted their children to be bilingual, but they differed in the way they went about it. Mrs. Fernández and Mrs. Durán thought that parents should teach their children to speak Spanish, not the schools; schools, according to them, should focus only on English. Mrs. Santana and Mrs. Vázquez maintained that all children should have access to bilingual education. Mrs. Santana's grandson had been in bilingual classrooms since kindergarten, but Mrs. Vázquez put her children in Catholic schools because the local public schools were very bad, and she consequently regretted that none of her children were able to speak Spanish. She said she spoke Spanish with me because she liked to listen to my, as she put it, *español bonito* (beautiful Spanish) from Spain in contrast to her Puerto Rican Spanish. This perception of her Spanish as of a lower quality than mine may have contributed to her decision not to talk to her children in Spanish. In contrast, although Dominican Spanish is stigmatized, primarily because of its deletion of <s> at the end of syllables (Zentella, 1997b), none of the Dominican parents belittled it. They all emphasized the importance of being able to communicate with family members in the Dominican Republic; Tony's grandparents and the Vázquezes also pointed out that it was important to speak more than one language for employment purposes. But no one mentioned the importance of being able to read and write in Spanish, so those skills were sacrificed to emphasize literacy in English.

CHILDREN'S INTERACTION WITH PRINT
IN THEIR EVERYDAY LIVES AT HOME

The children explored literacy in different ways before and after entering kindergarten, confirming a previous study of three preschool Dominican children (Rodríguez, 1999). Before starting school, the children in the current study explored reading and writing by initiating and organizing literacy activities whenever someone was involved in reading and writing in front of them or literacy materials were nearby. For example, the youngest child, Andrew (age 3), explored print when someone left a book on the sofa. He picked it up, turning pages while whispering to himself. He also got a piece of paper and a pen that were nearby and tried to scribble.

Homework

All the children regularly observed their siblings doing homework. Mrs. Vázquez reported that Matthew (age 4) and Andrew liked to get close to their siblings when they were doing homework, but she did not allow them to because she thought they distracted their older brothers. After the focal children started school, their main literacy activity at home was doing homework. Each child organized himself or herself in a different way. Some liked to do their homework immediately after coming home from school (e.g., Juan Carlos); others liked to do other activities beforehand, such as having a snack, watching TV, or playing. They did their homework lying or sitting on the floor, bed, or sofa; at the kitchen or living room table; while watching TV; or while having a snack. As in a previous study of three Dominican families with less formal education (Rodríguez, 1999), all the mothers intervened in some way in their children's homework. They all made sure that their children did their homework by asking about it and checking their notebooks, and they tried to help when their children requested it. Some mothers were very disappointed when they could not help because the homework was in English or they did not understand the instructions. In those cases they asked siblings and me to help.

Other Literacy Activities

In addition to doing homework, which often included reading, writing, and spelling, some parents involved their children in special language activities. Joel (age 7) and his sister Luz (age 6) illustrated spoken stories, which Mrs. Fernández modeled for them. She would distribute paper and say, "*Vamos a hacer una historia*" (Let's do a story). Then she would draw the characters in a story while telling it. When she finished, she encouraged Joel and Luz to create a story. They would draw and talk about the characters in their stories and their actions. Mrs. Fernández listened and asked questions about the drawings, such as: Where does the story take place? Why does this dinosaur have such a big head? Is this a car for the baby dinosaur? Joel, who loved to draw and was an excellent artist, enjoyed this activity, and it enabled him to express himself using ways other than writing, a weak area for him.

Three families visited the library. Mrs. Fernández and her two children and Mrs. Durán and her three children went to the library regularly during summer vacation. Joel, and especially his sister Luz, loved scary stories. Luz read one story aloud with the narrator of the audiotape of the borrowed book, waiting anxiously and saying "*El* ghost *está cerca*" (The ghost is close) until the ghost appeared accompanied by a scary noise. Then Luz ran with Joel to their bedroom. She came back laughing and continued reading the story, delighted and waiting impatiently for the scary sound to recur. Mrs. Fernández told her that she would be afraid at night, but Luz replied that ghosts were not real.

A practice widely found in print-oriented families is reading aloud to children (Cochran-Smith, 1984; Heath, 1983; Taylor, 1983). Mrs. Vázquez took Matthew (at age 3) and Andrew (at age 2) to a reading-aloud program at a library, but she discontinued this activity because the library was too far away, she no longer had a car, and the children misbehaved. Her older children visited a local library regularly on their own. At home, Mrs. Vázquez often read to her younger children at bedtime in English and reported that Andrew would not go to sleep without "reading" a book or being read to by his mom. She audiotaped Matthew and Andrew looking at and talking about books. Except for Tony's grandparents, all of the families read aloud to their children every evening before bedtime. Mr. Fernández read stories in Spanish and Mrs. Fernández read in both English and Spanish to their children. In addition, Joel and Luz were encouraged to read on their own. Mrs. Durán read to her children in Spanish and tried to read them simple books in English.

Two families used computers. The Fernándezes did not own one, but Joel and Luz attended free computer workshops at a Bronx library on Saturdays. I asked their mother if they had access to the Internet on those computers, and she said that they did but that she did not want her children to learn about the Internet yet. Juan Carlos Durán (age 6) and Jessica Durán (age 5) had a computer at home that they used to play their CD-ROMs. They often fought because they could not play together, but they did not want to wait their turn either. On one of the few occasions when they sat together in front of the computer, they spoke knowledgeably, imitating their father. Jessica said: "Me doing my e-mail, me doing my e-mail" (while tapping into the keyboard). Juan Carlos answered: "That is not for e-mail." Jessica reacted by tapping several letters at the same time, ending their "computer talk."

WATCHING TV, PLAYING, SINGING, AND DANCING

Like most children their age, the participants' everyday activities included watching television, playing, and listening to music. All except the non-Spanish-speakers, Matthew and Andrew, were also observed singing and dancing the *merengue* and *bachata*, traditional Dominican dances.

Watching television was a daily activity in all four households, and everybody had cable service. Each family owned at least two sets, one in the living room and the other in the parents' bedroom. Some children also had a TV in their rooms. TV watching could occur simultaneously with eating, playing, doing homework, singing, or dancing. The Fernándezes and Duráns did not allow the TV to be on during homework sessions, and Mrs. Fernández forbade violent programs. Matthew, Andrew, Juan Carlos, and Jessica participated in interactive TV programs in English by answering questions and by singing along or telling the main characters where to find what they were looking for. Everyone's favorite programs were cartoons in English.

TV was often on in the background; the children's attention was triggered by music, dance, dramatic action, screaming or crying, commercials about toys and food, or commercials involving young children. Print did not discourage them from being attentive to the screen. Print is plentiful in commercials, especially those selling cereals, toys, and music, and print appears at the beginning and end of programs. The children were all observed focusing on the print when the credits were shown. In addition to reinforcing the importance of print, watching TV may have helped these children develop a sense of narrative structure (Snow, Nathan, & Perlmann, 1985). They tried to understand who the characters were, what objects were involved, where and when the action took place, what the main event consisted of, why the event occurred, and what the consequences of the event were.

The children often played with toys and with balls, and some played with words. Toys included small cars, planes, stuffed animals, and action figures of TV cartoon characters (e.g., Batman and Pokémon characters). At Christmas time, playing with new toys replaced watching television. Five of the six children had Nintendo and other video games. They all loved playing or watching their friends or siblings play Nintendo; Andrew watched his brothers play for as long as 50 minutes. Tony loved baseball, the national game in the Domican Republic, which has produced many stellar players. Often, he would get a ball and pretend he was pitching. Rough-and-tumble games were popular with everyone. Juan Carlos was the only child who played a word game that asked questions such as "Which letter does the word *king* end with?" or "Which letter does the word *fish* start with?" Jessica was often around when he played this, but she would not participate.

Music was highly valued by adults and children alike. It was central to their entertainment, and all the children were encouraged to listen to music, sing, and dance. Music for family entertainment was often in Spanish, but children also listened to music and sang in English when they watched TV. For Joel, Tony, Juan Carlos, and Jessica, dancing was a favorite activity. Joel danced the *bachata*. Juan Carlos's favorite activities were singing and dancing. After doing homework or watching TV, he would turn on the radio, take anything handy to use as a make-believe microphone, and sing along and dance. Jessica often joined him in dancing. He also sang songs that he had learned in school. Tony pretended to play the guitar and danced.

Mothers often told their children to sing and dance for me. Listening to music and singing enriched the children's oral language; they helped in developing vocabulary, encouraging phonemic awareness, and understanding the schema of story, since songs sometimes have the format of a story. As Snow and Tabors (1993) have pointed out, "oral forms of language are in some sense prior to literacy language" and "oral language skills are the basis for the development of written language skills for children" (p. 6). Recent research has highlighted the importance of extending the young child's oral language and vocabulary in developing reading and writing skills (Dickinson & Tabors, 2001). The Dominican families involved all the children in oral musical activities, no matter what their ability level.

MOTHERS' CONCERNS ABOUT THEIR CHILDREN'S EDUCATION AND LITERACY DEVELOPMENT

Interviews and informal conversations disclosed the caregiver's major expectations and concerns regarding their children's education. All parents had high expectations; they hoped their children would attend college to pursue the careers of their choice. Two mothers confided that they had not had their parents' support when they were in school because they were girls. Consequently, they were very supportive of their daughters' education and encouraged them to do well. Tony's grandmother, concerned about his disability and the fact that she might not be alive to care for him as an adult, emphasized that she wanted her grandson to be independent. Everyone maintained that parents have an important role to play in the education of their children, which they understood to consist of the following:

1. Making sure their children went to school
2. Making sure they did their homework
3. Talking with their children about the importance of doing well in school

The mothers also shared their worries with me about the following: the assessment process, the quality of delivery of services to their children, the choice of language (English and Spanish, or only English) in the schooling of their children, and the need for guidance on how to help their children at home, especially with their homework.

Mrs. Vázquez was the only caregiver who did not express concern about the effectiveness of the special education assessment process and the delivery of services to their children. Mrs. Santana said she visited Tony's school often because if she were not on top of things, the child would not receive the services he was entitled to. For example, although Tony was supposed to have a para-educator to work one on one with him, the para-educator was often pulled out of the classroom to do other things. In her opinion, the quality of services deteriorated when Tony entered the public school system in kindergarten after attending a preschool special education center. Mrs. Durán's main complaint was that the special education personnel had tried too hard to convince her and her husband to enroll Juan Carlos in a full-time special education classroom that was full of children with more severe disabilities than Juan Carlos's and where he would not be challenged academically. She also resented the Individualized Education Plan's recommendation that her children be placed in bilingual classes when she and her husband had chosen monolingual classrooms. Lack of materials was also a concern. Mrs. Fernández felt that students with special needs should have reasonable access to computers (there was one computer for 12 children). She also thought that children with disabilities should not only be eligible for after-school programs but also encouraged to attend them.

The language of instruction was another major concern. All the mothers were aware of the issues related to the education of English-language learners who have disabilities, especially disabilities involving language impairments. However, as stated previously, their opinions varied as to which language should be used in speech and language therapy and for academic purposes. Mrs. Durán decided that her children should receive their language therapy in English even though she did not speak English well because she thought that English was easier for her children to learn and that using two languages would prove confusing for them. Mrs. Santana thought that her grandson should receive services bilingually because she did not speak English and she wanted to be able to communicate with him in Spanish. Mrs.

Fernández chose bilingual services for her son, even though she believed Spanish should only be taught at home, for practical reasons: She needed to help her son with his homework, and she could not provide help in English.

Mrs. Fernández offered the most poignant assessment of special education. It turned out that she could not read in English when Joel had initially been evaluated for special education services years before. I requested his initial report and re-evaluation, and when she finally read the information about her son that the teacher had given to the evaluator—information she had not known about—Mrs. Fernández said she felt "*impotente y humillada*" (impotent and humiliated). She added:

Por ahorrar tiempo y dinero, los padres no se enteran nada más que a medias de lo que está pasando con su hijo, cuando deberían saberlo todo para saber cómo lidiar con el problema. Cuando el padre desconoce información, inconscientemente agrega más al problema porque no trata al niño como debiera.	To save money and time, parents are only semi-informed about what is happening with their child, when they should know everything in order to know how to deal with the problem. When kept in the dark, a parent unknowingly adds to the problem because the parent doesn't deal with the child as he or she should.

Mrs. Fernández requested an independent re-evaluation because she did not trust the Board of Education or the teacher, who often complained about her son's behavior. Unfortunately, she was not informed of her right to request an independent re-evaluation free of charge as well as to receive the evaluation report in Spanish, the only language she could read at that time. As a result, she was forced to pay for the re-evaluation herself.

Mrs. Fernández was critical not only of the system but also of Latino parents. She believed that many think that good parenting only involves providing food, shelter, clean clothing, and keeping their children healthy. In her view, parents needed to do a lot more to educate their children adequately, especially those with special needs. Contrary to her opinion, I found that all the mothers wanted to work with their children, but they discovered how difficult it was to motivate them and keep them on task. Her own child and Jessica Durán, in particular, were easily distracted, and both resented being corrected. Mrs. Durán had an added difficulty, namely, helping her children in English, a language in which she was not proficient, although she placed them in English classes. The mothers were generally patient and loving, showering all children with affection equally, but they sometimes lost patience and recognized that they needed to know more about how to handle and teach their children with special needs. Their job is exhausting, since they shoulder the majority of the burdens, such as taking care of the children and dealing with the bureaucracy of the schools, the doctors, and special education services. Perhaps this explains why the mothers of five of the children attributed their disabilities to the husband's side of the family, as if to avoid shouldering that guilt. Clearly, educators and therapists can play a crucial role in easing parental burdens and resolving their concerns.

EDUCATING YOUNG DOMINICANS WITH DISABILITIES

Dominicans are the fastest-growing Latino group in New York City, and Dominican immigration to the United States is likely to increase. Because U.S. foreign policy and American economic needs helped create the conditions that spurred this immigration, it follows that our society has a responsibility to provide a sound basic education to the children of these immigrants, as it does to all children in the United States.

It has been convenient to blame both teachers and parents of minority children for not preparing the children for academic success. A recent and successful lawsuit in New York by the Campaign for Fiscal Equity, however, reveals a more fundamental reason for academic failure in the New York City public schools: disproportionately low allocations of state funds to New York City districts, where most minority children live. Tragically, these discriminatory allocations affect districts that have the highest numbers of uncertified and inexperienced teachers, as well as the most deteriorated school infrastructures. Coupled with other factors, these conditions have an additional consequence: a disproportionately high number of minority students in New York City have been classified as in need of special education services. In a well-funded and better-functioning school system with well-prepared teachers, many of these children's academic problems would have been resolved in the general education classroom instead of leading to their placement in special education settings. The real challenge, of course, is to make sure that children who really need special education services receive them and to avoid incorrectly evaluating children who merely need more time and help to learn a second language.

Those who claim that Latino parents contribute to their children's lack of success in school assume that they are not concerned about and involved in their children's education. The chapters in this book prove just the opposite, even though one of the Dominican mothers in this study echoed negative views of Latino parents' efforts. In truth, she and all the other parents are faced with many difficult decisions regarding their children's education, especially those with special needs, and they work hard at solving their problems with little support. They wrestle with whether to enroll them in bilingual or English-only classrooms, whether to use bilingual or monolingual special education services such as speech and language therapy, how to understand the bureaucracy and its evaluations of their children, and how to make their wishes known and respected by school personnel. Because parents make their decisions based on what they believe will be best for their children, they need the kind of research and outreach that will help them make informed decisions. In fact, all the mothers in the study were very aware of the difficulties in educating their children, and all said they needed more help to know how to assist in the process.

The participation of teachers and parents in the evaluation process is essential to avoid harmful placements. Standardized tests alone cannot measure the child's interests, behavior, and language skills in a variety of classroom contexts as well as the teacher who works with the child on an ongoing basis. Parents bring additional knowledge about their child's skills that complements the information provided by the teacher and the tests, making misdiagnosis and misplacement less likely. Teachers and clinicians have an important role in informing parents of the following:

1. Their rights; that is, their right to participate in the evaluation and to question the results of the evaluation and the placement of their child
2. The programs available in special education and bilingual special education
3. The disadvantages of using English as the language of instruction for Spanish-speaking children with disabilities

Children who are exposed only to English when they do not have their native language well established may experience language loss with serious implications for their family life and for the parents' involvement in their child's language development and education. In addition, teaching in a language that children with language difficulties do not understand deprives them of using their primary linguistic strength—the native language that allows them to make sense of the world around them (Rodríguez, 1998).

Despite their disabilities and poverty, and contrary to the typical findings of the limited research to date, the Dominican children I studied did have opportunities to explore literacy and develop language skills at home, with the help of caregivers of all ages. As within any group, there was variability in the literacy experiences of the individual families. Some children owned books and other literacy materials and were read to regularly by family members, while others sometimes lacked basic materials and were read to only occasionally. But all of the children who attended school did homework, went to the library, and read books. Two used computers. They were also involved in more unconventional literacy activities such as telling stories through illustration and narration, playing, singing songs, and watching both commercial and educational TV programs. These learning experiences should be considered as meaningful and effective as those routinely used in schools. An innovative and constructive approach would capitalize on these cultural practices in the classroom and acknowledge the parents' efforts, instead of assuming there are no meaningful learning experiences going on at home.

CHAPTER 9

Seeing What's There: Language and Literacy Funds of Knowledge in New York Puerto Rican Homes

Carmen I. Mercado

From 1996 to 1999, I collaborated with bilingual teachers in New York City (Mercado, 2003, in press) to identify funds of knowledge or intellectual, communicative, emotional, and spiritual resources for learning in Latino homes. For the most part these homes were not in communities usually identified with resources for learning. As we discovered, first impressions are deceiving, even for those of us who identify with these families. In keeping with the work of Moll and his colleagues (1995) in Arizona our study of funds of knowledge revealed a wide range of local knowledge, such as entrepreneurship, health care and medicine, music, and home repair and maintenance.

In this chapter, I re-examine data from 14 Puerto Rican households to understand how funds of knowledge are shaped by, and shape, language and literacy practices. Language (including literacy) is not just the means of acquiring funds of knowledge; language is a social, intellectual, and emotional resource that is shaped by and responds to social needs. This study makes clear what we could not see when we initially focused on funds of knowledge as disciplinary knowledge—that language is an invaluable fund of knowledge in its own right. Awareness of this finding can help address the fact that despite educational and economic advances and a growing professional class, U.S.-based Puerto Rican communities continue to experience a disproportionate percentage of high school dropouts and low college enrollment and retention. Language and literacy, researchers tell us, are at the core of these educational problems, but in order to achieve educational goals pursued by Puerto Ricans and other ethnolinguistic minorities, educators require tools and strategies to see what's there. The Funds of Knowledge approach provides the resources that educators need in order to see what escapes the uninformed observer. Because context is crucial in shaping language use, we begin by addressing the geographic and demographic context of the families.

HISTORICAL AND DEMOGRAPHIC BACKGROUND

New York's *El Barrio*, or East Harlem, home to 50% of the Puerto Rican households we studied, including the two featured in this chapter, is one of the largest Puerto Rican communities in the United States, stretching north from 96th Street to 125th Street and east from Fifth Avenue to the East River. East Harlem is at the crossroads of two worlds, bounded on the west by Harlem, with the nation's largest concentration of African Americans, and on the south by the Upper East Side, one of the nation's most affluent neighborhoods. New York City Puerto Ricans have had continuous and intensive contact with African Americans, whose linguistic influence contributes to the bilingual, multidialectal repertoire of children reared in East Harlem (Zentella, 1997a); the influence of their wealthy neighbors has not been documented. In a city as densely populated as New York, a subway ride creates contact zones and unexpected opportunities to witness mainstream socialization practices surrounding print; for example, I have observed read-aloud and shared reading on subway rides through affluent neighborhoods.

Puerto Ricans in East Harlem, unlike Puerto Ricans in other parts of the city or in other states, have the highest poverty rate, the lowest household incomes, and the lowest labor-force participation of nonimmigrant Latino groups (Mollenkopf, 1999). The median income for a family of four is about $15,000 in a city with a median family income of $50,000. Most New Yorkers ignore the economic and historical forces that have shaped the income of Puerto Ricans in the city, their reasons for leaving Puerto Rico, and the impact on families. Five little known factors distinguish Puerto Ricans from other Latinos: (1) a 100-year relationship with the United States, which imposed U.S. citizenship but rejected statehood; (2) decades of English-only policies in the island's public schools and the disparagement of Puerto Rican Spanish; (3) the "forced" migration of massive numbers of Puerto Ricans to New York after World War II; (4) the segregation of Puerto Ricans and African Americans in Harlem in the 1950s after the flight of the white middle class to the suburbs (Bonilla, 1985; Portes & Rumbaut, 1996); and (5) the displacement of Puerto Rican workers in the 1960s (including many females in the garment industry) due to the city's shift from a manufacturing to a service economy. These factors help explain the low incomes of Puerto Rican families, to which social scientists attribute the community's health, housing, and educational problems (Bonilla, 1985).

Puerto Ricans in New York City have been negatively affected by government policies, but they have not remained passive. One area where advocacy has resulted in unanticipated benefits is in educational reforms, including bilingual education. As a result, more Latino teachers and administrators work (and in some cases live) in East Harlem than in other areas of the city (Pedraza, 1997). Whether the activism and resulting policies have influenced language and literacy practices in East Harlem's households remains to be studied, but research and theory on language socialization (including literacy) over the past 20 years reorient our thinking and provide new ways of seeing what's there.

LITERACY AS SOCIAL PRACTICE

Social theories of literacy shed new light on what literacy means, what it looks like, and how it develops within particular groups and communities. According to Barton and Hamilton (1998) literacy practices "are the general cultural ways of utilizing written language which people draw upon in their lives" (p. 6). Also included are peoples' awareness of literacy; how they talk about and make sense of literacy; and the values, attitudes, feelings, and social relationships associated with it. Conceptions of literacy as social practice forge connections between the activities of reading and writing and the social structures in which they are embedded and which they help to shape.

Because language and literacy are not acquired apart from culture (Ochs, 1988), literacy is a cultural product embedded in an ideology that cannot be isolated and treated as neutral or merely technical (Street, 1984). Consequently, literacy is dynamic, changing to reflect the influence of family; friendship; social and institutional networks; and the social, emotional, economic, and communicative needs of individuals. Some scholars emphasize that literacy cannot be understood in isolation or in terms of self-enhancement skills. Historically, literacy has had a primary role in the transmission of morals, discipline, and social values, and recently it has been linked to social change and action (Graff, 1991).

As institutional agents, teachers bring to the study of local literacies what they have been conditioned to see. Del Valle (2002) explains that what we most value—although not necessarily practice—is the decoding of extended prose passages, such as the classics or *New York Times* best-sellers, or the production of expository writing. However, as I have found in other community-based studies (see Mercado, 2003), the uses of literacy in low-income communities respond to everyday needs of families and may exceed those typically emphasized in school.

Although everyday literacies are typically accorded lower social value, remaining invisible in institutions such as schools, they are, in fact, hybrid practices that draw on the media and official literacies, as well as the household's social networks. Consequently, the binary division that is made between academic and everyday literacies may be more imagined than real (Moje, Ciechanowski, Ellis, Carillo, & Collazo, 2004). Duranti and Ochs (1996) propose the notion of syncretic literacies to account for the ways in which the same language or code may be used for distinct cultural practices and the ways in which different cultural practices can be merged within the same literacy activity in linguistically heterogeneous communities.

TEACHER-RESEARCHER COLLABORATION

The teachers I collaborated with took on the role of social scientists, conducting two or three home interviews that engaged them in 3 to 6 hours of conversations with caregivers, guided by in-depth, open-ended questionnaires in the tradition of Funds of Knowledge research. They elicited information on language and literacy practices in Spanish and English, and learned about the family's migratory history, income-producing activities, and child-rearing practices and beliefs. My collaboration consisted of guiding documentation processes, debriefing field experiences, and analyzing emerging findings. Teachers organized their own research teams of two to four people, and I participated in seven home visits.

Given the dearth of research on bilingual researchers, one significant contribution of this study is the fact that more than half of the 103 teacher-researchers were Spanish–English bilinguals and multidialectal. They averaged 4 years of classroom experience in elementary schools in low-income communities. Many had been born in Puerto Rico, and some had lived in the communities where we interviewed families. I, too, was born in Puerto Rico and raised and educated in New York City, a product of its public schools. Shared language practices and cultural understandings and beliefs usually facilitated rapport and communication, but it did not always facilitate how we interpreted what we saw and learned.

Our home interviews were, as Ochs (1988) describes, culturally organized events that were complex, with overlapping and intertwined occurrences, although there were differences across households in terms of how home interviews were organized. For the most part, our discursive practices constructed and revealed shared cultural knowledge and a relationship of *confianza* (trust), which allowed for the easy exchange of information and the expectation that this information would be used to help the students and/or teachers (Mercado & Moll, 1997). Home interviews also gave direct glimpses of language socialization practices between caregivers and children, as this excerpt from one team's field notes on the interruptions that were allowed during Ita Alegría's interview illustrate:

> In all three interviews there were children and their friends present, conversing with us, too. This part of the interview was crucial because there was mutual language involvement. What each of us said was important because it was spontaneous. *A cada rato teníamos interrupciones. Ita estaba al tanto de todo. Mantenía todo en control mientras los hijos pedían ayuda mientras hablábamos. La televisión siempre estuvo prendida aunque los niños no le ponían atención. Preferían hablar y dibujar, mientras H. ponía una pared.* (There were many interruptions. Ita was aware of everything that was going on. She kept everything under control as her children asked for help while we spoke. The TV was on while we were talking but the children didn't pay attention to it. They preferred to talk and to draw while H. [her 17-year-old son] installed a wall.)

This bilingual journal entry reflects the teacher-researcher's level of comfort with and appreciation of the type of spontaneity and language involvement she experienced in this household. In general, the bilingual teacher-researchers were highly conscious of and sensitive to the role of language in establishing personal relationships. They also recognized that nonbilinguals who may not understand or be used to bilingual and multiparty interactions of this type may find them, at best, difficult to follow or, at worst, an indicator of disrespect.

Humor also built solidarity in our exchanges, exposing children to the ways in which the delivery, e.g., prosody and gestures, as well as the unexpectedness of an utterance or response fostered rapport, as in the following dialogue between the teacher-researcher (T-R), and Ita (IA), and analysis:

1. *T-R: ¿Ayudan los niños a cuidar los animales?* (Do the children help take care of the animals?)
   IA: Sí. (Yes)
   T-R: ¿Cómo? (How?)
   IA: ¡Poniendo gritos en el cielo! (By screaming at the top of their lungs!)
2. I asked her, how many languages does she speak? She said, "Spanish, English and *jeringonza*" [*jerigonza*, a kind of pig Latin]. We began a conversation in *jeringonza*. We laughed. I remember the times I spoke *jeringonza* with my grandmother, mom, aunts, cousins and friends in Puerto Rico. . . . To my astonishment, her children speak

it, too. Her youngest daughter got into the conversation. It was fun!
(Field notes, 10/12/95).

Our ability to respond with laughter appropriately created *confianza* (trust)
and mutual respect, allowing caregivers to establish their authority on matters of home life and lessening the social distance between them and the professional Latina interviewers.

In this climate of trust, the life stories that were authored were very
different from narratives constructed or invented by social scientists, the
media, and institutional agents to explain or justify the low status of Puerto
Ricans. In the vignettes below, primary caregivers represent themselves as
they believe themselves to be: strong, hardworking, responsible, and devoted
mothers who know how to respond to adversity and who sustain the integrity of their families at all costs. They are also mothers who are concerned
about their children's *educación*, an education that emphasizes character
development, not just the acquisition of information and skills.

LANGUAGE AND LITERACY IN TWO PUERTO RICAN HOMES

Two case studies illustrate the distinct manner in which the mothers' personal characteristics and the lived experiences of their households shaped their
language and literacy. The households selected for this new analysis were
chosen because of the thoughtfulness with which teacher-researcher teams
documented and conducted the household study and because I have presented
other aspects of this work at conferences with members of these teams. The
two families were comparable in their valuing of education and schooling
and in their relationship to their children's school, where they were both
known. The two children who motivated the study of these households attended the same school, although they did not know each other, and both
had literacy-related problems in school.

Language and Literacy in the Navarro Home

Jaclyn Navarro (pseudonym), age 34, has lived between
two islands all her life—Manhattan and Puerto Rico. She
has attended schools in both, as have the four oldest of her
ten children. "*Yo nací en Puerto Rico y me crié aquí. Vine a
los cinco años, pero mi mamá era* back and forth." (I was
born in Puerto Rico and I came here when I was 5, but my
mother kept going back and forth.) She and seven of her
children (three females, ages 16, 10, 9, and four males,

ages 6, 5, 4, and 2) live in an immaculate six-room apartment in government-subsidized housing on the boundary
between Yorkville and Harlem. On one side of this boundary is some of the highest-priced real estate in the city; on
the other, some of the poorest. "The only thing bad about
living here is the racism," she emphasizes in Spanish.

Being bilingual is very important to Jaclyn Navarro, reflecting her experience of living between two islands. "I didn't get my diploma but I don't
forget English and I don't forget Spanish," she said in Spanish. Hers is a classic
example of the *va-y-ven* (go and come) pattern of Puerto Ricans in New York
City. Although circular migration stems from a quest for belonging and economic well-being and fosters cross-cultural adaptability, it can also be a disruptive influence, contributing to social and economic destabilization. Jaclyn
understands this very well, because of what happened to her. "*Mi mamá nos
tenía yendo y viniendo.*"(My mother had us going back and forth.) She told
her mother, "*Llevando y trayendo, nunca voy a terminar high school y tú
me estás metiendo en un revulú.*" (Going and coming, I'm never going to
finish school and you're getting me into a mess.) "*Me fui con el papá de mi
hija por no regresar a Puerto Rico con mi mamá por tantos viajes.*" (I ran
away with my daughter's father so as not to return to Puerto Rico because
of so many trips.) She dreamt of another life for her children, but she was
plagued by worries.

The Navarro family was the most isolated of the families we visited,
receiving little help from family—Jaclyn was estranged from her siblings,
friends ("Friends *es pa'* [are for] trouble"), and ex-husbands. "I have been
married three times and I have suffered three times, but I have learned a lot,"
Jaclyn explained in Spanish. "*Yo soy madre y padre a la vez.*" (I am mother
and father at the same time.) Her biggest fear—because her brother had been
an addict—was that her children would succumb to drugs, and her greatest
hope was that they would make it to the university. She knew that everything depended on her, and she was determined to be strong: "*No me dejo
caer, no me puedo enfermar porque mis hijos me necesitan.*" (I don't let myself
fall, I can't get sick because my children need me.) Immersed in realities often
beyond her control, Jaclyn exercised control where she could, especially over
her children's activities at home and in school and their language development. She continued to send her children to the bilingual school even after
relocating 30 blocks south because "if the kids are not bilingual, the transition between New York and Puerto Rico will affect them because New York
is only English and Puerto Rico is only Spanish. *Yo les enseño los dos idiomas
porque* you never know." (I teach them the two languages because you never

know.) As a result, the Navarro children were as bilingual as their mother, including the youngest school-age child, 6-year-old Charles.

Born and raised in New York without ever having visited Puerto Rico, Charles was described by his first-grade teacher as "a comedian who loves to take the limelight and prefers to speak in Spanish, although he understands English." Charles's behavior in school, playful to some and disruptive to others, led Jaclyn to become a school volunteer. Charles's kindergarten teacher could not handle him and asked Jaclyn for help. The 6-year-old had earned a reputation for being problematic. One teacher described Charles as a "troublemaker" and his family as "dysfunctional." Regular contact with the school subjected Jaclyn to cruel gossip, but it also presented unanticipated opportunities. Because of her strong social skills and biliteracy, she sometimes interviewed parents who came to enroll their children, completing many forms and applications. She discovered skills and abilities that were suitable to teaching, which she longed to develop: "*Yo miro, yo observo y capto las cosas. Quiero aprender más. Me gustaría meterme en un salón de una maestra para aprender.*" (I watch, I observe, and I pick up things. I want to learn more. I would love to go into a classroom to learn.) Jaclyn remained an unpaid volunteer.

Evidence of the school's influence on language socialization in the Navarro home included the fact there was a lot of didactic teaching, in part due to a pattern established by Jaclyn's stepfather. Jaclyn recalled that he "gave us lessons and also helped us with our schoolwork," using a book called *Basic English*. Similarly, Jaclyn "taught" her children at home in both languages, with the aid of methods and materials borrowed from school and her entrepreneurial activities; she reinforced facts and concepts on a chalkboard purchased when she was selling AmWay products. Large-size Open Court phonics cards seemed out of place as wall covering in the room shared by three boys, but they were a powerful reminder of the value accorded literacy practices associated with school. Thus, Jaclyn, with assistance from her oldest daughter, María, responded to Charles's need for help in reading and other academic subjects through varied activities at home and at school.

Literacy helped Jaclyn shape and control the moral and spiritual development of her children, reflecting a historical and primary use of literacy (Chapter 5, this volume; Graff, 1991). The family prayed and read the Bible together at night, a ritual that reportedly included interpreting the biblical passages. The children went to church on Sundays, where they read and memorized songs as members of the choir. Religious influences were also evident in verbal exchanges, as Jaclyn occasionally cited scripture in Spanish to make a point: "*La Biblia dice que nosotros somos hermanos y tenemos que ayudarnos unos a los otros.*" (The Bible says that we are all brothers and sisters and that we have to help one another.) Quotations from the Bible communicated the power of the text as a source of moral authority and helped show children the way.

Worldly entertainment was also part of daily activities. The family had a well-stocked media center, which Jaclyn controlled. There was a TV, a Nintendo, a VCR, and a library of children's videos, including Disney films and educational videos such as *Barney* and *Sesame Street*. So few books and magazines for children or adults were visible that we might not have believed that literacy was valued and practiced in this home if we had not delved deeply into the family's funds of knowledge.

Jaclyn herself emphasized "entertaining" her children—playing games, telling jokes, and telling stories—to maintain an open dialogue with them. This was important, she said, because "children change" in New York, abandoning traditional customs. As an antidote, she offered many *"consejos,"* (advice-laden conversations), a valued Puerto Rican cultural practice. *"Yo les digo lo que les conviene y lo que no les conviene."* (I tell them what is in their best interest and what is not.) *"Tú tienes que defenderte. No le cojas nada a nadie."* (You have to defend yourself. Don't take anything from anybody.) She encouraged literacy and language development, but teaching them the difference between right and wrong was also central.

Primarily with the support of her children, this young mother took admirable care of her large family's physical, emotional, intellectual, and spiritual needs. Jaclyn's strengths as a caregiver contradict the image of the Puerto Rican "welfare queen" popularized by mainstream social scientists and reinforced in the media, which she confronts daily. Jaclyn uses literacy as one means of countering this image, trying to prove her worth as a human being and as a fit parent, *"para que no hablen mal de mi"* (so others do not talk badly about me).

Literacy in the Alegría Household

Ita Alegría (pseudonym), age 41, arrived from Puerto Rico in 1962 at the age of 7. For 7 years she has lived with her second husband, Luís, and her five children (21- and 17-year-old sons, and 20-, 13- and 9-year-old daughters) on the fourth floor of a tenement near the overpass to the commuter train to the wealthy suburbs. The railroad apartment is small, everything appearing to be scaled down in size. "Ita's world is like Macondo," writes the teacher, commenting on the impoverished living conditions she did not expect "here in America." For this teacher, Macondo, the setting for the novel *One Hundred Years of Solitude*, is symbolic of poverty. "Why bother to fix this apartment," Ita explains in Spanish. "If there's a fire, everything is lost."

Ita was forced to repeat the first grade in New York after starting school in Puerto Rico, a common practice affecting Puerto Rican children in New York City. Some of us were surprised to learn that she married at 13 and had her first child at 14. When we met, Ita had been with her Cuban-born second husband for 10 years; he was a licensed electrician, construction worker, and building superintendent. As the superintendent's wife, Ita learned to paint walls; install windows, locks, and electrical wiring; and repair electronic equipment. Curiosity led her to learn how to run a neighbor's printing press, and community interest led her to volunteer for a local politician after she sought help for a family problem. Ita described herself: "*A mi me encanta saber, me gusta explorar.*" (I love to learn, I love to explore.) Contrary to the initial image conjured up by a woman who had a child before most of us entered high school, her values and disposition shaped her mothering and the literacy practices in her home in positive ways.

"I am bilingual like my children," she proclaimed, tying her bilingualism to her relationship with the children. Ita needed to know English to keep up with what they were doing. "I speak in English and I speak *español*," she said, stretching out the syllables in accented English with delight. "*Me encanta hablar inglés.*"(I love to speak English.) I learned English because when I was 7; all I knew how to say was '*pollito*/chicken, *gallina*/hen, *lápiz*/pencil, *y pluma*/pen' (a school rhyme used to teach English in Puerto Rico and in New York City). I called the principal 'stupid' and got into trouble because a kid fooled me into thinking it meant 'good.'" Not having to depend on others for translations proved a strong incentive to learn English, but English was taking over the household. Although she continued to value Spanish, her children favored English: "My children speak English, but I speak to them in Spanish; they answer me in English even when I speak to them in Spanish."

Speaking English served specific purposes in Ita's life: "If I am very angry, I speak English so that my neighbors don't understand what we are saying. *La vecina es muy chismosa; está pendiente de todo.*"(My neighbor is a gossip and is alert to everything.) For the same reason, Ita also taught her children *jerigonza*, a form of language play that involves the systematic addition of a syllabic pattern like *chi* before each syllable. English and *jerigonza* provided invisibility and privacy in cramped quarters because walls were paper-thin and following the saga of other people's lives was popular entertainment. English had less emotional content than Spanish for Ita. "*Me relaja hablar inglés porque si una persona me va a insultar, suena más fuerte en español.*" (Speaking English relaxes me because if someone is going to insult me it sounds harsher in Spanish.) Different languages encode different emotional dimensions (González, 2001), and English was the more neutral language for Ita.

Wide reading in Spanish brought the world to Ita's door. "Every day I have to read something. I love to read the newspaper, magazines, everything. I read the novels that come from Mexico. I read love stories that are a bunch of lies. I read gossip. If I am interested, I read even a Brazilian magazine [in Portuguese]." She subscribed to *Las Américas* and read New York's *El Diario* as well as *El Nacional*, from the Dominican Republic, "*para cuando tenga una conversación saber de lo que estoy diciendo*" (so when I have a conversation I know what I am talking about). Literacy helped connect Ita to *El Barrio*'s growing Dominican and Mexican population. It also enabled her to help her children intellectually: "If my kids ask me something and I don't know the topic, I look it up in a book. . . . The children have many books, from storybooks to mechanic manuals, even about the private [intimate] life of a person." Cooking was an exception; according to Ita, reading recipes was for people who did not know how to cook.

Ita found books and magazines on her own and convinced neighbors and local merchants to donate others. The library was another source, and Ita encouraged her children to go even if she did not accompany them, explaining "*¡No me puedo estar quieta!*" (I can't sit still!) She cautioned her daughter to take care of books: "*¡Ay, mami, cuida mucho los libros porque los libros son como buenos amigos.*" (Oh, honey, take care of your books because books are like good friends.) Once, her two youngest daughters read aloud from magazines about Latino personalities, displaying their biliteracy with pride, to the surprise and delight of their mother and teacher. Facing the disparity in competence displayed by her student at home in relation to the child's performance in school prompted the teacher to reconsider why Ita's children had trouble reading in school. Planting the seed of doubt was the first step toward being able to explain the discrepancy.

Using literacy to connect to others in the modest homes we visited creates networks of support that may be activated with neighbors from other countries should an unexpected need occur. In addition, turning to books for information may be one way of countering the view that the low educational attainment of Puerto Ricans students is due to their lack of valuing or engaging in reading. Unlike Jaclyn, who seeks validation as a fit mother, Ita seeks to establish herself as an intellectual, someone who knows what she's talking about. Literacy is central to that identity, and books and magazines help her enact it. She is proud of her bilingualism and biliteracy, and it is one of her most important gifts to her children. Teachers can certainly identify with Ita's love of learning and admire her children's biliteracy. It should give them pause that the children are not doing well in school and encourage them to seek to understand the problem with the help of the parents and the students. In addition to Ita's support, the teacher can count on what she saw as a result of her visits: "Her [Ita's] children reflect what she reflects: a positive attitude toward the world and toward others."

SEEING WHAT'S THERE: LANGUAGE AND LITERACY PRACTICES IN LOCAL PUERTO RICAN HOUSEHOLDS

The two households featured in this chapter make abundantly clear that families in East Harlem value literacy. The majority of their literacy practices are about making sense of and responding to lived experience, supporting the theory that literacy mediates our interaction with the world. Literacy practices addressed a range of needs that included (1) health and nutrition, (2) legal issues affecting family members, (3) one's identity and the identities of those who are new to the community, and (4) spiritual comfort and guidance. In most of these activities, print and talk were seamlessly interwoven, making it difficult to separate one from the other. For example, community members addressed health issues affecting family and friends by seeking or being given technical literature available in hospitals or clinics and by engaging in conversations with experts—from neighbors with firsthand knowledge to medical doctors and friends who have studied the issues. Interaction with other symbolic media was also possible, for example, television programs or informational videos such as the one Jaclyn Navarro viewed to help her brother deal with his drug addiction. Together, these practices comprise what is referred to in school as informational reading—only in this case it is on matters critical to family health rather than on topics identified by teachers.

Caregivers who lead transnational lives also read newspapers and magazines in English and Spanish in order to stay current and connected locally and nationally, to get news from Puerto Rico, or to learn about the origins of new community members. Reading the newspaper is a valued practice that has a long history in *El Barrio*, but this may not be evident to teachers because newspapers and magazines may be read in transit—at a friend's home, on the subway, or at a clinic—rather than purchased individually. Literacy is restricted through class advantage (Del Valle, 2002) because reading materials are often costly and because there are few public libraries in low-income communities like East Harlem, which has only one. However, sense-making literacy is not likely to be visible through questions teachers typically ask, as we did in the home interviews: What kinds of things do you read? Are there books in the house?

As predicted by social theories of literacy, activities influence the character of literacy practices engaged in by family members. For example, primary caregivers participated in the building's tenants' patrol, in the local parent association, and as school volunteers; participation in these groups required a range of literacies. Jaclyn Navarro filled out police reports as part of her tenant patrol duties, and as a school volunteer she filled out admissions and registration forms for parents and translated documents from English to Spanish. Teachers did not expect some of the literacy practices we found in these homes, such as reviewing the Open Court phonics charts, writing words and numerals on a chalkboard, and viewing educational videos. They also became aware of the distinctive role that language and literacy socialization practices played in character development, especially in fostering responsibility, honesty, compassion, and service to others, whether attained through reading the Bible together or conversations intended to provide moral guidance. It was, in part, teachers' lack of familiarity with the day-to-day lives of families that made seeing what was there so challenging, even for experienced educators.

IMPLICATIONS FOR EDUCATORS

As this chapter makes clear, teachers must come to know the schools and communities in which they teach because "teaching occurs within a particular historical and social moment and is embedded within nested layers of context, including . . . language uses of the community and its web of historical, political, and social relationships to the school" (Cochran-Smith, 1995, p. 504). Because the Funds of Knowledge approach assumes that there are important cultural resources for teaching in the school's immediate community, knowledge of the U.S. Puerto Rican community, especially its intellectual and literary tradition, is essential background information. The library and archives of the Center for Puerto Rican Studies at Hunter College of the City University of New York (www.centropr.org) is an invaluable resource. Knowing that such a history has been documented and where informational resources are available is a first step in helping teachers look at curriculum and Puerto Rican students differently. Since our perceptions are conditioned by what we know, acquiring prior knowledge sets up expectations that may help us to see what is there. As learning theory makes clear, we do not see what we do not expect to find.

Recently, much attention has been given to the importance of home–school collaboration, yet the character of this collaboration remains vague. Similarly, teachers are now expected, if not required, to plan literacy instruction using research-based practice. The Funds of Knowledge approach responds to both concerns. It provides educators with an inquiry-based process for creating meaningful home–school partnerships and the tools to generate research-based knowledge through participant observation in local households. Entering students' homes as learners (researchers), rather than teachers, and treating family members as authorities who have important knowledge to share with teachers is a radical departure from the way educators typically relate to working-class Latino families. Not surprisingly, these experiences become a positive force in fostering mutually beneficial relationships between teachers and families, enabling teachers to develop pedagogical knowledge that bridges home–school uses of language and literacy in ways that build on and acknowledge the strengths of families. In effect, direct contact with and systematic study of students' homes and communities becomes the basis for curriculum planning and instruction, rather than unfounded generalizations or unconfirmed information.

Fittingly, our study of Puerto Rican households is the first to emphasize language as a fund of knowledge. We found that field studies help teachers understand how youngsters are socialized to use both English and Spanish for social, emotional, religious, and intellectual purposes; they also encourage teachers to build on and support bilingualism, multidialectalism, biliteracy, and language play for learning in the school. Teacher-researcher Vivian Garcilazo (2001) provides inspiration that comes from the wisdom of practice:

> As teachers . . . we are, alternately, told by administrators to use children's cultures and home life in our teaching or to ignore what children have at home because we can't have an effect on that. I have discovered that it is not in our hands. Children's cultures and home lives come to school every day in the form of five through twelve-year-olds. To actually go to the home is to make the choice to embrace and learn from the home and then be able to teach the child. (p. 12)

The Funds of Knowledge approach enables us to learn from families what they know, and what they may need to know, so that we may be better able to teach their children.

CHAPTER 10

The Language Socialization Experiences of Latina Mothers in Southern California

Ana María Relaño Pastor

The language ability and level of English proficiency of Latino communities in the United States are subjected to racial categorization; assigned racial meanings; and associated with poverty, marginalization, and negative stereotypes. Spanish-speakers are often stereotyped as non-white, and weak English-speakers are viewed as inferior (Suárez-Orozco & Páez, 2002; Chapter 1, this volume). Reports in popular media often blame Latinos "for making no effort to assimilate, for not learning English, and for lacking the ambition to excel beyond low-wage jobs where they are exploited and discriminated against" (Navarrete, 2003, p. B6). This corresponds to what Santa Ana (2002) calls the "metaphorization" of Latino life and languages in the United States, referring to the processes by which public discourse in the United States makes sense of who Latinos are as citizens, as immigrants, and as non-English-speakers.

Almost 8.5 million of the 31.5 million Californians who are 5 years old or over are Spanish-speaking; 4.3 million of them reported speaking English less than "very well" (U.S. Bureau of the Census, 2000d). Language proficiency is related to birthplace. The percentage of Mexican-origin residents born in San Diego County over 5 years old who speak English "not well" or "not at all" is 8.7%, a rate much lower than that of the Mexican-born San Diegans, 43% of whom do not speak English well. Speaking English "well" continues to be one of the main challenges facing Latino immigrants and their children. Their ability to learn English well is not just a matter of taking classes and/or applying themselves; it is influenced by their experience with English and English-speakers.

This chapter focuses on the role that language plays in the settlement and socialization experiences of a group of Mexican and Central American immigrant mothers in southern California. Research on language socialization in bilingual and multilingual communities has highlighted the difficulty of maintaining Spanish in the United States (Schecter & Bayley, 2002; Vásquez, Pease-Alvarez, & Shannon, 1994; Zentella, 1997a) as well as the need to investigate immigrant parents' language and learning ideologies (Pease-Alvarez, 2003; Pease-Alvarez & Vásquez, 1994). Little is known about the connection between Latina mothers' personal language socialization in the United States and their language socialization practices with their children.

The "communicative competence" (Hymes, 1972) of the mothers in this study was influenced primarily by their socialization as Spanish-speakers in their countries of origin (Mexico, El Salvador, and Guatemala). They did not speak English well when they migrated to the United States, and they encountered numerous communication difficulties in schools, stores, workplaces, hospitals, administrative offices, and even at church and at home (Relaño Pastor, 2002). Consequently, the values, beliefs and ideologies about "the social and moral rules of conduct" (Ely & Gleason, 1995, p. 254) transmitted to them in Spanish were evaluated, then abandoned or embraced—sometimes transformed—in the United States.

Parental experiences with language in the homeland and in the United States inevitably influence their children's socialization "to" and "through" Spanish and English (Chapter 1, this volume), particularly the *moral language order* transmitted to children. I define *moral language order* not as a ranking or set of rules about language but as the values that immigrant mothers believe should be associated with Spanish, English, and bilingualism, values that result from their moral reflections on their language experiences and their acceptance or refusal of the dominant society's language attitudes. The moral language order includes immigrant mothers' views of what is a fair and respectful appreciation of their linguistic proficiency and attitudes. As Garret & Baquedano-López (2002) point out, "notions of morality are negotiated through linguistically mediated understandings of daily life and events and of one's place in the world, both as an individual and as part of a collectivity" (p. 352). Language is the medium by which notions of morality are conveyed, and notions of morality are connected to specific languages and dialects as well as language behaviors.

This chapter analyzes the resulting *language moralization* or socialization based on the moral language order of immigrant mothers, reflected in 76 accounts of language socialization experiences between 23 Latinas and their children. Moralization is understood in this chapter as the process by which Latina mothers transmit moral lessons drawn from their language experiences to their children. The analysis contributes to the dismantling of stereotypes of Latino parents, often accused of not making any effort to learn English and participate in their children's education, by addressing the moral attitudes they associate with their English-language ability, bilingualism, and *respeto* (respect) (Valdés, 1996) for Spanish maintenance.

THE LANGUAGE EXPERIENCE

Two previous studies provide the data for this chapter. One studied the experiences with miscommunication of five Mexican and Central American (Guatemalan and Salvadoran) working-class mothers living in Los Angeles (Relaño Pastor, 2000), and another analyzed narratives of intercultural communication experiences among 18 Mexican immigrant mothers in San Diego (Relaño Pastor, 2002). The latter were connected to *La Clase Mágica* (The Magic Class, cf. Vásquez [2003], a bilingual/bicultural after-school computer program) as site coordinators or participants.

My personal experience drew me to these women and this topic, but our experiences were vastly different. As a Spanish-speaking, English-as-a-Second-Language learner, academic, and foreigner (from Spain), I had always experienced life in English as a rewarding challenge once I managed to master its linguistic system. I thought "effective communication" was primarily a matter of producing the language accurately, until I encountered the experiences of Latina immigrant women in southern California. I soon realized that their continuous efforts to learn English, including English as a Second Language classes in neighborhood schools, was not the ideal language experience I had had. The interviews I conducted became conversations about language *and* discrimination, language *and* race, language *and* their children's school performance, language *and* emotions, language *and* respect (Relaño Pastor, 2000).

The stories the mothers told about their language experiences displayed a high degree of emotional involvement (frustration, anger, sadness, shame) that was related to different moral stances about language use at home, lack of English, bilingualism, and the devaluation of Spanish in the Southwest. Their response to me, a speaker of Andalusian Spanish, wavered between distance and closeness during the course of the interviews. At first my Andalusian Spanish and blonde features created a sense of geographic, cultural, and racial displacement among these women. They started out thinking that I was *una Americana* (an American) who spoke Spanish very well, but as I got deeper into the discussion, it became a co-construction of explanations and evaluations on topics such as language discrimination, conflicts about language at home, and decisions about the use of Spanish and English in different social settings. The interview became a safe discursive space in which to tell their stories, authenticate and validate their language experiences, and "defend" themselves (Relaño Pastor, 2002). A total of 56 hours of audiotaped data were transcribed, including 76 language accounts involving Mexican and Central American mothers and their children. My analysis focuses on the moral viewpoints embedded in the evaluations of these accounts.

Sociolinguistic (Labov & Waletzky, 1967) and discourse analytic (Ochs & Capps, 2001) perspectives on narratives of personal experiences define *evaluation* as encompassing moral reflections on the events. Essentially, "conversational narratives are never simply informative; they are imbued with moral meanings" (Ochs & Capps, 2001, p. 242). The construction of morality in personal accounts of language experiences is particularly worthy of analysis in the case of immigrant mothers because understanding their moral perspective on English, Spanish, and bilingualism may contribute to effective ways of teaching their children.

The recurring themes of their language accounts were as follows:

- Spanish maintenance and language use at home (32% of the cases)
- Spanish language as a sine qua non of Mexican and Central American identities (18%)
- Value of bilingualism and home literacy activities in Spanish and English (17%)
- Language ridicule of Spanish-speaking children at school (9%)
- Language mixing (7%)
- Language use at *La Clase Mágica* (7%)
- Children as language helpers (5%)
- Language respect at church (5%)

All these themes invoked moral evaluations. The *moral evaluations* reflected an array of fundamental language ideologies (e.g., the values, beliefs, and attitudes) about the status of Spanish and English in the Southwest. Furthermore, moral evaluations constructed the mothers' identities in the "storyworld" (Ochs, Smith, Taylor, 1989; Ochs, Taylor, Rudolph, & Smith, 1992; Rymes, 1995) as they positioned themselves and other story characters according to a particular sense of what constituted good language socialization practices.

In the following sections, I focus on the moral evaluations of language accounts that took place in three socialization sites: home, school, and church. By socializing their children to an alternative moral world, this group of mothers was resisting the dominant language order imposed on them from the moment they arrived in the United States and morally relocating themselves in U.S. society (Relaño Pastor & De Fina, in press).

Language Lessons at Home

Language accounts centered on the home environment reflected a moral order based on respect for the maintenance of Spanish and Mexican and Central American cultural practices as well as the value of bilingualism. Some of the factors that shaped decisions about language choice in the home environment were generation, place of origin, and age of arrival in the United States; parents' language ideologies developed over time (cf. Chapter 2, this volume). The women were first-generation immigrants who came to California as adults, except for three who arrived at ages 3, 5, and 7; therefore, their shared determination to maintain Spanish at home was influenced by their own socialization to the value of Spanish as their mother tongue. For example, Luisa (all names are psuedonyms), who was 17 when she came from Mexico and had been in the United States for 20 years at the time of the interview, explained the importance of Spanish maintenance at home to her 9- and 4-year-old children. For Luisa, the boundaries between her language and theirs are determined by maternal and national loyalties:

Mi lengua, de mi mamá, que me enseñó mi mamá, de donde yo vengo, es el español. La lengua de ustedes aquí es la de inglés porque están en el país que se va a hablar inglés.

My language, my mother's [language], [the language] that my mother taught me, where I am from, is Spanish. Your language here is English because you are in the country where English is spoken.

Even when the primacy of English in their children's lives was acknowledged, the mothers shared a commitment to speak Spanish to their children, coupled with an effort to socialize them to Latino/Mexican cultural traditions. Lucía had been in the United States for 32 years and was a fluent bilingual. She encouraged her 10- and 6-year-old daughters to speak English well, but she also fostered Spanish as a social resource to maintain Mexican cultural traditions and pride in the family's ethnic identity and language, lest they consider themselves *totalmente americana* (totally American) in the monolingual English sense:

O sea, lo más que puedo enseñarles a ellas de su cultura, trato de hacerlo. Yo tengo familiares que viven en Tijuana entonces yo las llevo . . . o sea, yo no quiero que ellas se crean totalmente que

I mean the more I can teach them about their culture, I try to do it. I have relatives who live in Tijuana so I take them . . . I mean, I do not want them to think of themselves as totally Americans because they

porque una nació en Estados Unidos
una es totalmente americana. Ellas
me dicen a veces, la más chiquita
dice "OH! ¿Será that I forgot to
say that in Spanish?*" Le digo*
"¡CÓMO QUE SE TE OLVIDA
ESO EN ESPAÑOL SI TÚ ERES
MEXICANA!" Entonces yo pienso
que en eso tenemos que estar
reforzándolo "¡Tú puedes hacerlo!,
¡ES HERMOSO poder hablar los
dos idiomas!"

were born in the United States
Sometimes, they tell me, the
youngest tells me "OH! Maybe I
forgot to say that in Spanish?" I tell
her "WHAT DO YOU MEAN
YOU FORGOT THAT IN SPAN-
ISH IF YOU'RE MEXICAN!" so I
think that in that sense we have to
be reinforcing it. "You can do it! IT
IS BEAUTIFUL to speak two
languages!"

Because mothers viewed Spanish as central to Mexican and Central American culture, they feared for their children's language loss. In the next example, Ana, who had arrived in San Diego from Mexico 9 years earlier, when she was 16, explains her struggle to keep Spanish as the language of the home.

Llego a la casa y mi niño me trata
de hablar inglés y "¡M'hijo, no te
entiendo!" [Hijo: "¿Cómo que no
me entiendes?"] "M'hijo es que
aquí en la casa yo nomás hablo
español" . . . y es porque ellos
están perdiendo un poco el hablar
en español y no quiero que lo
pierdan.

I get home and my child tries to
speak English to me and "Sweetie, I
do not understand you!" [Son:
"How come you don't understand
me?"] "Sweetheart, it's just that at
home I only speak Spanish" . . .
and it is because they are losing the
ability to speak Spanish a little and
I do not want them to lose it.

Ana's fear is justified given the cognitive and educational consequences of losing the primary language because "what is lost is no less than the means by which parents socialize their children" (Wong Fillmore, 1991, p. 343). Most of our examples illustrate that *the moral language order* to which immigrant mothers socialize their children at home is based on respect for and recognition of Spanish. The latter was the topic Latina mothers emphasized most (32%), far outpacing other language themes.

School Struggles: *Vergüenza y Orgullo*

From language socialization research we learn that "as young children interact with their caregivers in socializing activities, they acquire linguistic and social skills as well as a culturally specific world view" (Garret & Baquedano-

López, 2002, p. 342). How is their worldview altered when children witness their mothers' struggles to make themselves understood in United States schools? The moral evaluations drawn from language experiences at school suggest a moral world in which mothers resist *vergüenza* (shame) for not speaking English well, while encouraging *orgullo* (pride) in Spanish among their children. Latina mothers construct themselves as *active* subjects in their English learning experiences, challenging dominant English-only ideologies that insist on fast-English language policies as the magical solution for economic success in the United States (Zentella, 1988). These ideal ideologies usually overlook immigrants' everyday efforts to learn English and communicate in different social settings despite their paradoxical bind: They need access to networks of English-speakers but they need English to get that access (Norton, 2000).

Latina mothers struggled continuously to understand issues concerning their children's education and to relieve their sense of guilt for not having learned "good English" or not having learned English at all. Amalia's efforts to get the information she needed from school were painful:

Algunas veces me he sentido frustrada y enfadada conmigo misma porque no he logrado aprender inglés y para ayudar a mis hijos en la tarea me siento que no puedo, y por ejemplo, las conferencias todo bien pero ya un problema más serio, ¡Me cuesta!, ¡Me cuesta!, pero ¡Como sea, yo no me vengo de la escuela si yo no estoy clara o si ellos no están claros! Pero ya cuando salgo me siento enojada, triste de todo, pero como sea me busco estar clara, busco la ayuda como sea y digo "OK, el hecho de que yo no nací aquí, OK si no tengo derechos, pero mis hijos sí." Por ellos yo sigo, yo sigo y digo que a mí que me hagan lo que quieran pero a ellos no.

Sometimes I have felt frustrated and mad at myself because I have not managed to learn English and I feel I cannot help my children with their homework, and for example, at parent meetings everything's OK but when it is a more serious problem, it is hard! It is hard! But no matter how, I do not come back from school unless I am clear or if they are not clear! But once I leave I feel angry, sad about everything, but no matter how, I make sure I understand, I find help no matter how and I say "OK, because I was not born here, it's OK if I do not have rights, but my children do." It is for them that I keep on, I keep on and I say they can do anything they want to me but not to them.

Amalia shows how daily communication is emotional (frustration, anger, disappointment, guilt) and due in part to the "ambiguous, conflicting nature of migration losses" (Falicov, 2002, p. 277). The tension between adapting to a new social environment and the cultural ties to their homelands result in "mixed feelings" towards their place in United States society ("It's OK if I do not have rights, but my children do"). Amalia pushes on, empowered because her children need her help and because they have rights. Falicov suggests mixed feelings can be overcome by building on family ties, social supports, and cultural strengths; Spanish and bilingualism are crucial to all three. The fight against being ignored because of poor English skills is one of the immigrants' cultural-adaptation strategies. Amalia insists on communicating in English despite what Americans think about her language abilities:

A mí no me importa, no me importa, o sea cuando uno dice "Could you please talk very slowly because I don't speak good English?" *sometimes they look um . . . El hecho de que uno no habla bien inglés ya eres poca cosa, ¿verdad?, ya te ignoran y a mí la verdad me cuesta.*	It does not matter to me, I don't care, I mean when one says "Could you please talk very slowly because I don't speak good English?" sometimes they look um . . . The fact that you do not speak English well, so you are nothing, right?, so they ignore you and to tell you the truth it's hard for me.

Urciuoli (1996, p. 107) notes that not speaking English well is "a powerful social fact," one that challenges the symbolic domination of languages considered legitimate, especially in school settings, because they are "correct in the framework of ideological orientations connected to social, economic and political interests" (Heller & Martin-Jones, 2001, p. 2). Mothers like Amalia who speak up despite their weak English constitute a powerful challenge to those interests.

   Children become aware at an early age of their mothers' difficulties understanding the symbolic capital of good English as compared to the impoverished status of Spanish in the United States. Much language socialization research emphasizes the efforts made by "experts" (mothers in our case) to socialize children, but the reactions and responses of children have usually been overlooked, although socialization is "a joint achievement between experts and novices . . . who negotiate their differences through interaction" (He, 2003, p. 129). In the following emotional narrative, language ideologies supporting the value of Spanish are contested by Amalia's 7-year-old and countercontested by his mother:

Yo siento que a algunos niños les da como pena hablar español. Ya ve, en la escuela que están Lisa y	I feel some children are ashamed of speaking Spanish. You see, at Lisa and Ale's school, you see that there

Ale, ya ve que son puros anglos. Yo digo que puros anglos y yo digo que solo cuatro o cinco latinos, los demás son anglos y yo siento que ellos se sienten diferentes porque hablan español. Yo he notado cuando iba a las fiestas o de voluntaria, yo siempre [hablaba] español. A mí no me importa que las americanas me queden viendo así como diciendo "¿Qué hace esta aquí?" ¿Verdad? A mí no me importa, yo le hablo español a mi hijo y entonces él un día me dijo "Mami no hables aquí español porque no me gusta," entonces yo le dije "¿SABES QUÉ? ¡YA ME VOY!" [Él dijo:] "¿POR QUÉ? ¡NO TE VAYAS!" Le digo "porque tú nunca tienes que sentir vergüenza por tu idioma porque ¡ES TU IDIOMA! y naciste aquí porque ya tuvimos que venir aquí pero es tu idioma así que no tienes que sentir vergüenza" y se quedó triste y me fui. Luego en la casa le dije "¡NUNCA TIENES QUE SENTIR VERGÜENZA PORQUE TÚ HABLAS ESPAÑOL!" Le digo "Al contrario,¡TÚ ESTÁS MEJOR QUE ELLOS porque sabes los dos idiomas!"

are only Anglos. I'd say only Anglos, I'd say four or five Latinos, the rest Anglos and I feel they feel different because they speak Spanish. I've noticed when I used to go to the parties or as a volunteer I always [spoke] Spanish. I don't care when the Americans look at me like saying, "What is this [woman] doing here?" right? I don't care, I speak Spanish to my son, and then one day he told me "Mommy, don't speak Spanish here because I don't like it," then I told him "YOU KNOW WHAT? I AM LEAVING!" [He said:] "WHY? DON'T LEAVE!" I tell him "because you never have to feel ashamed of your language because IT'S YOUR LANGUAGE! And you were born here because we had to come here but it's your language so you don't have to feel ashamed" and he got sad and I left. Then at home I told him "YOU NEVER HAVE TO FEEL ASHAMED BECAUSE YOU SPEAK SPANISH!" and I tell him "on the contrary YOU ARE BETTER OFF THAN THEM because you know two languages."

Linguistic stress is one of the sources of conflict between immigrant parents and their children (Porter & Hao, 1998; Wong Fillmore, 1991). Children learn English quickly at school, often preferring the dominant language and rejecting Spanish because it makes them feel different from the rest of their peers. Their reactions are in conflict with mothers' efforts to socialize children to the value of Spanish, which these women respond to as moral issues. Amalia and the other mothers imbue their United States born children with *moral lessons* born from their own struggles with the language shame and language pride dilemma; that is, shame—*vergüenza* or *pena* in Mexican Spanish—for speaking English poorly or with an accent, and pride in their defense of Spanish. They recognize that their communication problems are not only linguistic but also ideologically charged by public anti-immigration, anti-Latino, anti-Spanish discourses, obvious in California since the passing of the official state language law in 1986 and culminating in the virtual end of bilingual education in 1998. Defending the right to speak and teach their children Spanish and socializing children to the benefits of bilingualism are crucial elements of Latina mothers' moral language order.

Language Lessons at Church

Religion adds an important dimension to the language and ethnicity equation; it also strengthens the moral language order communicated by immigrant parents. Those who attend mass in Spanish manifest a stronger Mexican identity (Hidalgo, 2001, p.19), and the Catholic Church's literacy activities help shape Mexican identities (Baquedano-López, 1997; Farr, 2000b; Guerra & Farr, 2002). Some Protestant denominations connect Spanish with being on God's path (Chapter 5, this volume). But in many churches there are bilingual celebrations in which English is privileged and Spanish hardly used. Lola, who had been in the United States for 18 years, criticized this practice as a lack of respect:

A veces los sacerdotes quieren obligar a la gente a escuchar sus sermones o sus homilías o sus aparentes celebraciones bilingües, donde nomás dicen un canto en español o dicen un "Padre Nuestro" en español y todo lo demás es en inglés. A mí se me hace como una falta de respeto y discriminación y es casi decir, "Pues no eres tan importante para mí. No te voy a hablar en el idioma que tú puedes entender o lo que tú necesitas saber."

Sometimes the priests want to force people to listen to their sermons or homilies or their supposed bilingual celebrations, where they just sing a song in Spanish or say one "Our Father" in Spanish and the rest in English. For me it's a lack of respect and discrimination. It's like saying, "You are not so important to me. I am not going to speak to you in the language that you can understand or I am not going to tell you what you need to know."

Lola not only sharply criticizes the purported bilingual policy; she also takes action by leaving a Holy Week service, *moralizing* her children, by her words and actions, to the role that language should play in making people feel part of the church community.

Ahora, en Cuaresma, en mi comunidad surgió algo ... me di cuenta que todo lo que estaba pasando allí era puro inglés y no llegué a la mitad porque me SALÍ BIEN ENOJADA, porque sentí que era un INSULTO para la raza y así como que tú no eres importante. Yo que estoy atendiendo ahí me estoy sintiendo excluida porque no lo hayan hecho bilingüe. Cuando miré que el párroco, que el diácono, el que habla español, cuando iba a dar la lectura en español, la dió en inglés, me sentí que era una CELEBRACIÓN RIDÍCULA ... y me salí TAN ENOJADA que les dije a mis hijos "¡VÁMONOS, VÁMONOS!" "¿Qué pasa?" [preguntaron.] "¡VÁMONOS!" Y ya cuando salimos les dije "Me sentí que esa celebración no era para nosotros, por eso la dieron en inglés. No era para el pueblo, para la gente, para los hispanos" ... No me sentí bien y me salí, y luego ya no sé cómo estuvo que hablando ya con los niños, les digo "No sé hasta qué punto está mal que yo haya hecho eso, no me siento mal ni me siento bien, pero no se me hace justo que hay mucha gente que NO habla inglés, que no entiende inglés y nomás están ahí y se van mejor, entonces ESO NO ES SER COMUNIDAD.

Recently during Lent in my community something happened ... I realized that everything that was going on over there was in English only and I did not even stay for half of it because I LEFT REALLY MAD, because I felt that it was an INSULT for my own people as if you are not important. I, who am attending, am feeling excluded because they did not make it bilingual. When I saw that the priest, the deacon who speaks Spanish, when he was going to do the reading in Spanish he did it in English, I felt it was a RIDICU-LOUS CELEBRATION! ... and I left SO ANGRY that I told my children 'LET'S GO! LET'S GO!" "What's wrong?" [they asked.] "LET'S GO!" and when we were outside I told them "I felt that celebration was not for us, that's why it was in English it wasn't for the people, for the community, for Hispanics" ... I did not feel good, and I left, and then I don't know how but talking to my children, I told them "I don't know to what extent what I did was bad, I don't feel bad nor do I feel good." But I don't think it's fair that there are many people who DO NOT speak English, who do not understand English and they are just there, and it's better they leave, so THAT IS NOT BEING A COMMUNITY.

Lola acts on her anger at the church's decision to conduct all the religious services solely in English when so many in the community speak Spanish. In her moral language order, the church is not fostering community when it excludes the language of so many parishioners. Her children internalized this view and acted on it two days later. Lola could not go to the religious service, but her 17-year-old daughter Sara went to mass with the rest of the family, including Lola's mother, who was visiting from Mexico, and her brother and sister-in-law, none of whom were proficient in English. When they arrived, they learned that the same priest was going to conduct mass in English. Lola recounted how Sara confronted the priest:

Y dice, "Yo me quedé así con un coraje que fui a buscar al señor cura y le dije '¿Por qué estás haciendo la misa solamente en inglés? Los mexicanos, los hispanos, los que no hablan inglés, ¿QUÉ?'" Y dice que se le volteó y le dijo "¡OH! Si yo voy a México a mí nadie me va a decir la misa en inglés," dice, "Se me hizo mami ¡TAN RIDÍCULO!" Así me contestó, "Se me hizo tan ridículo que él me haya contestado eso, que se me hizo como si una tontada" dijo. "'Además estás en Estados Unidos y tienen que saber inglés' dijo y 'va a ser en inglés'" y dijo Sara que se volteó y le dijo "¡PUES ESTO ES INCORRECTO!"

And she says "I got so angry that I went to look for the priest, and I told him 'Why are you having mass in English only? What about Mexicans, Hispanics, those who do not speak English, WHAT ABOUT THEM?'" And she said that he turned around and told her, "OH! If I go to Mexico nobody is going to say the mass in English for me." She says, "It was SO RIDICULOUS mommy!" That's what she said, "I found it so ridiculous that he answered that, it was like non-sense" she said. "'Also you are in the U.S. and you have to know English,' he said, and 'it is going to be in English'" and Sara said that she turned to him and told him "WELL, THIS IS WRONG!"

This is a clear example of how children learn from their mothers' language experiences and adopt their moral language order. Sara reproduced her mother's language ideology, calling for language respect and fair treatment at church, where a sense of community and right and wrong should be most honored. By denouncing, reacting, resisting, Lola effectively socialized or moralized her child to challenge injustice, even in the church.

LATINA MOTHERS' MORAL LANGUAGE ORDER: EDUCATIONAL IMPLICATIONS

This chapter has presented a world in which communication is not merely about being understood in a grammatical sense, but about language struggles that are contested, moralized on, and transmitted to children. "The infamous language barrier" (Chapter 1, this volume), does not get resolved when immigrants learn English because their socialization as English-speakers and English-novices in U.S. society intersects with mainland language ideologies that dismiss Spanish-accented English and the value of maintaining Spanish. Immigrants try to hold on to the moral language order of the homeland, which stresses the primacy of Spanish in the family and the economic value of bilingualism in the outside world. As soon as Latina mothers start carrying out daily communicative transactions in different social settings, they reshape their views about the value of Spanish in the United States and struggle daily with shame about not speaking English well versus pride in defending and maintaining Spanish. Bilingualism changes from being an isolated economic goal into a skill that can help them maintain respect at home while demanding it outside the home.

Latina mothers not only overcome language barriers; they also resist them and draw moral lessons from them, constructing a moral order that they transmit to their children. In this chapter, I have been referring to this process as *language moralization*. I agree with Villenas (2001) that "Latina mothers are key to providing children with the cultural integrity to resist their deficit framing as minority students in English-speaking/non-bilingual schools" (p. 22). The cultural integrity that is central to Latina mothers' socialization of their children includes a recognition of their struggles as non-English-speakers and respectful acceptance of their linguistic repertoires, either as monolingual speakers of Spanish, as non-proficient English-speakers, or as fluent English-speakers.

Educators can benefit by paying attention to how mothers' and children's internalization of moral dilemmas are enacted in daily communicative exchanges with school administrators and social workers. In particular, a little knowledge of Spanish can go a long way. In addition to not "essentializing" (Chapter 1, this volume) Latinos by ignoring their multilingual and multidialectal diversity, teachers should consider the moral order associated with the varieties of English, Spanish, and bilingualism that Latino children bring from home so as to create optimal learning environments in their classrooms. The language accounts in this chapter make clear that learning and speaking a language are morally charged with multiple meanings to which teachers must be sensitive. Despite the negative message of the wave of antibilingual education initiatives, which have already passed in California, Arizona, and Massachusetts, teachers can still foster enriching learning environments that support children's choices of language in the classroom, allowing space for Spanish, English, and code-switching. Because these choices reflect the moral language order of Latino families, teachers who honor the importance of Spanish and the communicative power of code-switching will be more successful in helping students acquire excellent proficiency in English, which is also valued by the family. In addition, teachers can be nonjudgmental and patient with parents' accented English. Despite parents' limited English proficiency, teachers should encourage and welcome parents to be well informed about issues concerning their children's education. By the same token, knowledge and validation of Latina mothers' language experiences and the moral lessons they draw from these experiences can build bridges of understanding between teachers and Latino parents.

CHAPTER 11

Children in the Eye of the Storm: Language Socialization and Language Ideologies in a Dual-Language School

Norma González

The second generation of work on language socialization has focused on community and family interactional patterns and expanded to study larger institutional settings such as schools, which are often sites for multiple layers of language ideologies. This chapter examines the language used by and to children within a context of competing discourses in a dual-language school in the borderlands of Arizona. We need to remember that the word *socialization* is a kind of metaphor, implying that children can be moved from a place outside the "social" to a place within the social. Yet do we ever consider how children—or adults, for that matter—can be outside the "social," however defined? What is this place they are moved from, and where is this place that they are moved toward? Does the matrix within which "subjects" (i.e., our status and category) and "subject positions" (i.e., those spaces that we occupy) are formed assume children to be as-yet-unfinished subjects? For poststructuralists, subjects are constructed by and through circulating discourses. For some (Butler, 1993) this construction occurs as the reiteration of dominant discourses produces particular identities for subjects. What does this imply for children, though, who have experienced a relatively short temporal exposure to discourses and competing discourses? As Garrett and Baquedano-López (2002) point out in their overview of language socialization, "This attention to linguistic detail has not precluded attention to the historicized subject as language socialization researchers have sought to make visible the ideologies and power relations that underlie socializing interactions. . . ." (p. 343). Language socialization inevitably focuses on children, but except for language, children have been long neglected in many areas of research.

Theory and theorists rarely assume that children may construct their own lived experiences in qualitatively different ways. How can we capture the voices of children, seeing them within their own social worlds without imposing our adult gaze onto their "otherness"? Children are the ultimate "others," subjects who are constructed as being voiceless because their voices are viewed as unformed and consequently uninformed. They are essentialized not only by racial, ethnic, and linguistic discourses but also by their very childhood. Because, as adults, we cannot penetrate a child's world, we often resort to an artificial insertion of ourselves into their lives or a reflection on our own childhood. In this chapter, I raise the question as to whether adult subjectivities, as well as ideologies and intentionality, can be captured from a child's perspective. A focus on children, moving them from the margins to the center of inquiry, can shift our theoretical lens in unexpected ways. Most language socialization studies have recognized the co-construction of child and caregiver interactions and the dialogical nature of language use between novices and the more experienced, but the asymmetry of the relationship is rarely questioned, nor is the fact that the adult end of the interaction is more heavily laden. Schools can be sites for both taking up and contesting these asymmetries.

LANGUAGE IDEOLOGIES

This chapter is based on a 3-year study of the relationship between language ideologies and biliteracy development in a dual-language school. The research was made possible by a grant from the Spencer Foundation; the principal investigators were Luis Moll and Norma González. The study began in 1999 when the school was the Bilingual Magnet school for the school district. During the time of the fieldwork, Proposition 203, an initiative aimed at dismantling bilingual education, was voted on and passed. Because the data were collected prior to the implementation of Proposition 203, this chapter is written with reference to the dual-language program as it existed at the time.

The basic research question addressed here is: How do language ideologies influence the implementation of this dual-language program? The first challenge is to define *ideology*. Despite different traditions of language study and social theory, "what most researchers share, and what makes the term useful in spite of its problems, is a view of ideology as rooted in or responsive to the experience of a particular social position" (Woolard & Schieffelin, 1994, p. 58). In other words, an ideology can be considered as a set of beliefs that are tied to our social category.

For the French philosopher Louis Althusser, nothing exists outside of ideology, and the school is a potent example of a dominant ideological state apparatus. Further, ideology functions by naming and forming subject positions, "hailing" or "interpellating" them:

> ... ideology "acts" or "functions" in such a way that it "recruits" subjects among the individuals (it recruits them all), or "transforms" the individuals into subjects (it transforms them all) by that very precise operation which I have called *interpellation* or hailing, and which can be imagined along the lines of the most commonplace everyday police (or other) hailing: "Hey, you there!" (Althusser, 1971, p. 174).

Thus, at the moment someone is "hailed" and acknowledges the identification, ideology has recruited the individual and transformed him or her into a subject constructed through ideologies. Within this deterministic framework, identities are formed as subjects of the ideological apparatuses of the state. There is no room for the individual self outside of ideological formations, or for agency, as the interpellation project is ongoing and ever-present. Applied to language, this type of ideology is unconscious, but it maintains social stratification via particular speech practices. From a more Durkheimian perspective, ideology can refer to any body of assumed notions expressed through implicit or explicit metalinguistic discourse (Woolard, 1998), but in this chapter "ideology" implicates power, the exercise of power, and the reproduction of dominant–subordinate relations.

Ideologies do not laminate perfectly onto processes of language socialization, but language socialization is never completely free from ideological underpinnings; that is, it is important to stress, as Garrett and Baquedano-López (2002) do, "the recursive, mutually constitutive nature of the relationship between social structure and individual agency" (p. 344). In other words, language can both construct and be constructed, and language socialization is unavoidably a dialectical process. The articulation between micro-level interaction and macro-level patterns can be studied in schools by examining what children say, who they say it to, and under what circumstances. Also crucial, on the other hand, are circulating metadiscourses about language, about the purpose and use of language, about learning about language, and about learning through language.

COMPETING METADISCOURSES AT THE SCHOOL SITE

The elementary school that is the site for this research is the Bilingual Magnet School for a large urban school district in the southwestern United States. As a magnet school that welcomes students from across the district, the school receives funds for music and art specialists, a counselor, a librarian, a curriculum specialist, as well as a fully staffed extended-day program. The music program is particularly stellar, producing amazingly polished guitar and mariachi ensembles. Between 25% and 30% of the city's population is Latino, primarily of Mexican origin, and the school is located in the heart of one of the older Mexican *barrios* (neighborhoods). Classes were taught only in English for many years, until the school became the district's first bilingual magnet school in 1981. A maintenance bilingual education program was implemented; teachers were expected to use Spanish as the vehicle for instruction 50% of the time and English 50% of the time. Soon recognized for excellent and innovative bilingual instruction, the school attracted a great deal of media attention, and it won five prestigious state and national awards (Smith, 2000). Despite these successes, by the mid-1980s some teachers had begun to question the overall effectiveness of the bilingual maintenance model. Although students who entered the program dominant in Spanish exited in fifth grade as bilingual and biliterate, those who entered the program dominant in English seemed to make little progress toward becoming productive bilinguals. Even students who could understand Spanish quite well did not speak Spanish in school, and English became the dominant language of formal and informal settings in the school.

After examining different bilingual education program models and goals (Murphy, 1999), a teachers' study group advocated a new model, currently referred to as the Dual-Language (DL) Immersion Program, *el Programa de Inmersión en Dos Idiomas*, which was implemented in 1993–1994. In DL, all students, regardless of language background, receive instruction in Spanish during their first two years (K–grade 1), with an increase in English as the language of instruction in subsequent years, but never going below 70% Spanish. All students are immersed in literacy experiences in Spanish first. Approximately 65% of the students are magnet students; that is, they do not live in the neighborhood. Most of the magnet students are English-dominant, and 70% of the students are Latino, coming in as both *barrio* and magnet students. A significant percentage of the Latinos are third- or fourth-generation Mexican-origin children. They enroll for a variety of reasons, including the strong ancillary programs, but many families cite a desire for their children to recapture the Spanish language, often erased by English-only instruction. The faculty makes a conscious effort to privilege the minority language so that students can exit the program fully proficient in two languages, going to extraordinary lengths to promote Spanish as the language of academic, administrative, and social interaction. Visitors are asked to respect this fore-grounding of Spanish, and signs in the hallways proclaim *"Estamos orgullosos de ser bilingües, por eso hablamos español"* (We are proud to be bilingual, that is why we speak Spanish). From their first day at school, when the many reasons why it is important to be bilingual are explained at an assembly, the students learn respect for multiple ways of expressing oneself.

The privileging of a minoritized language and a reflective critical mass of teachers and parents have created an independent school that is the object of both awe and envy. Parents demonstrated their independence when they kept half of the first graders home on the day of mandated standardized tests. Their children, they explained, were too young to be subjected to the stress of high-stakes testing. This action elicited a reprimand from the school district and caught the attention of the local media. The local newspaper quoted one parent, a former elementary school teacher: ". . . high standards and expectations are not synonymous with standardized testing. . . . Oftentimes the right thing is not the popular thing to do. . . . They're learning to read and write in the first grade. For a student that is not doing well, can you imagine the frustration he'd feel?" (Corella, 2001, p. B1). Clearly, this is a school where teachers as well as parents are deeply committed to "raising a child, not a test score" (Smith et al., 2002).

EXITO BILINGÜE (BILINGUAL SUCCESS)

In the spring of 1997, the members of the teachers' study group began to express frustration with the disparate Spanish literacy skills in the classes as well as organizational problems. For example, some students in first grade were still learning color words in Spanish while others were reading Spanish chapter books, English-dominant newcomers without previous bilingual education or Spanish literacy were entering the program in the intermediate grades, and districtwide plans called for a new "balanced literacy" approach.

The faculty decided to create a schoolwide multiage interactive literacy program in Spanish to better meet the needs of students at all levels of Spanish literacy development, with district support. In the fall of 1998, *Exito Bilingüe*—a nonscripted, negotiated curriculum that integrates the professional expertise of faculty and the interests and strengths of all students from first through fifth grade—was born (for a complete description of *Exito Bilingüe*, see Smith & Arnot-Hopffer, 1998).

LANGUAGE IDEOLOGIES IN THE BORDERLANDS

When we first conceptualized the study, we could not foresee a series of events that would crystallize language ideologies within media and public discourses, leading to Arizona's version of California's antibilingual education initiative in the November 2000 election. Proposition 203 stipulated: "Children in Arizona Public Schools shall be taught English by being taught in English and all children shall be placed in English Language Classrooms. Children who are English Learners shall be educated through Sheltered English Immersion during a temporary transition period not normally intended to exceed one year." The Arizona version is draconian in its sanctions: "Any school board member or other elected official or administrator who willfully and repeatedly refuses to implement the terms of this statute may be held personally liable for fees and actual and compensatory damages by the child's parents or legal guardian, and cannot be subsequently indemnified for such assessed damages by any public or private third party." Spearheaded in Arizona, as in California, by Ron Unz, the Silicon Valley millionaire, under the auspices of "English for the Children of Arizona," Proposition 203 passed by a margin of 65% to 35%, underscoring again how ideologies can drive classroom practice and pedagogical methodology. We must not assume, however, that language ideologies are coherent across communities and that only xenophobia is at work. Indeed, the segmentation of language ideologies *within* the Latino community, highlighted by the media, was a pivotal factor in the debate. No firm data on the Latino vote on Proposition 203 are available, although local school district data indicate strong support for bilingual education from Latino parents.

What is the effect on children of this volatile and contentious debate? What discourses do children hear? How do they interpret them? What of the impact of other forms of media on children? For instance, in Spanish-language television programming—which many Latinos watch, including those in English-dominant households—advertising for *Inglés Sin Barreras* (English Without Barriers), an expensive English-language instruction program, promises success and riches as a consequence of learning English. English is "a jewel that no one can take away from you" and "the passport that no one can rescind," claim the ads. Children are sometimes portrayed overhearing their parents' discussions about their lack of employment opportunities and advancement due to lack of English, as the commercials claim that "every day that goes by without speaking English is money that is lost." These metadiscourses resonate within another language ideology, stemming from economic and social stratification, wherein language, rather than political hegemony, is seen as the barrier to economic security.

The confluence of these language ideologies, the market value of English, the influence of English-only campaigns, and a legacy of linguistic purism and linguistic insecurity due to the erasure of Spanish in their parents' generation all influence children profoundly. Children's interpretations of language use emerge from contested and contesting language ideologies within the historically situated context of the borderlands. In the borderlands, ideas about language and child rearing are neither uniform nor fixed (González, 2001), are not necessarily a coherent and integrated whole, and are sometimes contradictory sites for the push and pull of language-in-context. Many second- and third-generation borderland parents feel linguistic insecurity in Spanish because of the erasure of their native-language skills in the English-only schools they attended. They are reluctant to engage foreign-born Spanish-speakers in a conversation where there is no recourse to English, and they restrict use of Spanish to particular domains. Their insecurity is due to a sociohistorical legacy of language purism that treats anything but a standard language form as a socially stigmatized, uneducated form of expression, as well as to the absence of Spanish-language instruction in schools. The derogatory form *pocho*, used by Mexican nationals to refer to second generation Mexican-origin residents of the borderlands, is primarily a linguistic indictment, a stinging barb leveled at those who "should" speak standard Spanish, but cannot. An ideology of linguistic purism and prescriptivism has engendered a generation of parents who feel that the Spanish they speak is substandard. Gloria Anzaldúa (1987), the poet laureate of language use in the borderlands, addresses the theme she describes as "linguistic terrorism":

> Chicanas who grew up speaking Chicano Spanish have internalized the belief that we speak poor Spanish. It is illegitimate, a bastard language. And because we internalize how our language has been used against us by the dominant culture, we use our language differences against each other. (p. 58).

Borderlands language ideologies spill over into the training of bilingual teachers and are part of the contested mix that children are exposed to. The majority of the teachers at the DL school were trained in the Bilingual Block of the University of Arizona, where they encountered high standards for expanding registers in Spanish in order to be able to teach bilingually (Smith, 2000). As products of the effects of these complex ideologies, the teachers strive to nurture language use in all contexts at the school.

Due to its status as a magnet school, the ideological commitment of the faculty to the development of dual languages, its geographic location in the borderlands, and the demographics of the student population, the school has multiple layers of language ideologies and circulating discourses. During the course of our fieldwork, Proposition 203 led to the alternate hardening and blurring of language ideologies as they met and collided within the school setting and in the community. As implicit ideologies became explicit discourses, children found ways to talk back, to repel the interpellation of hailings and dominant discourses, and to constitute for themselves their own organic perspective of what the fuss was actually about. Examples that range from the minute to the momentous illustrate that children can be the best critical theorists because they have not yet overcome their "amazement at what everyone else seems to take for granted" (Eagleton, 1990, p. 34).

COUNTER-INTERPELLATIONS OF LANGUAGE IDEOLOGIES

In the dialogic process between nationalist antibilingual education discourse and local modes of self-representation, children can and do construct their own spaces for the discursive productions of identities and ideologies. In the following examples, children's voices come to the foreground in unexpected ways.

Students in one classroom are discussing the concept of opposites. The teacher asks for a word in Spanish that means the opposite of the word they are given, and students go around in a circle. When the teacher says *"Bilingüe"* (bilingual), there's a moment's hesitation and thought before the student blurts out *"Tonto"* (stupid, foolish), clearly refusing interpellations that construct bilinguals as in need of remedial or compensatory programs. This child inverts the deficit discourse of bilingual education and recasts those who do not have skills in more than one language as lacking academic achievement. Through the activity of articulation this child can subvert the rationale of hegemonic discourse and relocate an imposed negative identity.

The voices of the children plumb the depths of how adult discourses have the power to disrupt the only kind of schooling they have known—and love. Mariela (all names are pseudonyms), a second grader, expresses her fear concerning the possible passage of the proposition: *"Si pasa la ley, no vamos a poder hablar más en español."* (If they pass the law, we won't be able to speak in Spanish anymore.) And then she adds *"porque no entienden"* (because they don't understand). The subject *they* is not defined, but we can assume that she is referring to the voters who would vote in favor of the bill. *Porque no entienden* is a plaintive acknowledgment that as transparent as the issue is for her, her subjective understanding is not refracted onto dominant ideologies that seek to "hail" her as a subject of a monolingual state. Although as a child she is voiceless in terms of resisting the actual implementation of the law, she is not voiceless in apprehending the deeper structural/ideological current that has swept her and her classmates away. Those who favor Proposition 203 don't understand, *"no entienden,"* how this school has created a space for children of both English-speaking and Spanish-speaking families to come together to attain high academic goals in not just one, but two, languages. Similarly, an English-dominant student laments "Laura can get English anywhere, but I can only get Spanish here," incisively pinpointing her insight that the minority language is circumscribed to a space outside of official discourses and that without the protection and sustenance of her nascent second-language ability at the school, she will not attain another voice.

As we can see, schools can be a space for counter-interpellations as well as the formation of emergent subjectivities that can exercise a critical agency.

Another example reveals how the school can create a space for children to choose from repertoires of identities and subjectivities by providing them with ideological spaces for trying on and trying out multidiscursive practices, or ways of combining language styles. I analyze this through the lens of "syncretic literacy" practices, which Duranti and Ochs (1996) define as "an intermingling or merging of culturally diverse traditions that informs and organizes literacy activities (p. 3).

One fifth-grade teacher, *Señora* MacDonald, is a European American bilingual teacher who has been at the school for more than 15 years. As part of her literacy routine, she sits in a wooden rocking chair and lights a small candle before she starts reading. She is reading Harry Potter to the students, alternating between English and Spanish. She affects a Scottish accent whenever Hagrid speaks, and as she intones these inflections, several students giggle. She ends story time with a decidedly un-British ending, the traditional rhyme for ending Mexican stories, *Colorín Colorado, este capítulo queda cerrado* (Ruddy red, this chapter has been sent to bed).

What are we to make of this hybridity? Some commentators have lamented the impact of Harry Potter, attacking "the nation of dweebs that has emerged in the wake of a decade of geek ascendancy" and claiming that "Hogwarts school of witchcraft and wizardry appears to be just another under-integrated private school in the suburbs. . . . It's all quite white, in the end, which almost always portends blandness" (Stuever, 2001, p. C1). This particular circulating discourse about Harry Potter fans hardly fits the children in this dual-language class, who are seen with Harry Potter memorabilia. Their parents are hardly the tofu-eating generation who "played Chopin through Walkman headphones stretched across Mommy's belly" (Stuever, 2001, p. C1)." And yet, through a process of allowing multidiscursive practices in the classroom, there is a space for English learners to appreciate the wizardry of muggles and Quidditch. By ending the reading with the traditional story ending, *Colorín, Colorado, este capítulo queda cerrado*, the teacher reinforces the Spanish narrative structure that can be applied to a decidedly culturally incongruent form of literature and the fact that the borderland is also a space for play and fantasy, a space for imagining identities that are not reproductions of another generation's discursive practices. They create, instead, child-centered, child-focused, child-emergent forms that adults have little appreciation of. Indeed, these same children voted to have a magic day, inspired by Harry Potter, in which they concocted spells and potions and made name tags with designs of moons and stars.

Thus, children in this dual-language school have access to a polyphony of voices, an opportunity to engage with texts in multidiscursive ways. Their broad repertoire of language socialization is evident in the following letter, written by one of the students who had been in the first cohort of the dual-language immersion program. Now a junior high school student, she was asked to write an essay on a time in her life when she felt distressed or sad. She penned this essay, recalling special events that led up to St. Patrick's Day:

My Tiny Friend

The first time I heard Michael, my heart filled with excitement. The squeak of his voice echoed through the loudspeaker of our kindergarten classroom, soft at first, then with growing strength. "Top of the mornin' to ya boys and girls, this is Michael." It struck me with awe how Michael could be in two places at once; I was astonished that he was so swift, so mysterious. I'd never really had a personal experience with a leprechaun before Michael. Of course I knew they existed, but I never quite knew the magic they possessed.

Our class leprechaun was full of surprises. Everyday [sic] throughout the beginning of March, Michael would greet us through the intercom, and occasionally check up on us throughout the day. We soon found that Michael loved potatoes. I was amazed when I came in from recess one day to find a darling pair of emerald-green St. Patrick's Day sunglasses neatly tucked beneath my chair. If you brought a nice potato and placed it underneath your chair, during recess Michael would snatch the potato with his miniscule hands and put a fun little gift in its place. . . . I had a whole picture painted in my mind of exactly what Michael looked like. He was small, about the size of my thumb, with brilliant green eyes. He had a pointy nose and ears, and wore green clothes with miniature black booties and a black belt. His hair was red as well as his beard, which just covered the edge of his face.

When March 17 rolled around, Michael announced to us through the intercom that this would be his last day with us. He explained to us that he took pleasure in being with us, but that the time had come for him to return home to the other side of the rainbow. He told us we could visit him anytime, he even gave us his address. "Goodbye children! Always remember to search for that pot of gold at the end of the rainbow, and when ya find it, I'll be there waitin!"

By the end of the day, I was in tears. I knew that I would never see Michael again. My best friend Theresa and I stood outside of our classroom, hugging and crying, talking about all of the good times we had with Michael, and how much we would miss him. This was the first time I truly felt sorrow. It is amazing how something that small could fill me with such joy. Now he was gone, I would never again feel that immediate burst of warmth when I heard his squeal welcome

us to school. The more I thought about him, the more I cried. I
didn't know how to say goodbye. He was more than just our
class-leprechaun; he was my truest and greatest friend."

Clearly, this student, a Latina magnet student who participated in both the
mariachi orchestra and the folkloric dance troupe and who scored high at
the end of the fifth grade in both English and Spanish, is open to the possibility of many discourses, some in her background and some not. In spite of
the school's privileging of Spanish, the door was not closed on multiple repertoires of language socialization. That this student remembered this incident as being a formative event in her life gives us pause to remember that
children are creative and selective, not mere pawns of ideologies, interpellations, or even of schooling. She imagines alternative definitions of ethnic
identity within everyday narratives of self and other. As children encounter
discourses freighted with ideological contradictions, a place-based identity
rooted in a school can help us (re)imagine the changing public face of schooling.

One final example reminds us that children, despite their creative agency,
are substantially disempowered simply because of their status as children.
The incident took place at the rodeo, or *Fiesta de los Vaqueros*, a community-
wide event that emphasizes the community's cowboy past; school is let out
for 2 days. The week is marked by all the trappings of horse gear and horse-
manship, but there is a syncretism of the type noted by Jane Hill (1993a,
1993b). She cites the rich ranching and herding lexicon of the Southwest,
whose roots in Spanish are glossed over or ignored. The origins of words
such as lasso, lariat, chaps, and mustang—indeed, the very word rodeo—
were subject to linguistic erasure due to syncretic practices of the Anglo settlers who preferred parodic and hyperanglicized pronunciations of the Spanish
words. Given this backdrop, one teacher–student interaction becomes particularly significant. The first-grade class was at a Rodeo picnic, where typical cowboy fare—hot dogs and chili beans—was served. When one child went
up to the teacher and asked where the salsa was, the teacher looked at him
in surprise and remarked, "Salsa! There's no salsa at this picnic, *mijo* (my
son). This is a rodeo holiday, not a Mexican holiday." In this one interaction, the discursive history that has formed the teacher's utterance is weighted
in a way that the child's cannot be. Because of a temporal sequence of reit-
erating dominant discourses, the teacher is "spoken by" circulating discourses
about what constitutes "Mexican" and "American" traditions, eliding the
uniquely Mexican history of the cowboy rodeo. The asymmetry of this interaction between child and adult, which subsumed a child's perspective
beneath a cultural overlay, occurred in spite of the schools' overt ideological
privileging of cultural and linguistic multiplicities, and in spite of the teacher's
own sensitivities and awareness of and support for this ideological privileg-

ing. Freighted utterances such as the one in this example can truncate the emergence of multidiscursive practices in students and harden the boundaries between categories of identities and subjectivities.

SYNCRETIC SOCIALIZATION

This example of syncretic practices can be extended to a concept of syncretic socialization (Hirschfield, 2002). Children, while inhabiting the same space as adults, experience and interpret their spaces in very different ways. "A child's goal is not to become a successful adult, any more than a prisoner's goal is to become a successful guard. A child's goal is to be a successful child" (Harris, 1998, p. 198). Syncretic socialization does not assume that one laminates adult ways of being/thinking onto child ways of being/thinking. In fact, as exemplified by the above examples, children contested, modified, adapted, and redefined adult discourses. However, in other instances, they are not collaborators in a collective enterprise but rather subjects interpellated by historical discourses. We can further comprehend how children are able to learn in an ideologically permeable context, countering reproductionistic notions of cultural transmission.

As we continue to nuance processes of language socialization in communities and in schools, our notions of language socialization must consider children and children's voices as fully as we can. Because children's metapragmatic commentary may not be transparent to adults, we have to take children as the "other" into account, not ventriloquate their language processes. This requires affirming at every moment that although they are active and creative agents of language processes, their utterances may not bear the weight of the discursive histories that speak through adult utterances. Our theorizing of language socialization must begin with a theorizing of children and their voices, or we risk imposing adult interpellations on children's social worlds.

Finally, it is important to note, in this day of one-size-fits-all curricula, that schools and parents can still have a voice in children's schooling. This school site provided an ideological space not only for the development of bilingualism and biliteracy but also for multidiscursive practices and readings of the world (see González & Arnot-Hopffer [2003] for further examples of children's critical biliteracy skills). The solidarity of teachers, parents, and administrators forged the school's unique identity, in contradistinction to circulating public discourses, about the meaning and significance of language abilities. There is no doubt that schools can be sites of interpellation, reproducing dominant discourses of power and control. But they can also be sites for reimagining the role of public education, for fostering informed citizenship, and for listening to the voices of students. This is the promise of educational institutions, a promise often forfeited in exchange for quick-fix solutions. For the children at this school, bilingualism is an unquestioned asset, a resource that they can draw on to expand their "repertoire of identities" (Kroskrity, 1993), because they are nurtured and encouraged in their nascent language abilities and given every opportunity for high academic achievement in two languages. The teachers, not content to import models that had been fashioned in different contexts and different circumstances, used their own funds of knowledge to create *Exito Bilingüe*. By theorizing their own practices, they became producers rather than passive consumers of knowledge and pedagogy. For all teachers and those of us who study language socialization, listening to the voices of the children will help us look deeper and more closely into how language completes us as unfinished subjects.

Building on Strength
con *Educación, Respeto, y Confianza*
(with Education, Respect, and Trust)

Ana Celia Zentella

These are difficult times for teachers, beset as they are by the imposition of top-down policies and statewide standards on the one hand and on the other by an increasing number of students whose languages and ways of speaking they do not understand. The tendency is to reassure teachers by offering a one-size-fits-all solution, like No Child Left Behind, but they are only more frustrated when it fails. Many educators are eager to rethink their methods, curricula, and evaluations with Latinos and other ethnolinguistic minority children in mind, but they are stymied by the complexity of the relationship among language, culture, and education, and unsure about how to proceed. For teachers who do not speak Spanish, which frustrates their communication with Latino parents, or teachers who do not understand the ethnic varieties of English that their students speak, the differences may seem greater than they are. The walls between lower-working-class Latino families and those who live in the American mainstream make polarized models of "We Americans do/believe this" but "They (Latinos) do/believe that" seem believable. The contributors to this volume reject such a model and complicate the notion of culture in order to make it more comprehensible and more useful. Although not designed to be a how-to text, each chapter suggests ways for teachers to build on the strength of language and literacy socialization in Latino families and communities. Succesful approaches, including transformative inquiry (Chapter 6) and the Funds of Knowledge (Chapter 9), should prove especially helpful. In our experience, once teachers become disposed to question the role of the school and their own views, they find additional solutions that meet their particular needs.

We also speak directly to Latinos who realize that they must educate their communities about the mainstream institutions' practices and expectations as well as about the experiences of the nation's recent Latino arrivals— of their own and other backgrounds—to be better able to educate others. Broad Latino participation is vital to correct the false impression that the needs and skills of all Latinos are the same. Latina mothers, including my own, take center stage in these pages, in part because Latinas shoulder the heaviest burdens related to their children's education. The voices of Latino fathers, brothers, and sons are fainter in these pages, but also concerned, and we expect them to grow stronger as the more traditionally gendered divisions of labor are blurred. In my own life, my father, whose elementary schooling was interrupted by the Mexican revolution, never attended a parents' association meeting (whereas my mother became vice president), but his exceptional bilingual skills and cultural activism guided my linguistic and sociopolitical development as well as complemented *mami*'s direct interventions. Together, well-informed Latinas and Latinos can help their children more and help their schools and communities more.

MANY VOICES

Traditionally, Latino parents send their children to school with the admonition that "*la maestra es tu segunda mamá*" (the teacher is your second mother), expecting teachers to sustain and expand the values of the home (Reese, Balzano, Gallimore & Goldenberg, 1994). On the other hand, teachers believe that parents are the child's first teachers, expecting them to introduce and reinforce language and literacy skills at home. Both parties see their responsibility as shared with the other, yet neither fully realizes what is expected of them. Mutual efforts to break down the walls that separate Latino families and educators can be encouraged by honoring *educación, respeto, y confianza*.

Although education in the sense of learning new information is only one of the meanings of *educación* (see below), one of our main objectives is to educate and inform readers about the diversity within the Latino community. Accordingly, we have highlighted differences in national and ethnic origin, regional settlement, generations, legal status, religion, class, and race in the hope that readers will question sweeping generalizations about "Hispanic parents" or "Latino students." Latinos are in a state of flux, moving from Latin America to all across the United States and sometimes back again, forging syncretic language and literacy practices intergenerationally and transnationally. Children are falling in love with Big Bird, leprechauns, and muggles while reaffirming their devotion to *salsa, merengue*, and *mariachis*. Caregivers may mix bald-on-record imperatives with justified directives, multiparty teasing with direct teaching, and individualism with familism (Chapters 3 & 4). Lessons learned in church sometimes contradict and sometimes support the lessons learned at home and at school (Chapter 5). Nowhere are diversity, movement, and syncretism more evident than in the varieties of languages and dialects spoken by Latinos, and their ways of speaking them.

"Spanish" and "English" are at once too broad and too narrow as labels for the languages of Latinos. They erase other, predominantly indigenous languages, such as the four dialects of Mayan spoken by Guatemalans in Los Angeles, and obscure the many varieties within Spanish and English that identify the regional and generational background of their speakers. Spanish monolinguals learn to distinguish *cipote, patojo, chamaquito, escuintle*, and *nene*—all terms for "child"—depending on the regional origin of their neighbors. They recognize Caribbean speakers by their deletion or aspiration of the /s/ that ends syllables, and when they hear *vos* they identify Central Americans. Many borrow some lexical, phonological, or grammatical forms from another nation, but intimate, unequal contact results in code and identity transformations that foreground dominant groups, like Mexicans, and make others, like Central Americans, feel like they are "speaking in silence" (Chapter 6).

Among the new ethnic varieties of English enriching the English landscape, which are the first (and sometimes only) languages for many second-generation Latinos, only Chicano and Puerto Rican English have begun to be studied in depth (Bayley & Santa Ana, 2004; Fought, 2003; Santa Ana & Bayley, 2004; Urciuoli, 1996). These English dialects incorporate aspects of the Spanish spoken by the first generation and the English of African American and Anglo neighbors, but they signal specific Latino identities. Latino youth who tap into several dialects in several languages for varied communicative purposes, often alternating between them, belie charges of verbal deprivation or limited language proficiency (Zentella, 1997a).

In one or more varieties of Spanish and/or English, Latinos speak to children in ways that challenge the stereotype of overburdened caregivers who communicate little with their children, provide few explanations, and place their needs and wants before the child's. Within any group, seemingly contradictory styles may coexist. For example, western Mexico's *rancheros* see no conflict between very direct one-on-one speech and confusing wordplay that can be multiparty; toddlers are involved in both (Chapter 3). Some Latino parents may favor the situation-centered model of language socialization that they were raised with, but older children bring new ways learned outside the home, and parents also change as a result of personal and school-related influences (Chapter 4). The Latino banner is a patchwork quilt made up of many voices.

SEEING WHAT'S THERE, *CON RESPETO*

For those voices to be heard clearly, it is necessary to look beyond stereotypes with genuine *respeto* (respect) to see what's really there. The family members in these pages endure many damning labels: illegal alien, welfare queen, pregnant teenager, unwed mother, gang member, language-disabled, non-English-speakers, *mocho*, *pocho*, Spanglish-speaker. But in all these homes, and those where parents do not read to their children, like mine, we found evidence of a strong commitment to a better life for the children and concrete efforts to foster language and literacy. The comfort of our stereotypes is ultimately destructive because the anger, shock, and/or dismay they produce blind us to the resources for learning that exist in all homes and to the possibilities for growth in everyone.

Seeing what's there includes recognizing everyday language and literacies: personal letters and greeting cards (via snail mail and e-mail); communications in/from banks, schools, and government offices; doctrine classes; church choirs; Bible reading at home; Scrabble games; family entrepreneurial efforts that involve buying, selling, cooking, and serving; volunteer work for tenant patrols, the school office, or church committees; print on TV, on video boxes, and in computer programs; memorizing and reciting poems and prayers; and the narrative structures in popular music. Everyday literacies are everywhere (Chapters 8 and 9) once we look beyond a family's access to books and computers or even paper and pencils, which has more to do with the parents' economic situation than with their commitment to education.

EDUCACIÓN AND EDUCATION

The Latino commitment to education cannot be fully appreciated without understanding how *educación* is defined. For Latinos, *educación* is linked with a good upbringing and based on *respeto* as the foundation for learning. Moral and academic aspects are fused in *educación*, not just the formal schooling stressed in "education." Rooted in an agrarian model of human development that arose in societies requiring collective work and the supervision of elders, aspects of the traditional model help Latinos adapt to difficult new circumstances that threaten the cohesion of the family in the United States (Reese et al., 1994). Some critics complain that Latinos privilege behavior over books, but Reese and colleagues' (1994) longitudinal study of Latino families in Los Angeles found that the Latino and mainstream models of *educación* and education are not in opposition:

> . . . agrarian-origin values that differ from the academic-occupational orientation of school personnel . . . do not necessarily work to the disadvantage of

students. To the contrary, under certain conditions, the values may be complementary to those of the school and in fact serve to support educational adaptation and achievement. (p. 59)

Families that emphasize filial piety and reciprocity can and do encourage doing well in school in order to signal respect for their elders' wishes and to contribute to the family's progress. Moreover, family cohesion supports school success.

BUILDING *CONFIANZA*

Parents worry about how and what the school teaches, and they need to know more because the information that schools send out is often inadequate, unintelligible, and/or confusing—breeding a lack of *confianza* (trust) between parents and teachers. Much of the information is in English with no translation provided, even of crucial documents such as evaluations of a child's disability (Chapter 8), or it is in a formal Spanish that makes it difficult to comprehend translations of "primary language program", "mainstream", "percentile", or "language acquisition." Adding to the confusion is the proliferation of labels and acronyms, such as ELLs, Bilingual Education, Dual Language (DL), Two-Way Bilingual, Structured English Immersion (SEI), or Mainstream English Language Development (MELD, California's euphemism for English-only classrooms). As a result, some parents do not know what kind of program their child is in or how it works. They may reject bilingual education for the wrong reason, even if they cannot speak to the teacher in the English-only class or help with the homework, because they fear bilingual education does not teach English. Although the great majority of Latino parents want their children to learn Spanish, many end up sacrificing their children's bilingual future, especially literacy in Spanish, on the altar of misinformation about the best way to learn English (Chapters 2, 3, 8).

School information sessions are often formal, one-way, and top-down transmissions of program labels, or "you should's." Latinos, whether they speak English or not, can understand educational methods and goals if educators communicate with them regularly—informally as well as formally—in the appropriate language(s). Parents want to be informed about how their kids are behaving *and* learning, and schools that build *confianza* by ensuring two-way discussions about the children's progress and the parents' language and academic goals can count on helpful volunteers and stalwart supporters. But even in Miami, where Cuban numbers and economic power should translate into widespread educational support for bilingualism in cooperation with parents, effective school programs are hard to find (Chapter 7).

THE ANTHROPOLITICAL HOPE

Teacher and parent groups, working with student input, can come up with creative methods for tapping into children's multilingual proficiencies, families' ways of speaking, and other funds of knowledge—methods that translate into academic success. From an anthropolitical perspective, however, we hope not only for increased test scores and improved graduation rates but also for a profound rethinking of the purpose and impact of schooling, with particular attention to the role of language and literacy. A school (administrators, staff, teachers, parents, students) that takes its power seriously and commits itself to guard against recruiting Latino children to be complicit subjects in their own devoicing and failure must challenge anti-Latino stereotypes and expose the many disguises of the dominant discourse of English hegemony (Chapter 11). Since not only children are recruited, but all of us, it takes collective vigilance and action to mount a successful counteroffensive against misrecognizing Latino abilities, practices, and dreams. Bourdieu (1991) highlights the central role of "misrecognition" in constructing complicit subjects:

> . . . the language of authority never governs without the collaboration of those it governs, without the help of the social mechanisms capable of producing this complicity, based on misrecognition, which is the basis of all authority (p. 113).

Another aspect of our anthropolitical hope is that the language of authority of the school may be used to disrupt the collaboration of teachers, parents, and children in their own silencing by recognizing bilingualism and multidialectalism as assets instead of liabilities, and by becoming multilingual in vision and practice. This requires challenging educational policies that have been decided by referenda instead of by educators for the first time in the history of the nation, as in California and Arizona, making it illegal for children to be taught in their heritage language even when they are also being taught English.

The dismantling of bilingual education programs and the increased linguistic profiling that results from laws disallowing government services in languages other than English (27 states now have them) foment linguistic insecurity among speakers of other languages, with insidious results. A consistent but contradictory Latino refrain claims pride in Spanish along with the fear that it holds Latinos back; Spanish is considered important for family cohesion and cultural identity, but not very useful for learning and writing and good jobs. These messages become part of Latino children's language socialization, along with shame about Spanish accents or nonstandard grammar. As a result, some children ridicule their parents' English, stop responding in Spanish, and even try to stop their parents from talking Spanish to them in public (Chapter 10). Despite attempts to extol bilingualism and the value and beauty of Spanish, the most powerful linguistic message transmitted to children at school and at home is the symbolic power of English to determine who is worthy of respect.

But children can learn a contrasting, empowering lesson from educators who honor parents' desires to help their children succeed in school without sacrificing the cultural and linguistic cohesion of the family. The maintenance of Spanish is central, because it facilitates intergenerational *consejos* (advice) and because it creates healing cultural spaces, the "pockets of remembrance" that psychotherapist Celia Falicov (2002) has found essential to the well-being of immigrants who struggle with the trauma of dislocation. Spanish is not enough, however; according to Falicov the healing "dual vision" that facilitates continuity with past traditions and the change required by distinct traditions in the United States involves Spanish *and* English, for caregivers and their children. Classrooms with a dual vision, in which students and teachers are constructing a multilingual culture with an international perspective, will achieve both the educational outcomes valued by local communities and those needed for social, economic, and political participation in today's simultaneously expanding and shrinking world. Most important, the powerful love that children feel for the schools and teachers that celebrate the polyphony of their voices, expand their repertoire of identities, and encourage them to embrace a limitless future can nurture them throughout life. We honor teachers who accept the challenge; *y estamos a sus órdenes* (and we are at their service).

Colorín Colorado, este cuento se ha acabado.

References

Ada, A. F., & Campoy, F. I. (2004). *Authors in the classroom: A transformative education process*. Boston: Pearson, Allyn & Bacon.

Allard, R., & Landry, R. (1992). Ethnolinguistic vitality beliefs and language maintenance and loss. In W. Fase, K. Jaspaert, & S. Kroon (Eds.), *Maintenance and loss of minority languages* (pp. 171–195). Amsterdam: John Benjamins.

Alonso-Zaldívar, R. (2003, June 19). Latinos now top minority. Retrieved on June 19, 2003, from: www.LATimes.com/news/nationworld/nation/la-na-latino19jun19.1.4254451.story?coll=la-home-headlines

Althusser, L. (1971). Ideology and ideological state apparatuses. In *Lenin and philosophy and other essays* (pp. 127–186). New York: Monthly Review Press.

Anzaldúa, G. (1987). How to tame a wild tongue. In *Borderlands/La frontera: The new mestiza*. San Francisco: Spinsters/Aunt Lute.

Aponte, S. (1999). *Dominican migration to the United States, 1970–1997: An annotated bibliography*. (Dominican Research Monographs). New York: City University of New York, Dominican Studies Institute.

Auer, P. (1984). *Bilingual conversation*. Amsterdam: John Benjamins.

August, D., & Hakuta, K. (Eds.). (1997). *Improving schooling for language-minority children: A research agenda*. Washington, DC: National Academy Press.

Bailey, B. H. (2001). The language of multiple identities among Dominican Americans. *Journal of Linguistic Anthropology, 10*(2), 190–223.

Baquedano-López, S. P. (1997). Creating social identities through *doctrina* narratives. *Issues in Applied Linguistics, 8*(1), 27–43.

Baquedano-López, S. P. (1998). Language socialization of Mexican children in a Los Angeles Catholic parish. Unpublished dissertation, University of California, Los Angeles.

Barragán López, E. (1997). *Con un pie en el estribo: Formación y deslizamientos de las sociedades rancheras en la construcción del México moderno*. Zamora, Michoacán, México: El Colegio de Michoacán.

Barton, D., & Hamilton, M. (1998). *Local literacies: Reading and writing in one community*. London, UK: Routledge.

Baugh, J. (2000). *Beyond Ebonics: Linguistic pride and racial prejudice*. New York: Oxford University Press.

Bayley, R., & Santa Ana, O. (2004). Chicano English: Morphology and syntax. In B. Kortmann & E. Schneider (Eds.), *A handbook of varieties of English*, vol. 2 (pp. 168–183). Berlin: Mouton de Gruyter.

Bayley, R., & Schecter, S. (Eds.). (2003). *Language socialization in bilingual and multilingual societies*. Clevedon, UK: Multilingual Matters.

Bayley, R., Schecter, S., & Torres-Ayala, B. (1996). Strategies for bilingual maintenance: Case studies of Mexican-origin families in Texas. *Linguistics and Education, 8*, 389–408.

Bernstein, B. (1986). A sociolinguistic approach to socialization with some reference to educability. In J. J. Gumperz & D. Hymes (Eds.), *Directions in sociolinguistics: The ethnography of communication* (pp. 465–497). New York: Blackwell.

Billings, D. (2000). Organizing in exile: The reconstruction of community in the Guatemalan refugee camps of southern Mexico. In J. Loucky & M. Moors (Eds.), *The Mayan diaspora: Guatemalan roots, new American lives* (pp. 73–92). Philadephia: Temple University Press.

Bonilla, F. (1985). Ethnic orbits. *Contemporary Marxism*. San Francisco: Synthesis Publications.

Boswell, T. D. (2000). Demographic changes in Florida and their importance for effective educational policies and practices. In A. R. Roca (Ed.), *Research on Spanish in the United States: Linguistic issues and challenges* (pp. 406–431). Somerville, MA: Cascadilla.

Bourdieu, P. (1991). *Language and symbolic power* (J. B. Thompson, Editor, G. Raymond & M. Adamson, Trans.). Cambridge, MA: Harvard University Press.

Brimelow, P. (1995). *Alien nation*. New York: Random House.

Butler, J. (Ed.). (1993). *Bodies that matter: On the discursive limits of sex*. New York: Routledge.

Cárdenas Negrete, D. (1967). *El español de Jalisco: Contribución a la geografía lingüística hispanoamericana. Revista de filología española (Anejo 85)*. Madrid: Instituto Miguel de Cervantes, Consejo Superior de Investigaciones Científicas. Patronato Menéndez y Pelayo.

Chavez, L. (2000, September 21). Why José doesn't graduate. *Jewish World Review*. Retrieved Sept 21, 2003 from: www.jewishworldreview.com/cols/chavez092100.asp.

Clarke-Stewart, A. (1973). *Interactions between mothers and their young children: Characteristics and consequences*. Chicago: University of Chicago Press.

Clements, C. (1984). *Witness to war: An American doctor in El Salvador*. Toronto: Bantam.

Cochran-Smith, M. (1984). *The making of a reader*. Norwood, NJ: Ablex.

Cochran-Smith, M. (1995). Uncertain allies: Understanding the boundaries of racism in teacher education. *Harvard Educational Review, 65*(4), 541–570.

Corella, H. (2001, April 4). Davis parents say first graders are too young to be assessed. *Arizona Daily Star*, p. B1.

Crawford, J. (1992). *Hold your tongue: Bilingualism and the politics of English-only*. Reading, MA: Addison-Wesley.

Cummins, J. (2000). *Language, power, and pedagogy: Bilingual children in the crossfire*. Clevedon, UK: Multilingual Matters.

Davis, M. (2000). *Magical urbanism: Latinos unite the U.S. big city*. New York: Verso.

Delgado-Gaitán, C. (1990). *Literacy for empowerment: The role of parents in children's education.* New York: Falmer.

Del Valle, T. (2002). *Written literacy features of three Puerto Rican family networks in Chicago.* Lewiston, NY: Edwin Mellen Press.

Dickinson, D. K., & Tabors, P. O. (Eds.). (2001). *Beginning literacy with language: Young children learning at home and in school.* Baltimore, MD: Brookes.

Domínguez Barajas, E. (2002). *Reconciling cognitive universals and cultural particulars: A Mexican social network's use of proverbs.* Unpublished doctoral dissertation, University of Illinois, Chicago.

Duranti, A. (2003). Language as culture in U.S. anthropology. *Current Anthropology, 44(3),* 323–335.

Duranti, A., & Ochs, E. (1996). Syncretic literacy: Multiculturalism in Samoan American families. Retrieved August 13, 2003 from: http://www.ncela.gwu.edu/miscpubs/ncrdsll/rr16/index.htm

Eagleton, T. (1990). *The significance of theory.* Oxford, UK: Basil Blackwell.

Ebaugh, H. R., & Chafetz, J. S. (2000). *Religion and the new immigrants: Continuities and adaptations in immigrant congregations.* Walnut Creek, CA: AltaMira Press.

Eisenberg, A. (1986). Teasing: Verbal play in two Mexicano homes. In B. Schieffelin & E. Ochs (Eds.), *Language socialization across cultures* (pp. 182–198). Cambridge, UK: Cambridge University Press.

Ek, L. (2003, April). *Socialization and resistance in an immigrant Latino Pentecostal Sunday school.* Paper presented at the annual meeting of the American Educational Research Association, Chicago.

Ek, L. (2004, April). *Literacy socialization in a Latino/a immigrant Pentecostal church.* Paper presented at the annual meeting of the American Educational Research Association, San Diego.

Ely, R., & Gleason J. B. (1995). Socialization across contexts. In P. Fletcher & B. MacWhinney (Eds.), *The handbook of child language* (pp. 251–259). Cambridge, MA: Blackwell.

Erickson, F. (1984). School literacy, reasoning, and civility: An anthropologist's perspective. *Review of Educational Research, 54(4),* 525–546.

Ervin-Tripp, S (1976). Is Sybil there? The structure of some American English directives. *Language in Society, 5,* 25–67.

Falicov, C. J. (2002). Ambiguous loss: Risk and resilience in Latino immigrant families. In M. Suárez-Orozco & M. Páez (Eds.), *Latinos: Remaking America* (pp. 274–289). Berkeley: University of California Press.

Farr, M. (1993). Essayist literacy and other verbal performances. *Written Communication, 10(1),* 4–38.

Farr, M. (1994). Echando relajo: Verbal art and gender among *Mexicanas* in Chicago. In M. Bucholtz, A. C. Liang, L. A. Sutton, & C. Hines (Eds.), *Cultural performances* (pp. 168–186). Proceedings of the Third Women and Language Conference, April 8–10, 1994. University of California, Berkeley.

Farr, M. (2000a). ¡A mí no me manda nadie! Individualism and identity in Mexican ranchero speech. In V. Pagliai & M. Farr (Eds.), Language, Performance and Identity [Special issue]. *Pragmatics, 10(1),* 61–85.

Farr, M. (2000b). Literacy and religion: Reading, writing, and gender among Mexican women in Chicago. In P. Griffin, J. K. Peyton, W. Wolfram, & R. Fasold (Eds.), *Language in action: New studies of language in society* (pp. 139–154). Cresskill, NJ: Hampton Press.

Farr, M. (in press). *Ways of speaking and identity: Rancheros in Chicagoacán.* Austin: University of Texas Press.

Farr, M., & Domínguez Barajas, E. (2005). Latinos and diversity in a global city: Language and identity at home, school, church, and work. In M. Farr (Ed.), *Latino language and literacy in ethnolinguistic Chicago* (pp. 3–32). Mahwah, NJ: Erlbaum.

Feagans, L. (1982). Narratives for school adaptation. In L. Feagans & D. C. Farrans (Eds.), *The language of children reared in poverty* (pp. 95–114). New York: Academic Press.

Fought, C. (2003). *Chicano English in context.* New York: Palgrave Macmillan.

Freire, P. (1998). *Pedagogy of freedom: Ethics, democracy, and civic courage.* Oxford, UK: Rowman & Littlefield.

Fry, R. (2003). *Hispanic youth dropping out of U.S. schools: Measuring the challenge.* Washington, DC: Pew Hispanic Center.

García, O. (1999). Latin America. In J. Fishman (Ed.), *Handbook of language & ethnic identity* (pp. 226–243). New York: Oxford University Press.

García, E., & Hurtado, A. (1995). Becoming American: A review of current research on the development of racial and ethnic identity in children. In W. Hawley & A. Jackson (Eds.), *Toward a common destiny: Improving race and ethnic relations in America* (pp. 163–184). San Francisco: Jossey-Bass.

García Bedolla, L. (2003). The identity paradox: Latino language, politics, and selective dissociation. *Latino Studies, 1,* 264–283.

Garcilazo, V. (2001, June 15) *Funds of knowledge: Inquiry-oriented approach to professional development.* Paper presented at the First Annual Conference on Teaching Diverse Learners, sponsored by the Educational Alliance at Brown University.

Garrett, P., & Baquedano-López, P. (2002). Language socialization: Reproduction and continuity, transformation and change. *Annual Review of Anthropology, 31,* 339–361.

Getting the message out to young Latinos. (2002, September 5). *San Diego Union-Tribune,* p. C1.

Gibson, M., & Ogbu, J. (Eds.). (1991). *Minority status and schooling: A comparative study of immigrant and involuntary minorities.* New York: Garland.

Giles, H., Bourhis, R. Y., & Taylor, D. M. (1977). Toward a theory of language in ethnic group relations. In H. Giles (Ed.), *Language, ethnicity, and intergroup relations* (pp. 307–348). New York: Academic Press.

Goelman, H., Oberg, A., & Smith, F. (1984). *Awakening to literacy.* Portsmouth, NH: Heinemann Educational Books.

Goffman, E. (1974). *Frame analysis: An essay on the organization of experience.* New York: Harper & Row.

González, L. (1974). *San José de Gracia: Mexican village in transition.* Austin: University of Texas Press.

González, L. (1991). Del hombre a caballo y la cultura ranchera. *Tierra Adentro, 52,* 3–7.

González, N. (2001). *I am my language: Discourse of women and children in the Borderlands.* Tucson: University of Arizona Press.

González, N., & Arnot-Hopffer, E. (2003). Voices of the children: Language and literacy ideologies in a dual language immersion school. In S. Wortham & B. Rymes (Eds.), *Linguistic anthropology of education* (pp. 213–243). Westport, CT: Praeger.

González, N., Moll, L. C., Tenery, M., Rivera, A., Rendón, P., & González, R. (1995). Funds of knowledge for teaching in Latino households. *Urban Education, 29*(4), 443–470.

Graff, H. J. (1991). *The legacies of literacy.* Bloomington: Indiana University Press.

Griffith, A. (1995). Mothering, schooling, and children's development. In M. Campbell & A. Manicom (Eds.), *Knowledge, experience, and ruling relations: Studies in the social organization of knowledge* (pp. 108–122). Toronto: University of Toronto Press.

Guerra, J., & Farr, M. (2002). Writing on the margins: The spiritual and autobiographical discourse of two Mexicanas in Chicago. In G. Hall & K. Schultz (Eds.), *School's out: Literacy at home, at work, and in the community* (pp. 96–123). New York: Teachers College Press.

Guerra Vásquez, G. (2003, Fall). CentroAmericAztlan: Contact, *convivencia, conocimiento y confianza* in California's millenial cultural projects. *La Gente, 33,* 18–19.

Gutiérrez, K., Asato, J., Santos, M. & Gotanda, N. (2002). Backlash pedagogy: Language and culture and the politics of reform. *The Review of Education, Pedagogy and Cultural Studies, 24*(4), 335–352.

Gutiérrez, R. J. (2000). Part-time Salvi. In *Izote voz: A collection of Salvadoran-American writing and visual art* (pp. 28–29). San Francisco: Pacific News Service.

Hamilton, N., & Chinchilla, N. S. (2001). *Seeking community in a global city: Guatemalans and Salvadorans in Los Angeles.* Philadelphia: Temple University Press.

Harris, J. R. (1998). *The nurture assumption: Why children turn out the way they do.* New York: Free Press.

Hart, B., & Risley, T. R. (1995). *Meaningful differences in the everyday experience of young American children.* Baltimore, MD: Brookes.

He, A. W. (2003). Novices and their speech roles in Chinese heritage language classes. In R. Bayley & S. Schecter (Eds.), *Language socialization in bilingual and multilingual societies* (pp. 128–147). Clevedon, UK: Multilingual Matters.

Heath, S. (1982). What no bedtime story means: Narrative skills at home and school. *Language in Society, 11*(1), 49–76.

Heath, S. (1983). *Ways with words: Language, life and work in communities and classrooms.* Cambridge, UK: Cambridge University Press.

Heath, S. (1986). Sociocultural contexts of language development. In California State Department of Education (Ed.), *Beyond language: Social and cultural factors in schooling and language minority students* (pp. 143–186). Los Angeles: California State University, Evaluation, Dissemination and Assessment Center.

Heller, M., & Martin-Jones, M. (Eds.). (2001). Voices of authority: Education and linguistic difference. *Contemporary Studies in Linguistics and Education* (Vol. 1). London: Ablex.

Herrnstein, R. J., & Murray, C. (1994). *The bell curve: The reshaping of American life by difference in intelligence*. New York: Free Press.

Hidalgo, M. (2001). Spanish language shift reversal on the U.S.–Mexico border and the extended third space. *Journal of Language and Intercultural Communication*, *1*(1), 1–40.

Hill, J. (1993a). Hasta la vista, baby: Anglo Spanish in the American Southwest. *Critique of Anthropology*, *13*(2), 145–176.

Hill, J. (1993b). Is it really no problemo? In R. Queen & R.Barrett (Eds.), *SALSA 1: Proceedings of the First Annual Symposium about Language and Society* (pp. 1–12), Austin, Texas.

Hirschfield, L. (2002). Why don't anthropologists like children? *American Anthropologist*, *104*(2), 611–627.

Hoff-Ginsberg, E. (1991). Mother–child conversation in different social classes and communicative settings. *Child Development*, *62*, 782–796.

Huntington, S. P. (2004). *Who are we?: The challenges to America's identity*. New York: Simon & Schuster.

Hymes, D. (1972). Models of interaction of language and social life. In J. Gumperz & D. Hymes (Eds.), *Directions in sociolinguistics: The ethnography of communication* (pp. 35–71). New York: Holt, Rinehart & Wiston.

Hymes, D. (1974). *Foundations in sociolinguistics: An ethnographic approach*. Philadelphia: University of Pennsylvania Press.

James, N. P. (1998). *Directory of Dominicans*. (Dominican Research Monographs). New York: City University of New York: Dominican Studies Institute.

Johnson, F. (2000). *Speaking culturally: Language diversity in the United States*. Thousand Oaks, CA: Sage.

Judd, E. (2004). Language policy in Illinois: Past and present. In M. Farr (Ed.), *Ethnolinguistic Chicago: Language and literacy in the city's neighborhoods* (pp. 33–49). Mahwah, NJ: Erlbaum.

Kaye, K., & Charney, R. (1981). Conversational asymmetry between mothers and children. *Journal of Child Language*, *8*, 35–40

Kerr, L. A. N. (1976). *The Chicano experience in Chicago, 1920–1970*. Unpublished doctoral dissertation, University of Illinois, Chicago.

Klass, P. (1995, April). Home remedies: A book a day. *Parenting*, pp. 71–72.

Krashen, S. D. (1999). *Condemned without a trial: Bogus arguments against bilingual education*. Portsmouth, NH: Heinemann.

Kroskrity, P. (1993). *Language, history and identity: Ethnolinguistic studies of the Arizona Tewa*. Tucson: University of Arizona Press.

Labov, W. (1972a). *Language in the inner city*. Philadelphia: University of Pennsylvania Press.

Labov, W. (1972b). *Sociolinguistic patterns*. Philadelphia: University of Pennsylvania Press.

Labov, W., & Waletzky, J. (1967). Narrative analysis: Oral versions of personal experience. In J. Helm (Ed.), *Essays on the verbal and visual arts: Proceedings of the 1966 Annual Spring Meeting of the American Ethnological Society* (pp. 12–44). Seattle: University of Washington Press.

Lamm, R., & Imhoff, G. (1985). *The immigration time bomb*. New York: Dutton.

Landry, R., & Allard, R. (1994). Diglossia, ethnolinguistic vitality, and language behavior. *International Journal of the Sociology of Language, 108*, 15–24.

Lanehart, S. L. (2002). *Sista, speak!: Black women kinfolk talk about language and literacy*. Austin: University of Texas Press.

Lauria, A. (1964). Respeto, relajo and interpersonal relations in Puerto Rico. *Anthropological Quarterly, 37*, 53–67.

Lavadenz, M. (1991). *Post traumatic stress disorder in Central American immigrant children*. Unpublished master's thesis, California State University, Northridge.

Lavadenz, M. (1994). The effects of war trauma in Central American immigrant children. In N. Stromquist (Ed.), *Education in urban contexts* (pp. 219–235). Philadelphia: Praeger.

Lavadenz, M., & Martín, S. (1999). *Developing a sociocultural/constructivist framework for teacher education: Reconstructing theory and practice*. Paper presented at the annual meeting of American Educational Research Association, Montreal, Canada, April.

Lee, C. D. (1995). A culturally based cognitive apprenticeship: Teaching African American high school students skills in literary interpretation. *Reading Research Quarterly, 30*(4), 608–631.

Lee, C. D. (1997). Bridging home and school literacies: Models for culturally responsive teaching, a case for African American English. In J. Flood, S. B. Heath, & D. Lapp (Eds.), *A handbook for literacy educators: Research on teaching the communicative and visual arts* (pp. 334–345). New York: Macmillan.

Levitt, P. (2002). Two nations under God? Latino religious life in the United States. In M. Suárez-Orozco & M. Páez (Eds.), *Latinos: Remaking America* (pp. 150–164). Berkeley: University of California Press.

Light, J., & Kelford-Smith, A. (1993). The home literacy experiences of preschoolers who use augmentative communication systems and of their non-disabled peers. *Augmentative and Alternative Communication, 8*(1),10–25.

Lipski, J. (1994). *Latin American Spanish*. London: Longman.

Logan, J. R. (2001). The new Latinos: Who they are, where they are. Retrieved November 20, 2002, from: http://www.albany.edu/mumford/census/

López, D. (1996). Language: Diversity and assimilation. In R. Waldinger & M. Bozorgmehr (Eds.), *Ethnic Los Angeles* (pp. 139–163). New York: Russel Sage Foundation.

López, D., Popkin, E., & Telles, E. (1996). Central Americans at the bottom, struggling to get ahead. In R. Waldinger & M. Bozorgmehr (Eds.), *Ethnic Los Angeles* (pp. 279–304). New York: Russell Sage Foundation.

Loucky, J., & Moors, M. M. (Eds.). (2000). *The Mayan diaspora: Guatemalan roots, new American lives*. Philadephia: Temple University Press.

Malmkjaer, K. (Ed.). (1991). *The linguistics encyclopedia*. New York: Routledge.

Marvin, C. (1994). Home literacy experiences of preschool children with single and multiple disabilities. *Topics in Early Childhood Special Education, 14*(4), 436–454.

Marvin, C., & Mirenda, P. (1993). Home literacy experiences of preschoolers enrolled in Head Start and special education programs. *Journal of Early Intervention, 17*(4), 351–367.

Marvin, C., & Ogden, N. (2002). A home literacy inventory: Assessing young children's contexts for emergent literacy. *Young Exceptional Children, 5*(2), 2–10.

Marvin, C., & Wright, D. (1997). Literacy socialization in the homes of preschool children. *Language, Speech, and Hearing Services in School, 17*(4), 351–367.

Menjívar, C. (2000). *Fragmented ties: Salvadoran immigrant networks in America.* Berkeley: University of California Press.

Menjívar, C. (2002). Living in two worlds: Guatemalan-origin children in the United States and emerging transnationalism. *Journal of Ethnic and Migration Studies, 28*(3), 531–545.

Mercado, C. I. (2003). Biliteracy development among Latino youth in New York City communities: An unexploited potential. In N. H. Hornberger (Ed.), *Continua of biliteracy* (pp. 166–186). Clevedon, UK: Multilingual Matters.

Mercado, C. I. (in press). Reflections on the study of households in New York City and Long Island: A different route, a common destination. In N. González, L. C. Moll, & C. Amanti (Eds.), *Theorizing practice: Funds of knowledge in households and classrooms.* New Jersey: LEA.

Mercado, C. I., & Moll, L. C. (1997). The study of funds of knowledge: Collaborative research in Latino homes. *CENTRO, the Journal of the Center for Puerto Rican Studies, IX*(9), 26–42.

Moje, E. B., Ciechanowski, K. M., Ellis, L., Carillo, R., & Collazo, T. (2004). Working toward third space in content area literacy: An examination of everyday funds of knowledge and discourse. *Reading Research Quarterly, 39*(1), 38–70.

Mollenkopf, J. H. (1999). Urban political conflicts and alliances. In C. Hirschman, P. Kasinitz, & J. DeWind (Eds.), *The handbook of international migration: The American experience* (pp. 412–422). New York: Russell Sage Foundation.

Montejo, V. (2001). *El Q'Anil: Man of lightning.* Tucson: University of Arizona Press.

Morales, M. (2000). Always say you're Mexican. In K. Cowy Kim & A. Serrano (Eds.), *Izote voz: A collection of Salvadoran American writing and visual art* (pp. 66–67). San Francisco: Pacific News Service.

Morgan, M. (2002). *Language, discourse and power in African American culture.* New York: Cambridge University Press.

Moss, B. (1988). *The Black church sermon as literacy event.* Unpublished doctoral dissertation, University of Illinois, Chicago.

Moya Pons, F. M. (1995). *The Dominican Republic. A national history.* New Rochelle, NY: Hispaniola Books.

Mulder, G. (1998). La pragmática lingüística del español: Recientes desarrollos. In H. Haverkate & G. Mulder & C. F. Maldonado (Eds.), *Diálogos hispánicos* (22) (pp. 237–275). Amsterdam: Rodopi.

Murphy, E. (1999, April). *Where do we go from here? Participatory learning and action in a teacher study group*. Paper presented at the annual meeting of the Society for Applied Anthropology, Tucson, AZ.

Navarrete, R. (2003, May 28). Latino and European immigrants. *The San Diego Union Tribune*, p. B6.

Newport, E. L., Glietman, H., & Glietman, L. R. (1977). Mother I'd rather do it myself. Some effects and non-effects of maternal speech style. In C. Snow & C. Ferguson (Eds.), *Talking to children: Language input and acquisition* (pp. 109–149). Cambridge, UK: Cambridge University Press.

Norton, B. (2000). *Identity and language learning: Gender, ethnicity and educational change*. New York: Longman.

Ochoa, A. (2003, July 30). Succeeding in America. *San Diego Union-Tribune*, p. G1.

Ochs, E. (1988). *Culture and language development*. New York: Cambridge University Press.

Ochs, E. (1993). Constructing social identity: A language socialization perspective. *Research on Language and Social Interaction, 26*(3), 287–306.

Ochs, E. (2001). Socialization. In A. Duranti (Ed.), *Key terms in language and culture* (pp. 227–231). Malden, MA: Blackwell.

Ochs, E. (2002). Becoming a speaker of culture. In C. Kramsch (Ed.), *Language acquisition and language socialization: Ecological perspectives* (pp. 99–121). London: Continuum.

Ochs, E., & Capps, L. (2001). *Living narrative: Creating lives in everyday storytelling*. Cambridge, MA: Harvard University Press.

Ochs, E., & Schieffelin, B. (1984). Language acquisition and socialization: Three developmental stories. In R. A Shweder & R. A. LeVine (Eds.), *Culture theory: Essays on mind, self, and emotion* (pp. 276–320). Cambridge, UK: Cambridge University Press.

Ochs, E., & Schieffelin, B. (1995). The impact of language socialization on grammatical development. In P. Fletcher & B. MacWhinney (Eds.), *The handbook of child language* (pp. 73–94). Cambridge, MA: Blackwell.

Ochs, E., Smith, R., & Taylor, C. (1989). Detective stories at dinnertime: Problem-solving through co-narration. *Cultural Dynamics, 2*, 238–257.

Ochs, E., Taylor, C., Rudolph D., & Smith, R. (1992). Story telling as theory-building activity. *Discourse Processes, 15*(1), 37–72.

Olsen-Fulero, L. (1982). Style and stability in mother's conversational behavior: A study of individual differences. *Journal of Child Language, 9*, 543–564.

Orellana, M. F. (2001). The work kids do: Mexican and Central American immigrant children's contributions to households and schools in California. *Harvard Educational Review, 71*(3), 366–389.

Orfield, G. (2002). Commentary. In M. Suárez-Orozco & M. Páez (Eds.), *Latinos: Remaking America* (pp. 389–397). Berkeley: University of California Press.

Padilla, E. (1958). *Up from Puerto Rico*. New York: Columbia University Press.

Parodi, C. (2003). Contacto de dialectos del español en Los Angeles. In G. Perisonotto (Ed.), *Ensayos en Lengua y Pedagogía* (pp. 22–38). Santa Barbara: University of California Linguistic Minority Research Institute.

Pease-Alvarez, L. (2003). Transforming perspectives on bilingual language socialization. In R. Bayley & S. R. Schecter (Eds.), *Language socialization in bilingual and multilingual societies* (pp. 9–24). Clevedon, UK: Multilingual Matters.

Pease-Alvarez, L., & Vásquez, O. (1994). Language socialization in ethnic minority communities. In F. Genesee (Ed.), *Educating second language children: The whole child, the whole curriculum, the whole community* (pp. 82–102). New York: Cambridge University Press.

Pedraza, P. (1997). Puerto Ricans and the policy of school reform. *CENTRO, The Journal of the Center for Puerto Rican Studies, IX*(9), 74–85.

Perry, T., & Delpit, L. (Eds.). (1998). *The real Ebonics debate: Power, language, and the education of African-American Children*. Boston: Beacon.

Porter, A., & Hao, L. (1998). E pluribus unum: Bilingualism and loss of language in the second generation. *Sociology of Education, 71*(10), 269–294.

Portes, A., & Rumbaut, R. (Eds.). (1996). *Immigrant America: A portrait* (2nd ed.). Berkeley: University of California Press.

Potowski, K. (2005). Latino children's Spanish use and identity investments in a Chicago dual immersion classroom. In M. Farr (Ed.), *Latino language and literacy in ethnolinguistic Chicago* (pp. 157–185). Mahwah, NJ: Erlbaum.

Ramírez, D. (2001). *Testimony to the U.S. Commission on Civil Rights on No Child Left Behind: A blueprint for educational reform*. Washington, DC: U.S. Commission on Civil Rights.

Ramírez, D., Yuen, S., Ramey, D., & Pasta, D. (1991). *Final report: National longitudinal study of structured English immersion strategy, early-exit and late-exit transitional bilingual education programs for language-minority children*. (2 vols.) (Prepared for U.S. Department of Education). (No. 300-87-0156). San Mateo, CA: Aguirre International.

Ramírez, R., & de la Cruz, P. (2003). *The Hispanic population in the United States: March 2002*. [Current Population Reports.] Washington, DC: U.S. Census Bureau.

Reese, L., Balzano, S., Gallimore, R., & Goldenberg, C. (1994). The concept of educación: Latino family values and American schooling. *International Journal of Education Research, 23*(1), 57–81.

Relaño Pastor, A. M. (2000). *Latina positioning in narratives of problematic talk*. Unpublished master's thesis, University of California, Los Angeles.

Relaño Pastor, A. M. (2002). *La comunicación intercultural en la frontera de Méjico y Estados Unidos: Un estudio de casos a través de la narrativa de mujeres inmigrantes mejicanas*. Unpublished doctoral dissertation, University of Granada, Spain.

Relaño Pastor, A. M., & De Fina A. (in press). Contesting social place: Narratives of language conflict. In M. Baynham & A. De Fina (Eds.), *Dislocations/relocations: Narratives of displacement*. St Jerome Publishers.

Rickford, J., & Rickford, R. (2000). *Spoken soul: The story of Black English*. New York: Wiley.

Rodríguez, M. V. (1998). Problems and issues in the education of culturally and linguistically diverse preschool children with disabilities. *Equity and Excellence in Education, 31*(2), 39–46.

Rodríguez, M. V. (1999). Home literacy experiences of three young Dominican children in New York City: Implications for teaching in urban settings. *Educators for Urban Minorities*, *1*, 19–31.

Romaine, S. (1995). *Bilingualism* (2nd ed.). Oxford, UK: Blackwell.

Rossell, C. H., & Baker, K. (1996). The educational effectiveness of bilingual education. *Research in the Teaching of English*, *30*, 7–74.

Rymes, B. (1995). The construction of moral agency in the narratives of high-school drop-outs. *Discourse and Society*, *6*(4), 495–516.

Sagás, E. (2000). *Race and politics in the Dominican Republic*. Gainesville: University of Florida Press.

Sánchez, R. (1994). *Chicano discourse: Socio-historic perspectives*. Houston: Arte Público Press.

San Miguel, G., Jr. (2004). *Contested policy: The rise and fall of bilingual education in the United States 1960–2001*. Denton: University of North Texas Press.

Santa Ana, O. (2002). *Brown tide rising: Metaphors of Latinos in contemporary American public discourse*. Austin: University of Texas Press.

Santa Ana, O., & Bayley, R. (2004). Chicano English: Phonology. In B. Kortmann & E. Schneider (Eds.), *A handbook of varieties of English*, (Vol. 1, pp. 407–424). Berlin: Mouton de Gruyter.

Schecter, S. R., & Bayley, R. (1997). Language socialization practices and cultural identity: Case studies of Mexican-descent families in California and Texas. *TESOL Quarterly*, *31*, 513–541.

Schecter, S. R., & Bayley, R. (1998). Concurrence and complementarity: Mexican-background parents' decisions about language and schooling. *Journal for a Just and Caring Education*, *4*, 47–64.

Schecter, S. R., & Bayley, R. (2002). *Language as cultural practice: Mexicanos en el Norte*. Mahwah, NJ: Erlbaum.

Schieffelin, B. B., & Ochs, E. (1986). Language socialization. *The Annual Review of Anthropology*, *15*, 163–191.

Schieffelin, B., & Ochs, E. (Eds.). (1989). *Language socialization across cultures*. New York: Cambridge University Press.

Searle, J. R. (1976). A classification of illocutionary acts. *Language In Society*, *5*, 1–23.

Shweder, R. (2000). Rethinking the object of anthropology (and ending up where Kroeber and Kluckhohn began). *Items & issues: Social Science Research Council*, *1*(11), 7–9.

Silva-Corvalán, C. (1994). *Language contact and change: Spanish in Los Angeles*. Oxford, UK: Clarendon.

Smith, P. (2000). *Community as a resource for minority language learning: A case study of Spanish–English dual language schooling*. Unpublished doctoral dissertation, College of Education, University of Arizona, Tuscon.

Smith, P., & Arnot-Hopffer, E. (1998). Exito bilingüe: Promoting Spanish literacy in a dual language immersion program. *The Bilingual Research Journal*, *22*(2, 3, 4), 261–277.

Smith, P., Arnot-Hopffer, E., Carmichael, C., Murphy, E., Valle, A., González, N., & Poveda, A. (2002). Raise a child, not a test score: Perspectives on bilingual education at Davis bilingual magnet school. *Bilingual Research Journal, 26*(1), 103–121.

Smitherman, G. (1999). *Talkin that talk: Language, culture, and education in African America.* New York: Routledge.

Snow, C., Arlman-Rupp A., Hassing, Y., Jobse J., Jooster J., & Vorster, J. (1976). Mother's speech in three social classes. *Journal of Psycholinguistic Research, 5,* 1–20.

Snow, C., Nathan, D., & Perlmann, R. (1985). Assessing children's knowledge about book reading. In L. Galda & A. Pellegrini (Eds.), *Play, language and stories: The development of children's literate behavior* (pp. 167–181). Norwood, NJ: Ablex.

Snow, C., & Tabors, P. (1993). Language skills that relate to literacy development. In B. Spodek & O. Saracho (Eds.), *Language and literacy in early childhood education* (pp. 1–20). New York: Teachers College Press.

Solé, Y. R. (1995). Language, nationalism, and ethnicity in the Americas. *International Journal of the Sociology of Language, 116,* 111–138.

Solís, J. (2002). *The (trans)formation of illegality as an identity: A study of the organization of undocumented Mexican immigrants and their children in New York City.* Unpublished doctoral dissertation, City University of New York, New York.

Stoll, D. (1990). *Is Latin America turning Protestant: The politics of evangelical growth.* Berkeley: University of California Press.

Street, B. (1984). *Literacy in theory and practice.* New York: Cambridge University Press.

Stuever, H. (2001, November 23). Harry and the nation of dweebs. *Washington Post,* p. C1.

Suárez-Orozco, M. (1989). *Central American refugees in U.S. high schools.* Stanford, CA: Stanford University Press.

Suárez-Orozco, M., & Páez, M. (Eds.).(2002). *Latinos: Remaking America.* Berkeley: University of California Press.

Taylor, D. (1983). *Family literacy: Young children learning to read and write.* Portsmouth, NH: Heinemann.

Taylor, D., & Dorsey-Gaines, C. (1988). *Growing up literate: Learning from inner-city families.* Portsmouth, NH: Heinemann.

Thomas, W., & Collier, V. (2003). *A national study of school effectiveness for language minority students' long-term academic achievement.* Santa Cruz: University of California Center for Research on Education, Diversity and Excellence.

Tobar, H. (1998). *The tattooed soldier.* New York: Penguin.

Toribio, A. J. (2000). Language variation and the linguistic enactment of identity among Dominicans. *Linguistics, 38*(5), 1133–1159.

Torres-Saillant, S., & Hernández, R. (1998). *Dominican Americans.* Westport, CT: Greenwood.

Traub, J. (2000, January 16). What no school can do. *New York Times,* p. 57.

Urciuoli, B. (1996). *Exposing prejudice: Puerto Rican experiences of language, race, and class.* Boulder, CO: Westview.

Urciuoli, B. (2001). The complex diversity of language in the U.S. In I. Susser & T. Patterson (Eds.), *Cultural diversity in the United States: A critical reader* (pp. 190–205), Malden, MA: Blackwell Press.

U.S Bureau of the Census. (2000a). *The Hispanic population in the United States.* (File P20-535 March, 2001.) Washington, DC: U.S Department of Commerce, Economics and Statistics Administration.

U.S. Bureau of the Census. (2000b). *Foreign born immigrants in the United States.* Washington, DC: Bureau of the Census.

U.S. Bureau of the Census. (2000c). 100-percent data. Hispanic or latino by type. Los Angeles city, CA. (Summary File 1 SF 1). Retrieved August 14, 2004, from: http://factfinder.census.gov/servlet/QTTable?_bm=y&-geo_id=16000US0644000&-qr_name=DEC_2000_SF1_U_QTP9&-Tables=DEC_2000_SF1_U_QTP9&-ds_name=DEC_2000_SF1_U&-_lang=en&-redoLog=false&-_sse=on&-

U.S. Bureau of the Census. (2000d). Language spoken at home and ability to speak English for population 5 years and over by state (Table 4). Retrieved February 25, 2003, from: http://www.census.gov/prod/cen2000/doc/sf3.pdf

U.S. Bureau of the Census. (2000e). Race and hispanic or latino (Summary file, GCT-P6). Retrieved February 26, 2005, from: http://factfinder.census.gov/servlet/GCTTAble?_bm=y&-gepo_id=01000US&_box-head_n

Valdés, G. (1996). *Con respeto: Bridging the distances between culturally diverse families and schools: An ethnographic portrait.* New York: Teachers College Press.

Valdés, G. (1998). The world outside and inside schools: Language and immigrant children. *Educational Researcher, 27*(6), 4–18.

Vásquez, O. (2003). *La clase mágica: Imagining optimal possibilities in a bilingual community of learners.* London: Erlbaum.

Vásquez, O., Pease-Alvarez, S. L., & Shannon, S. S. (1994). *Pushing boundaries: Language and culture in a Mexicano community.* Cambridge, UK: Cambridge University Press.

Verhovek, S. H. (1995, August 15). Mother scolded by judge for speaking in Spanish: Language at home is issue in custody fight. *New York Times,* p. A12.

Villenas, S. (2001). Latina mothers and small-town racisms: Creating narratives of dignity and moral education in North Carolina. *Anthropology & Education Quaterly 32*(1), 3–28.

Warner, R. S., & Wittner, J. G. (Eds.). (1998). *Gatherings in diasporas: Religious communities and the new immigration.* Philadelphia: Temple University Press.

Wertsch, J. V., Del Rio, P., & Alvarez, A. (Eds.). (1995). *Sociocultural studies of mind.* Cambridge, UK: Cambridge University Press.

Willig, A. C. (1985). A meta-analysis of selected studies on the effectiveness of bilingual education. *Review of Educational Research, 55,* 269–317.

Wong Fillmore, L. (1991). When learning a second language means losing the first. *Early Childhood Research Quarterly, 6,* 323–346.

Woolard, K. (1998). Introduction: Language ideology as a field of inquiry. In K. A. Woolard, B. Schieffelin, & P. Kroskrity (Eds.), *Language ideologies: Practice and theory* (pp. 3–47). Oxford, UK: Oxford University Press.

Woolard, K., & Schieffelin, B. (1994). Language ideology. *Annual Review of Anthropology, 23,* 55–82.

Zentella, A. C. (1988). Language politics in the U.S.A.: The English-only movement. In B. J. Craige (Ed.), *Literature, language and politics* (pp. 39–63). Athens: University of Georgia Press.

Zentella, A. C. (1990). Lexical leveling in four New York City Spanish dialects: Linguistic and social factors. *HISPANIA, 73*(4), 1094–1105.

Zentella, A. C. (1997a). *Growing up bilingual: Puerto Rican children in New York.* Malden, MA: Blackwell.

Zentella, A. C. (1997b). Spanish in New York. In O. García & J. Fishman (Eds.), *The multilingual apple: Languages in New York City* (pp. 167–201). New York: Mouton de Gruyter.

Zentella, A. C. (2002). Latin@ languages and identities. In M. Suárez-Orozco & M. Páez (Eds.), *Latinos: Remaking America* (pp. 321–338). Berkeley: University of California Press.

About the Editor and Contributors

Robert Bayley is a Professor of Bicultural-Bilingual Studies, University of Texas, San Antonio. His research interests focus on sociolinguistics, language socialization, and second language acquisition. Recent publications include *Language as Cultural Practice* (with Sandra Schecter, 2002) and *Sociolinguistic Variation in ASL* (with Ceil Lucas and Clayton Valli, 2001).

Fazila Bhimji is a Lecturer in the Department of Humanities, University of Central Lancashire, United Kingdom. She received her Ph.D. from the University of California, Los Angeles, in Applied Linguistics, and her multiple research interests include language socialization in bilingual communities, language and identity, and the socio-cultural and linguistic experience of immigrant communities.

Elías Domínguez Barajas, Assistant Professor, Department of English, Texas A & M University, College Station, conducts research on the social and cognitive dimensions of language use among Mexican-origin populations in the United States. In addition to his work in linguistic anthropology, he also teaches Latino literature and literacy studies from an analytical perspective, examining the implications of using a particular language or dialect in people's lives.

Lucila D. Ek, who received her Ph.D. in Urban Schooling at the University of California, Los Angeles, conducts research on language, literacy, socialization, and identity in Latino immigrant communities. Her numerous awards include the University of California President's Postdoctoral Fellowship, at the University of California, San Diego. She was a Visiting Scholar at the Center for the Study of Urban Literacies, University of California, Los Angeles, from 2004–2005.

Marcia Farr is Professor Emerita of English and Linguistics, University of Illinois, Chicago, and Professor of Education and English, Ohio State University, Columbus. Her research and teaching focus on cultural variation in oral

197

language and literacy practices. Recent work includes a long-term ethnographic study of language and literacy among transnational Mexican families in both Chicago and Mexico, funded by the Spencer Foundation. Her book on this work, *Ways of Speaking and Identity: Rancheros in Chicagoacán*, is in press.

Norma González, an Associate Professor in the Department of Education, Culture and Society, University of Utah, is an anthropologist with specializations in anthropology and education, linguistic anthropology, and applied anthropology. Her publications include: *I Am My Language: Discourses of Women and Children in the Borderlands* (2001), and an edited volume, *Funds of Knowledge: Theorizing Practices in Households and Communities* (in press).

Magaly Lavadenz is Associate Professor of Education, Associate Director of the Ed.D. in Educational Leadership for Social Justice, and Coordinator of Bilingual/Bicultural Education at Loyola Marymount University, Los Angeles. She was born in Cuba and has many years of classroom experience in the United States and as a consultant to school districts nationally and internationally. Current research activities include bilingual teacher preparation, teacher action research and biliteracy, Central American immigrant children, public policy concerning language and education, and equitable assessment practices for language minority students. She served as President of the California Association for Bilingual Education from 2003–2005.

Carmen I. Mercado is Associate Professor of Literacy, School of Education, Hunter College, City University of New York. A former elementary school teacher, she conducts collaborative action research with teachers, students, and families on ways to improve the conditions for learning in low-performing schools. A major research interest is locating and understanding uses of language and literacy in bilingual, multidialectal homes and communities. She is also developing online curriculum resources using the archives from the Center for Puerto Rican Studies, Hunter College, on Puerto Rican communities in New York. The National Conference for Research on Language and Literacy elected Professor Mercado a member in 2004.

Ana María Relaño Pastor is a Postdoctoral Fellow, University of California, San Diego, sponsored by the Ministry of Education of Spain. She received a Ph.D. in English Philology from the University of Granada, Spain, and an M.A. in Applied Linguistics and TESL from the University of California, Los Angeles. Her research interests include language socialization in immigrant communities, intercultural communication experiences of Mexican immigrant women; and language, education, and identity of minorities in Spain.

Ana Roca is Professor of Spanish and Linguistics, Department of Modern Languages, Florida International University, Miami. Professor Roca's publications and teaching focus on sociolinguistic, pedagogical, and policy issues related to bilingualism and Spanish in the United States. Her books include Mi lengua: *Spanish as a Heritage Language in the United States* (co-edited with M. Cecilia Colombi, 2003) and *Research on Spanish in the United States: Linguistic Issues and Challenges* (2000).

M. Victoria Rodríguez, Assistant Professor, Department of Early Childhood and Childhood Education, Lehman College, City University of New York, worked for 20 years as a preschool, elementary, and special education teacher in Madrid and Barcelona, Spain, and in New York City. Her areas of interest include the training of para-professionals, early learning experiences of culturally and linguistically diverse students, and emergent literacy among Latino students with and without disabilities.

Sandra R. Schecter is a Professor of Education and Women's Studies, York University, Toronto. An ethnolinguist, her publications include *Language Socialization in Bilingual and Multilingual Societies* (edited with Robert Bayley, 2003) and *Multilingual Education in Practice: Using Diversity as a Resource* (edited with Jim Cummins, 2003).

Ana Celia Zentella, Professor in the Department of Ethnic Studies, University of California, San Diego, is an anthro-political linguist, whose primary focus is the linguistic diversity of Latino communities in the United States. Her award-winning book, *Growing Up Bilingual: Puerto Rican Children in New York* (1997) is an ethnographic study of Nuyoricans in El Barrio. Current research includes an NSF sponsored study of Spanish dialects in New York City (with Ricardo Otheguy, City University of New York Graduate Center), and a UC-Mexus sponsored study of border crossing students who live and study in Tijuana and San Diego.

Index